EVOLUTION'S END

EVOLUTION'S *End*

Claiming the Potential of Our Intelligence

JOSEPH CHILTON PEARCE

HarperSanFrancisco

A Division of HarperCollins*Publishers*

Harper San Francisco and the author, in association with the Rainforest Action Network, will facilitate the planting of two trees for every one tree used in the manufacture of this book.

FIRST EDITION

Library of Congress Cataloging-in-Publication Data

Pearce, Joseph Chilton.
Evolution's end : claiming the potential of our intelligence /
    Joseph Chilton Pearce. — 1st ed.
p. cm.
Includes bibliographical references and index.
ISBN 0–06–250693–5 (alk. paper)
1. Evolution. 2. Intellect. I Title.
B818.P33 1992   91–58899
128–dc20   CIP

92 93 94 95 96 ❖ RRD(H) 10 9 8 7 6 5 4 3 2 1

This edition is printed on acid-free paper that meets the
American National Standards Institute Z39.48 Standard.

To David Bohm

Contents

Acknowledgments

Marilyn Ferguson's *Brain/Mind Bulletin* was a major source for the materials of this book, and I am grateful to her. Many thanks to Michael Toms, of New Dimensions Radio—long-time friend, Acquisition Editor for Harper, and general adviser for this book. Thanks to Leela Heard for her help in the first major edits and reductions of the original manuscript, and to Janet Reed for her splendid copyediting. Thanks to Frank Nuessle, of Enhanced Audio Systems, for his constant support over the years. My special thanks to Julie Saiber-Heyman for her years of patient managing of my lecture tours about the world, wherein I worked out so many of the issues of this book, and from which audiences I received so much supportive material. My gratitude to my meditation teachers is immense, as is my gratitude to Bernadette Roberts for opening my mind to a whole new dimension as this book took its final shape.

Origins

In the beginning was neither existence nor nonexistence:

Neither the world nor the sky beyond. . . .
That one breathed, without breath, by its own impulse;
Other than that was nothing at all. . . .

In the beginning was love,
Which was the primal germ of the mind.
The seers, searching in their hearts with wisdom,
Discovered the connection between existence and nonexistence.

They were divided by a crosswise line.
What was below and what was above?
There were bearers of seed and mighty forces,
Impulse from below and forward movement from above.

Who really knows? Who here can say?
When it was born and from where it came—this creation?
The gods are later than this world's creation—
Therefore who knows from where it came?

That out of which creation came,
Whether it held it together or did not,
He who sees it in the highest heaven,
Only He knows—or perhaps even He does not know!

RIG VEDA[1]

Introduction

Several events come to mind when I am asked to summarize the ideas in this book. I recall, for instance, a talk I gave at the University of Adelaide in Australia, and a government chap telling me of his recent six-week tour of schools in the United States. "American schools," he said, "are in chaos, with everyone rushing around trying to sell their answer, while no one is asking the right question. Your talk," he said, "posed the right question and contained the answer." This struck me as funny since my talk was not about education. A wide variety of people find an equally wide variety of issues in my lectures and workshops. A member of Hawaii's criminal justice department heard a talk I gave at a university there, and asked me to address his entire department. They were baffled, he said, over the epidemic of violent crime and overstuffed prisons and needed to hear my "analysis of the cause and solution." My talk however, had been on this book's subject, which is not (to my knowledge) about crime and violence at all. Nor is it about child suicide, though after another talk a major television network asked me to consult on a proposed series on that unhappy subject.

My work inspires such a variety of responses because it explores some very fundamental issues about the human mind and our development as a species:

- how our experience of the world and of ourselves forms within the "ocean of neurons" in our heads;

- why the very nature of our brain/mind leads us to "dominion over" the physical world and then beyond that world's boundaries;

- why we fail to develop and so feel victimized by the world instead; and

- what simple steps we can take as individuals to complete our natural development and achieve the potential nature intended.

This book shows how a vague longing, which begins in our mid-teens, and our mounting personal and social problems are connected. Both result from a failure to develop our neocortex, or "new brain", the latest evolutionary achievement, lying largely dormant within us.

A growing number of research scientists agree that we use very little of this largest and newest part of our central nervous system, although others argue that since our brain operates as a unit we use all of it automatically. A new perspective opens when we consider the difference between use and development. I, for instance, use my muscles automatically, whereas the weight lifter develops his or hers very deliberately, and the difference is startling. Development of potential, not a semiconscious use, is the issue and challenge.

The first part of this book explores how unique personal experience is formed by our brain/mind translating from a common pool of potential, a "universal field" that is shared by each of us. Once one grasps the nature of this unified field and the play of unity and diversity within, one's perspective and attitude shift. To help explain and clarify this, I have used a wealth of scientific material, interwoven with living examples to make for easy reading. The opening section of the book is more tightly woven and perhaps more challenging than the second section, but for the latter to be fully meaningful, you need the former.

The frame of reference in which I have interpreted this material is quite different, however, from that of the researchers. My viewpoint was forged unbeknownst through decades of intense inner search, a "life of the spirit" as my first meditation teacher, George Jaidar, called it. This inner journey led me from a conventional southern background through the heady realms of poet William Blake and Christian contemplatives such as Meister Eckhart, to years of eastern meditation and vastly enriching retreats to a spiritual ashram in India, only to spiral back to a rediscovery and embracing of that camp of western contemplatives so loved in my younger years (a move rather catching me by surprise, as the inner journey is apt to do).

Seeing within changes one's outer vision. From such a changed perspective I find in scientific reports helpful facts on the one hand, even as I find, on the other hand, what I deplore—the deadly wrong and destructive view held by most of the scientific community of who we are and what life is about. Facts and truth, like use and development, are not necessarily the same. Many unexplained phenomena, dismissed by scientific people for not fitting their model, find explanation in the model of mind offered here. Recently, for instance, a medical doctor telepathically experienced a patient repeatedly calling to him in distress. Later the same day the doctor learned that the patient had been killed at the exact time of the doctor's experience in what might have been an avoidable accident. That a call of such clarity could reach him outside all physical means was hardly in keeping with his training and belief, and he wrote a moving letter to Marilyn Ferguson's *Brain/Mind Bulletin* asking if anyone could in any way explain this experience.

This book answers the doctor peripherally, just as it throws light on our epidemics of crime, violence, collapsing schools, broken families and so on. The real thesis of this book, however, is the magnificent open-ended possibility our higher structures of brain/mind hold, the nature of their unfolding, why many of them don't unfold, and what we can do about it. The good doctor, for instance, experienced but a fragment of a very practical intelligence, designed by nature to unfold in us at around age four, but disabled from doing so for reasons that will be made quite clear. Though they suffer the same fate, we have within us far more wondrous potentials, wherein evolution's next venture waits.

For years Karl Pribram, the grand patriarch of brain research, has championed "parallel processes" of brain/mind, viable functions over and above the usual textbook neural structures.[1] There are, as well, parallel processes over and beyond the higher brain centers themselves. These, too, are not available to ordinary research, yet they hold within them all that makes us human, and can, indeed, lead us from the human to the divine. All of our perennial philosophies, spiritual paths, religions, dreams and hopes, have spun out of an intuitive knowing that these higher intelligences exist, that life is more than just an economic knee-jerk reflex, that we are not just glorified

Skinner-box pigeons or naked apes. On the one hand we have divinized our potential, projecting who we are designed to be onto an abstracted cloud nine rather than fulfilling our evolutionary potential, and falling victim to the politics of that projection. On the other hand, and far more destructively, we have denied our evolutionary nature, grounding ourselves in the more primitive, physically bound modes of our brain/mind, and subjecting ourselves to the magician-priests who can best manipulate that physical realm.

Because nature builds new structures on the foundations of established ones, our huge "new brain", the one we seriously underdevelop, is built on the chassis of a quite ancient neural structure shared with all animals. This ancient chassis furnishes us with our physical experience of body and environment, and has skillful drivers of its own, programmed for millions of years to maintain the physical system they inhabit. These are intelligences in their own right, locked into our genes, they can't of their own nature relinquish the wheel. If we develop the higher structure of our brain/mind, it automatically integrates these lower ones into its service and employs the previous drivers to the best advantage of all. This, too, is the pattern of evolutionary progression, and in line with that progression we make marvelous humans on our way to divine heights. If, however, we fail to develop the higher and just use it by default, we invariably employ its intellectual capacity in the service of our more primitive "defense" systems. This means that those ancient inflexible drivers have fragments of the new power infused into their old ways, which proves devolutionary. The new potential is lost and, to compensate, we employ the old system in nefarious ways and make awful creatures, behaving as no decent "lower" animal ever has or will.

Split between these lower and higher neural systems, with evolution pressing to break through into its new modality, our situation can get precarious. Our personal awareness, with its ego-intellect, makes up an estimated 5 percent of the total intelligent energy of our brain/mind. (The rest provides the environment and maintains the conditions of, this personal 5 percent.) Yet with this paltry percentage we try to manipulate universal forces of unknown magnitude and then wonder why everything goes wrong. Over and again we hear the clarion call that we must take evolution in our hands and do that which bumbling nature, in its fifteen billion years of incredible creation, has obviously not had the intelligence to do. While the ego-intellect loves such arrogant, bootstrap nonsense, operations of this sort plunge us from one personal, social, and ecological catastrophe to another, and we are apparently incapable of catching on to our error. As architect Henry Bergman once said, "Each and every problem we face today is the direct and inevitable result of yesterday's brilliant solutions."

Evolution is neither in our hands, a blind groping, nor a "stately dance to nowhere" as Stephen Jay Gould elegantly put this safely academic and deadly wrong cliche.[2] Anyone looking at the nature of our three-fold brain and the direct parallel with it found in infant-child development will see a precise direction of evolution, a clear if stochastic[3] progression from the "concrete to the abstract" as Jean Piaget put it, or from matter to spirit as Henri Bergson said. Evolution completed its biological framework for this great venture long ago and we are it, complete and needing only to develop that which lies perfect but dormant within.

We are, nevertheless, the grounds of an evolutionary struggle, in effect, and precisely as myth and legend have projected: the struggle between "higher and lower forces." It is not one of a demonic netherworld and an angelic, heavenly realm but rather one between those ancient, well-established and vital neural structures functioning as intended, and our comparatively recent, largely unknown and undeveloped ones difficult to access. We have no choice at birth but to identify with those ancient functions since they provide our primary body and world experience. The unknown higher state, involving our most recent neural system, forms only as we participate with it, operates from a different frequency than our physical basis, and can't be approached as an object. It can only flow into, transform, and use lower neural systems. Such a nonphysical force is interpreted by the survival instincts of our maintenance system as tantamount to death. Since this ancient system controls our very sensory world and exerts its energy to keep a safe status quo, evolution's thrust is parried below our awareness. Our opening to a fuller humanity closes before we even discover it really exists, leaving us with an empty longing projected onto myths and dreams. Yet, as you will see, we can, with a bit of effort, confound this neural deadlock and open to this highest development. And though its inception is designed by nature for mid-adolescence, we can make this turn at any age. "The laborer coming to this vineyard at the eleventh hour gets the same wage as the one coming at the first hour." Once we are in line with evolution's intent, we have that intent's power behind us, access to other modalities opens within us, fear and anger disappear from our life and nothing is the same. Physician Larry Dossey writes powerfully along these lines.[4]

Part II traces how this evolutionary process develops in us from infancy, the awesome potentials it holds for us, where it is designed to take us, where it goes awry, and why it stops prematurely. The critical role played by a biological connection between heart and brain is explored here. A first, hormonal stage of this heart-mind dialogue is the key to the growth of our intellect and capacity to adapt. The massive evidence presented in this section shows that our schools have collapsed not from "bad" educational systems, which have always plagued us, but from a majority of our children having been neurologically damaged past the point of educability. This is not a popular or happy proposal, as I, father of five and grandfather of twelve can attest. The specific causes of this crisis in childhood are spelled out in detail, and include a discussion of five recent social-technological innovations that are the principle contributors.

A further "intelligence of the heart" is designed to unfold at adolescence, when the physical system is nearing completion. This stage would incorporate our intellect into its service, providing a foundation for the higher development made possible by our newest neural structures. The final two chapters are devoted to this highest journey that should open at adolescence and continue lifelong, were it given the appropriate nurturing environment. It may fail to unfold because of the relative newness and unknown nature of this capacity, rather than the moral shortcomings of society, as I long believed. No society or parent can give what they don't have or nurture what they have no knowledge of. These concluding chapters discuss what is known about this mature development, some of the ways to initiate it, and why this higher intelligence within us alone can alter our path from global and personal destructiveness.

You will find a distinction in what follows between intellect and intelligence. Intelligence, found in all life forms, strives for well-being and continuity; intellect, a human trait, strives for novelty and possibility. The opening prologue from the *Rig Veda* speaks of "impulse from below and forward movement from above." Intellect is that impulse within us to solve problems, generally of its own making, and explore possibility. Intellect is evolution's gamble, and it attempts to both entice us toward and prepare us for a new realm of being. Intellect involves the brain while intelligence involves the heart. Intellect may be likened to a "masculine" side of mind perhaps—analytical, logical, linear, inclined to science, technology, the search for external novelty and invention; while intelligence is more a "feminine" side, open to the intuitive and mysterious interior of life, seeking balance, restraint, wisdom, wholeness, and the continuity and well-being of our species and earth.

Creative discovery, like a creative life, arises from a coupling of intellect's passion with the unfathomable matrix of intelligence. Without intellect we would stagnate and evolution would pass us by; without intelligence we would lose our bearings, collapse into chaos and destroy ourselves, and evolution would lose its gamble. Developed without a corresponding intelligence, however, intellect doesn't move toward the unknown or help prepare for a new dimension. It digs deeper into that which is already known, using the creative imagination of our highest brain/mind to manipulate and change its surroundings rather than prepare us to move beyond them as designed. It manipulates its environment without concern for, or the foresight to determine the consequences of, its impulsive invention. Intellect, on the one hand, looks through its tunnel vision and asks only *Is it possible?*, and creates disaster. Intelligence, on the other hand, that mysterious "forward movement from above" asks *Is it appropriate?*, and will, if developed, use intellect to complete the movement from the "concrete to the abstract" as evolution intends.

Each of us, male and female, embody both intellect and intelligence, of course, and the complementary nature of these two polarities is the creative tension between mind and heart, the very spark of life. Disaster befalls us, however, when we develop intellect but not intelligence, as we have done for generations now. The fundamental complementarity then goes awry, and the principle polarity of life falls into petty but deadly struggles between ego positions—personal, social, and eventually global. The dying social body we see today is the outer display of just such an inner civil war.

A breakdown in male-female relations, epidemic among us, is a biological anomaly that has grown out of and is symbolic of the split between mind and heart in each of us. Intellect, trying to usurp nature and the wisdom of the heart for its own ends, has cut itself off from that heart. And like a child cut off from its mother, its entire development is at risk. Indeed, the mother figure is disappearing today, and an orphaned generation falls upon us. We humans do poorly without her. Matrix and guardian of our species, nurturer, source of strength and guidance for untold cycles of millennia, the mother has become the target of male intellect, swallowed up as a dollar commodity, leaving all of us, male and female, motherless, bereft, and lost. All around us we see the breaking of the bond of heart and mind. From that of mother and infant, child and family, child and earth, young person and society, to the male-female bond upon which life itself rests, we tear at our living earth—our greater mother and lifegiver—in an outward projection of our inner anxiety and rage. Should intellect win its battle with heart's intelligence, the war will be lost for all of us. We will be just an experiment that failed, evolution's end on a negative note. This book explains *how* this is so, why it *need not* be so, and how we might open to those dimensions within us as intended for us all along.

PART *one*

THE CEREBRAL UNIVERSE

CHAPTER 1

Idiot-Enigma

Paradox can be a threshold to truth.

GEORGE JAIDAR

Within that class of people called idiots there is a sub-group that used to be called idiot-geniuses, now called idio-savants, *savant* being French for "learned-one." Both terms are paradoxical since these people have an average I.Q. of 25. They are generally incapable of learning anything; few can read or write. Yet each has apparently unlimited access to a particular field of knowledge that we know they cannot have acquired. The identical twins, George and Charles, for instance, are "calendrical-savants."[1] Ask them on which date Easter will fall ten thousand years hence and immediately the answer comes, with all pertinent calendrical information such as the time of the tides and so on. Easter depends on both solar and lunar cycles and is a most difficult calculation, but George and Charles do not calculate, they simply respond to stimuli given, if that stimuli is resonant with their narrow spectrum of ability. Ask them for the date of some event before 1752, the year in which Europe shifted from Gregorian to Julian calendar systems, and their answers automatically accommodate to the appropriate system. They can range some 40,000 years in the past or future to tell you the day of the week of any date you choose. If you give them your birth date, they can state the Thursdays on which your birthdate might fall. In their spare time the brothers swap twenty-digit prime numbers, showing a parallel capacity not always found in savants. They can't add the simplest figures, however, nor can they understand what the word *formula* means. Ask them how they knew to accommodate to the change of calendrical systems in 1752 and they will be confused, since such an abstract question is beyond them as is such a term as *calendrical system*.

The twins, quite incapable of fending for themselves, have been institutionalized since age seven. Most savants are institutionalized, illiterate, uneducable, and male. (Eighty percent of all idiots are male, savant or not, which is not entirely beside the point though a separate issue.) During World War II the British employed two mathematical savants who served essentially as computers. They were, so far as is known, infallible. One mathematical savant was shown a checkerboard with a grain of rice on the first of its sixty-four squares and asked how many grains there would be on the final square were they doubled at each one. The answer took the savant forty-five seconds to deliver since that answer is a number greater than our estimate of the atoms in the sun. My mathematical friends tell me the answer is 1.8447×10^{19}, or 18,447,000,000,000,000,000. (The zeroes here represent place figures only in this quintillion number, since my friends did not have computers powerful enough to run the complete sequence.) Ask these savants how they get their answer and they will smile, pleased that we are impressed but unable to grasp the implications of such a question.

A musical savant, placed at an instrument with a sheet of music before him, will rattle off the music at top speed. Unless you turn the page for him, however, he will repeat the page over and over, unaware of the discrepancy. If you listen to this rapid playing you will find it lifeless and mechanical. On the other hand, a well-known blind musical savant can repeat, on the piano, a complex piece heard only once, in a perfect mirroring, including every emotional nuance of expression.

Savants are untrained and untrainable. The ones sight-reading music can't read anything else, yet display this flawless sensory-motor response to musical symbols. Missing are the essential inputs from emotion or any of the higher intelligences.

4

Savants have a multitude of capacities as a group, though seldom has a single savant more than one such ability. A savant whose specialty was automobiles was brought to Columbia University Medical Center in New York City for observation. He was asked to look out at the busy street below and then describe from memory the automobiles he saw. He could describe them all, in orderly fashion, by make, model number and year, including the latest items just hot off the press in Detroit or Tokyo. He is, of course, illiterate and uneducable.

Recently an excellent study of savants was published by a medical doctor, Darold Treffert, in his book, *Extraordinary People*.[2] His observations, made over many years, give us a large cross-sampling of this group. When all is said and done, however, savants remain an enigma. The answers come through them but they are not aware of how—they don't know how they know.

I once met a youngster labeled autistic who was fascinated with water heaters. He knew a remarkable amount about them, various brands, models, types and asked everyone he saw about their water heaters. He was uneducable and illiterate but was hardly an idiot. His questions were sharp, to the point, and he volunteered voluminous information about your water heater if you gave him the make or type.

Darold Treffert describes a savant with a conversational vocabulary of fifty-eight words, who can, if asked, give the population of every city and town in the United States that has a population over 5,000 (or any number); the names, number of rooms, and locations of two thousand leading hotels in America; the distance from any city or town to the largest city in its state; statistics concerning three thousand mountains and rivers; and the dates and essential facts of over two thousand leading inventions and discoveries. We might call this one a geographical savant.

The issue with these savants is that in most cases, so far as can be observed, the savant has not acquired, could not have acquired, and is quite incapable of acquiring, the information that he so liberally dispenses. If we furnish the savant with the proper stimulus, a question about his specialty, he gives the appropriate response, but he can't furnish himself with that stimulus, can't develop the capacity as an intelligence, and can't move beyond his narrow limits.

Poet William Blake understood what is at stake here when he wrote "Man is born like a garden ready planted and sown. This world is too poor to produce one seed."[3] Blake claims we bring everything with us when we come into this world. Howard Gardner proposes that we possess a multiple of independent intelligences, separate fields of capacity such as linguistic, musical, mathematical, spatial, inter- and intra-personal intelligences, and so on.[4] Each of these is its own independent grouping of potential and our brain translates from them in any learning. Our "peaks of activity in a population of neurons," are resonating with and from corresponding "fields" of intelligence. (Where these fields are is a matter for later consideration.)

A savant is pre-disposed to the intelligence of his specialty through some early infant-childhood experience that activates a "field of neurons" capable of translating from a "field of intelligence," within narrow limits. Just how this takes place is a major issue of the second section of this book. Walt Whitman furnishes us a clue to such predispositions:

> There was a child went forth every day,
> And the first object he looked upon, that object he became,
> And that object became part of him for the day or a certain part
>   of the day
> Or for many years or stretching cycles of years.[5]

The mother of George and Charles, our calendrical savants, had a perpetual calendar, an ingenious little brass gadget with various cogged cylinders. You could turn the one cylinder and they all turned until the proper alignment was made and you could determine a future or past date over a fairly wide period of time. The boys were fascinated with the gadget and played with it continually. That they couldn't read its coding and such is beside the point. The device acted as a stimulus that activated the corresponding "calendrical field," in much the same way that a mother's speech activates the phoneme response in an infant.

There is a savant who can make perfect, scale-model reproductions of any machine or device he has seen, using only brown paper from shopping bags and glue. He was born out of wedlock. His mother doted on him but the natural father, who lived with them, insisted the mother give him up for adoption. She refused for a year, during which she spent most of her time holding her infant and making models of automobiles—not a typical woman's hobby nor ordinarily a new mother's passion. Finally she gave in, the infant was sent to an agency and had a horrendous childhood, shunted from one foster home to another, ending, as one might expect, far below normal in development. He had, however, this knack for making accurate models of anything seen, out of the most unlikely materials. This ties in with the studies of doctors Thomas Verny, David Cheek, David Chamberlain, and others, who show how early experience imprints on some basic level and influences our future.[6]

That intelligence groups in universal or commonly shared fields explains many phenomena dismissed by classical, academic opinion and sheds light on the parameters of human thought. Physicists Russel Targ and Harold Puthoff, formerly at the Stanford Research Center in Palo Alto, California, have for many years, mostly under federal research grants, investigated "remote viewing."[7] Robert Jahn, former and long-time Dean of the School of Engineering at Princeton University, included remote viewing in his own ten-year research into "anomalies," phenomena falling outside the ordinary scientific "margins for reality."[8] In remote viewing a "receiver" sits in the laboratory, wired up to equipment that records brain-wave and body responses, while at a distant locale another person, the "sender," observes a "target" randomly selected from a large number of possible sites (such as objects or famous landmarks of the area). The receiver in the laboratory proceeds to describe or draw a sketch of his or her impression of what the target site is. Generally the person correctly identifies the target.

Robert Jahn found that often what appear to be misses are accurate reports misinterpreted by the research people, "misses" that prove more important than the hits. For instance, if the target were a particular front view of a building, the subject might see the building from any angle, from an inside room, or from behind, a random factor making validation far more complex and remote viewing far more revealing. Were the target a public fountain in a garden, the subject might pick up an individual sitting on a nearby bench reading a book. Such discrepancies lend authenticity to the experiments and give insight into how our brain-mind functions. In 1984, in an experiment with Targ, a Russian accurately described a merry-go-round, a target site randomly selected for viewing four hours later in San Francisco. Remote viewing of a future event can take place more easily, Targ thinks, because "the signal to noise ratio is better." That is, our systems are not ordinarily cued, or asked, to pick up future signals, so that area of potential is open, while the present is crowded with action and demands. The point is, the receiver senses that which the experiment itself sets up for viewing, whether present or future. The savant who could tell the make, model, and year of automobiles, including the most recent editions, was picking up information in essentially the same way.

Since the back side of a building might be "received" while the front side is being viewed and supposedly "sent," or, since the event can be anticipated by several hours before any "sending" takes place at all, we can seriously question whether "messages are being sent." Almost surely the direct viewer supposedly "sending" can be dispensed with; the overall experiment probably determines the result as much as anything else. Telepathy, for which people were originally testing, is no more involved in these experiments than in the following "theological discourse" given by my then five-year-old son. No "messages" are sent, as Abner Shimony finds in the actions of particles at a distance in quantum mechanics; a far more revealing function of brain-mind is being demonstrated. Terms like *parapsychology* muddy the waters and are no longer relevant, while such terms from quantum mechanics as *non-locality* and *fields of compatible-variables* are very much relevant as we shall see here.

When I was in my early thirties, teaching the humanities in a college, I was engrossed in the psychology of Carl Jung and theology. The issue of the God-human relationship occupied my mind to the point of obsession, and my reading on the subject was extensive. One morning as I prepared for an early class, my five-year-old son came into my room, sat on the edge of the bed, and launched into a twenty-minute discourse on the nature of God and man. He spoke in perfect, publishable sentences, without pause or haste, and in a flat monotone. He used complex theological terminology and told me, it seemed, everything there was to know. As I listened, astonished, the hair rose on the back of my neck, I felt goose-bumps, and, finally, tears streamed down my face. I was in the midst of the uncanny, the

8

inexplicable. My son's ride to kindergarten arrived, horn blowing, and he got up and left. I was unnerved and late to my class. What I had heard was awesome, but too vast and far beyond any concept I had had to that point. The gap was so great I could remember almost no details and little of the broad panorama he had presented. My son had no recollection of the event.

Here a bright, normal child underwent a kind of "savant episode" as he responded to a field of information that he could not have acquired. Terms such as *telepathy* are misleading; he wasn't picking up his materials from me. I hadn't acquired anything like what he described and would, in fact, be in my mid-fifties and involved in meditation before I did. Just as the standard intelligences Howard Gardner observes (mathematical, musical, and so on) are carried as "fields of potential" available to all brain-minds, experience in general also congregates as "fields." The more any phenomenon or experience is repeated, individually or within a society, the stronger its field-effect.

Years ago Karl Pribram proposed a "frequency realm from which our brain mathematically constructs its reality," viewing the brain as a micro-hologram of the larger macro-hologram of the universe.[9] Russel Targ proposed that we "live in a kind of holographic soup, closer in time-space than a naive realism allows." (By "naive realism" he means the concept of dualism separating mind from reality, which stems from the time of Descartes and rules most contemporary thought). That cosmic soup is highly organized, however, and any brain action selects from it logically. Targ's and Jahn's information arises not at random, but out of a clearly designed and purposeful testing situation. Even the time discrepancies, mixing future and present, are built into the nature of the experiment. They tested for just such possibilities, their "experiments" were careful arrangements setting up highly selective stimuli that elicited specific, selective responses precisely as our brain-mind does anyway, instant by instant, in constructing our ordinary experience.

My son's theological discourse was not random but squarely in keeping with my own passionate pursuits. Children, as Carl Jung observed, live in the shadow of their parents, and my son and I had a close rapport to begin with. Note that my son's report was direct and clear, like a savant's report, while the remote viewing person often describes the target in round-about ways, indicating that they are having to interpret, decode from a mixture of impressions. The correspondence between the subject and target is generally quite clear, there is no questioning of the validity of the reception, but what is described is often representative, analogous, or parallel, as in seeing the back rather than the front of the target. With the savant the information given is clearcut.

The ingredients of the cosmic soup on which our brain draws include ingredients we experience as matter, emotion, and knowledge. Whether giving rise to information, behavior, ability, or the phenomena of our material world, the same source is drawn on by all brains. The method of access to the fields determines the nature of what is then experienced from those fields. Whether we call this source a field of consciousness, categories of experience, a holographic soup, frequency realm, or collective unconscious, several generalizations can be made, giving insight into the workings of our own lived experience.

This source is not "unconscious" (collective or singular), but the very fountainhead of consciousness; however, we are largely unconscious of it. This source is intelligence itself; it gives rise to and powers our brain-mind and furnishes those potentials that we translate and live. This source arises as a single primary frequency that holds all variable frequencies within it—an infinite possibility for awareness-experience, a unity giving rise to endless diversity, a totality drawn on by the actions in the neural fields within us. The source is the universal, our response furnishes the needed individuality; yet each, individual and universal, diversity and unity, is "in" the other, as complements are. Whether drawn on in savant-fashion for a limited fact or as the great insights of a genius, the cosmic soup is the same; the difference lies in the medium sampling that soup.

In no way can we divide brain from source since only through our brain is that source available; all we can know of source is what our brain is doing. They are complementary, polar aspects of the same phenomenon or function; we can't have one without the other.

All functions in nature are dynamics: Each of our responses to this process dynamically feeds back into the source from which our potential springs. This feedback changes the content though not overall nature of the source. The soup-source is the same for all, but our personal development and the particular way in which each of us translates from that source determines our particular experience of it.

Since, as Targ's and Jahn's work shows, future events can be selectively perceived, and distance has nothing to do with the phenomenon, the soup-source frequency-realm obviously lies outside, cuts through, and/or is not limited to time-space. Quantum physicists use the term *non-locality* for those organizing forces that are not "temporal-spatial," not in time-space, and this term offers a way to explain this aspect of the frequency-realm.[10] We can't locate the potential, only our lived translation of it. Since the neural fields of our brain and the non-localized potential operate as a dynamic of resonant frequencies, our brain's neural-fields are obviously "quasi-temporal-spatial," both in and not in the time-space they give rise to. No research has been able to determine where in the brain perception actually takes place, because perception isn't localizable; yet every response we make to the stimulus of awareness changes the field from which our awareness springs. Our lived experience is a dynamic between a non-localized potential and our particular localizing of that potential as our perceived time-space world.

Targ's metaphor "soup" implies a random mixture of homogenized ingredients, but it is discretely categorized in clear groupings that give rise to the same nature of response. A study of creative discovery in the sciences, arts, or spiritual pursuits illustrates this. Review the classical steps of creative pursuit, as detailed by Marghanita Laski, Jerome Bruner, Peter McKellar, and many others:[11] First we are seized by a passionate commitment to some creative project, problem, or possibility; this prompts the search for the solution and means to find it. Eventually we exhaust the materials available, resulting in a plateau and stagnation—a time of gestation. The goal seems to elude us so we give up, quit, or perhaps just set the problem aside in frustration. This clears the decks for the arrival of the answer, the Eureka!, which comes "out of the blue," whole and complete, beyond thought, a revelation.

Most creative people, scientists, artists, and spiritual geniuses agree that the Eureka! answer seems given, a grace they can only receive, not of their own doing. Gordon Gould, inventor of the laser in 1957, gives this report: "The whole thing suddenly popped into my head . . . I was electrified. I spent the rest of the weekend writing down as much as I could and got it notarized. But the flash of insight required the prior twenty years of work I had done in physics and optics to put all the bricks of that invention in there. . . . I think the mind is unconsciously churning away, putting all these things together like a jigsaw."[12]

Dozens of like accounts have been collected,[13] and the issue remains: Who is unconscious of what here? Who or what continues to work out the infinite details of relationship, continually changing, shifting, reforming, and regrouping categories of possibility in that soup of categories until the right combination forms? There are striking cases of simultaneous discovery of a new mathematical or scientific process occurring by unrelated people on opposite sides of the globe. The Eureka! seems to spring from a cauldron of inner ferment, a springing forth that is about the same in Einstein as the idio-savant. The savant, however, can only give information; the genius can create something new. The difference lies not in the source but in the method of access and stimulus that brings about that springing forth. The savant's answer is nearly instantaneous; the answer to the passionate search of an artist, scientist, or saint, though it may take but an instant to spring forth, might take a lifetime to bring about. Creative answers tend to arrive in symbolic form and generally must be translated into the common domain. The capacity of the individual to translate the symbol into our common language or the language of the discipline involved is as critical as the actual value or meaning inherent within the symbol, and often determines the acceptance or rejection of the insight. Gordon Gould spent the weekend writing out (translating) as much as possible of what occurred in a single instant—just as mathematician William Hamilton spent fifteen years translating the great quaternions falling into his head in a single flash.

Generally the answer arriving out of the blue bears scant resemblance to the materials one has so arduously amassed in the search for the answer, though seldom does such an answer come without this painstaking preparation. True creation does not rehash the same old ingredients as invention often does, but gives new ones. The savant could never "translate" a symbolic answer for he doesn't have the symbolic structures of mind that are the marks of high intelligence. He never "solves problems" or gives a creative answer, only dry information. Producing 2^{64} power is computer stuff, not problem solving—not even remotely similar to such creativity as $E=MC^2$, the Benzene Ring, or the B Minor Mass.

The savant has a direct line of communication with one soup-category but only one, usually, while the rest of us can access a near-infinite number of categories, as many as we are attuned to by proper environment and guidance. Our generality is bought at the price of precision, however; we usually can't access our soup-source directly as does the savant. We undergo a long, involved development of intelligence, building up a capacity to handle limitless soup ingredients, draw selectively, and even create new ingredients out of them. Further, as we progress in any discipline, our skills, at first laborious, become more spontaneous. We develop a "sixth" intuitive sense that goes beyond information as itself. We move into process and are no longer limited to products.

We can access higher intelligences such as mathematics only as we can "correlate," carry over one ability into another such as reading, spatial intelligence, a sophisticated grasp of abstract symbols, and so on. We can even, to some extent, state our mathematical creations in verbal terms as well as the more restricted abstract symbolic languages. Areas of compatibility exist or are created between apparently non-related processes, none of which is available to the savant who can only be a channel for a specific ingredient of that soup-source.

Almost surely the savant's failure to develop multiple intelligences is what allows such direct openness to the single one he can access. His expertise digs its channel deep from lack of competition. His potential doesn't have to accommodate to anything and can come through with pristine purity—and profound limitation. The savant's lack of personal intellect-intelligence shows that the field accessed is intelligence itself, that intelligence does indeed group in compatible aggregates and is, on some level, independent of us, a "non-localized" conscious energy. So our individual intelligence, measurable perhaps on a testable scale, is our ability as an individual to correlate and synthesize actions between independent intelligences, any of which could, in its pristine form, pour through us in savant style.

Translating intelligences from their potential state into our personal experience of them is what infant-child development, and indeed our entire life, is all about, and will occupy the central portion of this book. Each intelligence or ability, as language, for instance, is a potential brought into our awareness through neural circuits in our brain as those circuits respond to stimuli of a like order from our environment. Through clear developmental steps this dynamic of stimulus-response brings about a structure of knowledge, an independent capacity we can call on at any time, a coherent and responsive "peak of activity in a population of neurons."

Nature's agenda unfolds these intelligences within us for their development at a time appropriate to each. Just as steak and champagne is not an appropriate lunch for a toothless infant and mother's milk not quite the diet for an adolescent, our developmental diet is equally specific. We can fail to nurture an intelligence by pushing for it too soon, waiting too long, or simply ignoring it. Being "built-in" as a potential is no guarantee of actualization. Jean Piaget felt that intuition unfolds as a capacity around age four. I have heard marvelous stories from parents about intuitive capacities in their children, and I could add many of my own, such as the one of my son's "channeling" of theological theory mentioned earlier. All the infant-child (and the adult as well) wants to do is what nature intended: learn, build those structures of knowledge. And all that is needed for this is an appropriate environment—being surrounded by a mature, intelligent intellect, open to mind's possibilities and tempered by heart's wisdom; recognizing that to the human all may be possible—but always asking, "Is it appropriate?"

CHAPTER 2

Fields of Neurons

Whether the desired information is the orientation or
the direction of motion of a visual stimulus, the time
interval between two particular sounds, or the location
of a sound source in space, the answer is always
represented as the location of a peak of activity within
a population of neurons.

ERIC I. KNUDSEN, ET AL. IN ANNUAL
REVIEW OF NEUROSCIENCE

Saul Sternberg of Bell Laboratories found in his ten-year study that
when asked a question that can be answered with yes or no (for instance), our brain takes as long to process a "no" as it does a "yes."
More intriguing, even when we come up with the appropriate answer
(yes, for instance), our brain continues right along processing all the
alternate aspects of that question—its "no" aspects and many in-
betweens. We are not aware of or involved in such homework. We
go on to other things, happily oblivious to the ferment of activity
going on in our busy head. In mathematical problem solving, long
after the mathematician has shouted "Eureka," written out the answer, and gone on to other things, the brain continues at full speed
apparently calculating every conceivable alternate aspect of that particular mathematical situation. Stretching things a bit, perhaps,
Sternberg has even estimated that the brain calculates about thirty
items or digits per second in this ongoing maneuver.[1]

That our brain-mind continues this action outside our awareness is
significant. Those parts of our brain involved in processing the mathematical problem, or whatever, continue to work out all the new

15

relationships which that problem and its solutions introduced. Meanwhile other areas go right ahead with other types of work. This lends weight to Howard Gardner's theory of independent intelligences.[2] Each field of intelligence acts as its own unique brand of soup within the larger soup-source and contains many separate ingredients within its own particular recipe. Any participation with that mathematical field, for instance, brings about a re-relating of each sub-section the general mathematical field has within it. All related fields involved (spatial, linguistic, etc.) must accommodate to the novelty introduced in order to maintain the unity or integrity of that overall mathematical intelligence.

According to research, our brain works by neural "fields"—groups of neurons operating in units.[3] A neuron is a large brain cell that vibrates at a certain frequency and dies if this vibration ceases. It vibrates only in relay with other neurons with which it is connected through slender thread-like extensions called dendrites and axons. Dendrites meet other cell connectors at points called synapses, where major exchanges of information-energy take place. In our neocortex, neurons are organized into fields of a million or so, relating through dendrites and axons. A single adult neuron connects with an average of ten thousand others to form such groups. The resulting networks create various forms of information-experience through exchange of frequency or "information" between neurons and fields. Each neuron or neural field has both its specialty, its particular category of soup-ingredient to process, and its generality: It can lend its specific services, its soup-ingredient specialty, to other neural fields to process other ingredients, make larger recipes, richer mixtures; a field's own wave-frequency modulates according to network needs in this relaying back and forth, giving an infinite flexibility to the whole system. And thus, sooner or later any single action will relate to the brain as a whole, though this might run long into the night.

Cells within a neural-field operate dynamically, and neural fields interact with each other as dynamics. A dynamic is a two-way flow of information or energy. All cells in a field are simultaneously sending and receiving the frequency potential being processed. The sum of the group action gives that field's unified output, which in turn adds its bit to the overall production from all the fields involved in that particular piece of the action; all of it being, or somehow ending as, our perception, our lived experience. Once set in motion we can't say a dynamic begins here and ends there. In a dynamic there are no static properties, everything exists only through movement, a feedback loop is always involved.

Neurons don't contain information any more than the transistors or tubes of a radio contain the shows they play, nor can they store information. They "translate" potential frequencies with which they are resonant and to which they have been "tuned" or keyed.[4] Since neurons survive only as frequency patterns or vibrating units, they maintain a constant low-amplitude vibration at all times, even while we are asleep or unconscious, as do all the muscles of our body—interlocked as they are with the brain-dynamic that guides them. Like an engine idling, our neural fields are abilities ready to fire into action when called on, and they interact on levels of which we are seldom aware.

New information, that is, frequencies of potential for which the brain has no established patterns for translation, must find uncommitted fields that are resonant or fields whose frequency can accommodate the new one economically—with a minimum of modulation of frequencies.[5] Fields can occasionally shift, rearrange their activities, interact and cooperate, organize new fields, and establish new connections to process new potentials. Some fields can compensate for each other and, within limits, take over activities of a related field should a particular brain area be damaged. A single field's ability increases as it interacts with other fields; its unique specialty can help process a multitude of related information by shifting communication from one field relation to another, just as a letter of our alphabet can take part in an endless variety of words. Any part of the brain implicates every part to some extent, sooner or later; the brain functions on highly specific, individual levels, in groups, and as a single integrated whole. Michael Gazzaniga spoke of this mass feedback system as a very "social brain."[6]

Research has centered, of necessity, on our perceptions of a physical environment—a staggering task. The real gist of our life, however, revolves around our emotional and mental environments, which aren't available to the same kind of research. Our human dilemma and major occupation doesn't revolve around issues of our living planet or biology nearly so much as around emotional-intellectual issues, beliefs, paradigms, images of self. My five-year-old produced that astonishing display of theological theory when a field of intelligence broke through, in typical "savant-style," in response to the stimulus of my obsession, which was his stimulus because of our close rapport. He was, as we shall see later, at the precise age for just this to happen. All this was, however, not apparent to either of us, and that such fields of intelligence operate independently of and yet in response to us both confirms Howard Gardner's theory and presents us with major challenges. To say we "process information"[7] means our brain constructs that information out of an unknown diverse set of frequency-potentials, an ongoing continuum of shared non-physical experience. Conventional quantum fields can account for our perceptions of a physical world; however, a corresponding range of emotional and intellectual fields is as evident, as important, and a greater problem. Our perceived environment or lived experience is an end-product to which we ipso facto attribute the source of that experience. This common-sense, rather inevitable observation is as fundamental an error as attributing the source of the television play being viewed to the machine itself.

Language learning offers a clear and simple example of the independence of intelligences, while development of it shows the nature of (and exemplifies) structural-coupling. Within the wide spectrum of sounds available to us there is a specific group of sounds that we term "phonetic." A phoneme is the smallest unit of sound out of which words are formed. Syllables and even the letters of our alphabet are forms of phonemes. We share a common "phoneme field" just as Poincare, Hamilton, or my daughter struggling with her multiplication tables share a common mathematical field. There are thousands of languages spoken at any time on earth, yet all are built out of, or draw on the same pool of some fifty phonemes, just as all systems of arithmetic use nine numbers and a zero. Not all languages use all the available phonemes, but the same phonemes selectively underlie all languages.

From the seventh month in utero all hearing infants respond with a precise muscular movement to each of the phonemes in each word spoken by the mother.[8] The same muscle moves in response to the same phoneme each time the phoneme sounds, with no time lag between sensory-input and motor-response. By birth these "sensory-motor structures" of language have stabilized, and the infant is ready for the next stage.[9]

Actual words are formed by drawing on the established "phoneme fields," and forming new neural connections grouping words themselves. These, in turn, group into related networks, or "sub-fields" based on emotional relation, sound similarities, and usage—nouns, verbs, and such. Each word must correlate with all words of its similar category, and a huge thesaurus of similarity is slowly built up through inter-relating neural fields. Each category encompasses sub-groups in turn: names sub-divide into fruits, flowers, faces, and so on. All fields and sub-fields interconnect, giving our language system. Occasionally a person will develop a tiny abscess or lesion in the brain that affects only one particular neural group. In vision, for instance, such a tiny loss can result in a blind spot, an actual "hole" in our outer visual world.[10] Similarly with language. One man lost his fruit-naming ability, for instance, and had a "hole" in his speech when that category was called on.[11]

Emotional similarity is a powerful influence: Scatological language, for instance, describes sexual-physical actions not ordinarily discussed in polite society, and so is primly kept in its privy place by our brain. In one famous case a gentleman developed a brain lesion that somehow activated that neural-field; each time he tried to speak he spewed forth unacceptable words against his will and to the embarrassment of all.

We add a new word to our vocabulary by finding its appropriate category. This, in turn, requires an ongoing shift of relations within all previously related categories, sooner or later involving the entire brain itself. The numerical weight of relations can be astronomical, but we have an astronomical possibility for field interactions in our heads.

Writing ushers in additional complexity. Symbols require their own network of similarities and relations, and writing involves fine-tuned muscular control. This abstract visual network must be related to spoken language while keeping its own action intact. Once we

have learned to read, and the automatic pilot takes over, we read anything in sight. When we come across a new word while reading, and
don't look it up in the dictionary right then, comprehension may
come to a halt, though we continue reading along on a surface level.
When that unknown word came into our ken our neural circuitry
began to search for a place for it.

As our chapter on language will prove, we don't teach language to
infants—language is as automatic as teething if a normal, hearing
infant is given a language environment. Learning language is a perfect
example of what Maturana and Varela call "structural-coupling" between the potentials of mind and environment.[12] Stimuli must be
given that resonate with a network of brain-cells that, in turn, can
resonate with the phoneme field and translate both ways, as found
in all phenomena. This innate phoneme field is a perfect example of
a field of compatible-variables (as each word category will later be):[13]
compatible in that a particular phoneme always gives rise to its precise muscle response in the infant and always leads to language (as no
other sound will); variable in that a different muscle responds to each
phoneme, or that an endless number of languages can be built out of
the results. Compatible in that all normal infants respond to
phonemes; variable in that no two respond to the same phonemes
with the same muscles. Compatible in that the same pattern of unfolding is followed regardless of language type; variable in that each
child develops at a slightly different time pace.

Infants born to deaf-mute mothers have no repertoire of muscular
movements to speech, cannot develop speech until such a repertoire
is established, and make no such movements until there is prolonged
and close contact with a speaking person or persons.[14] Nature's imperative, then, and her over-arching developmental rule, which has
enormous consequences, is that no intelligence or ability will unfold until or unless given the appropriate model environment. Mind
and environment give rise to each other through that new-born brain
only if the environment is there. Even our primitive instincts require direct, close contact with the necessary corresponding environmental stimuli. We are born into the world like a garden that has
been sown, but the seed must be nurtured and nourished by the appropriate environment. Further, the character, nature, and quality of

the model environment determines, to an indeterminable degree, the character, nature, and quality of the intelligence unfolding in the child. That a French-speaking mamma has a French-speaking child (or a German-speaking mother a German-speaking child, and so on), holds with all intelligences.

Kittens brought up in an artificial environment of vertical stripes can't perceive horizontal forms later, nor can they learn to. They will stumble into any horizontal object.[15] We humans are more flexible than kittens but still subject to the same model-imperative; the same structural coupling between mind and environment takes place. Our universe will be as big as the stimulus universe provided us initially, our range of participation as wide as our awareness of the dynamics involved.

Learning moves from broad generality to fine tuning. The infant in the womb responds to general sounds with general movements long before these become specific to phonemes.[16] In the same way, around the ninth month after birth the open phoneme field closes to, or becomes specific to, those phonemes used in the language spoken by the mother. Japanese infants, for instance, respond to all phonemes until about this time, when they begin to confuse the sound for *R* with the sound for *L*, as is typical of Japanese speech.[17] The model elicits the infant-response, activates the field, and then brings closure of the field on behalf of that model language.

Surely a wide range of known and unknown functions are involved in learning. Karl Pribram proposes "parallel processes" operating beyond such known observable ones as the synaptic junctions of dendrites. Researchers often refer to brain structures *myelinating,* as well, using the term to indicate some maturation or stabilizing of neural structure. A recent research paper has proposed an expanded and ongoing, continual role for myelin.[18] Based on this paper, which covered many aspects of development, I will use the term *myelination* figuratively to indicate the stabilizing or maturation of neural fields, recognizing the controversial nature of such use, and knowing that myelination is but one, at best, of many processes involved.

Several times in an infant-child's development the brain cleans house—releases a chemical that dissolves all unproductive, unused, or redundant axon-dendrite connections (and possibly various supportive cells as well), leaving the productive, developed neural fields intact. The trimmed up neurons will put forth new dendrites and axons as needed to establish new fields for new stimulus-responses. A field's imperviousness to this house-cleaning chemical seems to involve this fatty protein called *myelin*.[19] As learning takes place myelin forms an insulating sheath around the long axon connections of the neural fields involved and corresponding muscular nerves. Myelin is impervious to the chemicals used in house-cleaning; its sheathing somehow helps preserve that particular network, making that ability permanent. And it seems to assist in conducting the energy being exchanged between neurons, which speeds up the dynamic of information-flow; the more myelin, the more efficient that field. At first, many connections may be necessary, requiring far more concentration on our part. As learning develops, fewer connections can do the job. An initially slow, clumsy operation gets smooth and goes on "automatic pilot" when the myriad neural fields involved have myelinated enough to become a new intelligence or ability at our disposal, ready to fire into service when needed.

Repetition may stimulate myelination, as when the infant moves the same muscle in response to the same phoneme of the mother's speech. The more frequent the response, the more myelin forms; the thicker the myelin sheathing, the quicker information can be conveyed, requiring less energy for its conduction; the more firm and lasting the learning, the more efficient and compact that particular neural network becomes. That's why our primary language, though always more powerful, takes up far less room in the brain than a second language.[20] It is also why practice makes perfect and why, when once locked in or myelinated, a learning is generally lifelong. So we see that neural fields are brought into play by usage and made permanent by the extent of that usage.

Our self-sense is naturally "embedded" in a learning until that learning becomes autonomous, or partly so, by myelination of the neural fields. Any serious learning requires "all hands on deck," total attention and energy, and our ego-self, which directs the energies of our mind, temporarily identifies with the task, or is embedded in it. Maturation of the learning (its myelination, to use that single function to metaphorically describe all the complexities of a learning), frees our personal awareness from this embeddedment. Then we can

22

stand back from that ability, use it at liberty, and move on to other things. This cycle of psychic-embeddedment and freedom from that embeddedment plays a critical role in our life-long development and is our evolution in a capsule form. So long as we are embedded in a learning, or block of learnings—as those of early, middle, or late childhood—we can't grasp the possibility of any higher mode of operation.

Our brain and the frequency realm it draws on are complementary, an interlocked dynamic. The nature of our cosmic soup is that every time we sample that soup, our sample itself enters into the ingredients we sample. Ours is a participatory universe; each participation enters into the possibilities for further participation, reorganizing relationships between potential fields and the brain-fields that translate them.

When we invented the automobile, a new category formed in the fields of potential. The more we use automobiles, the stronger the category becomes, as happens daily with mathematics or chemistry. As we did with the automobile we are now doing with computers, an invention rapidly changing the whole set of our minds and shape of our society. Once set in motion any creative dynamic self-perpetuates, continually reinforced by its own output of events that dynamically feed back into their source, giving rise to a new display of the characteristics, which feeds back ad infinitum. The nature of our source is constant, its display infinitely varied. My mind maintains a steady image of my ego-self, while yet incorporating into it an inordinately complex new set of experiences, emotions, and thoughts. I have always been simply *me*, yet I realize that my five-year-old *me* and my current *me* have very little in common except that central agreement of always being *me*.

Set up a Pentagon in a war-time emergency, feed the bulk of your national energy into it for several traumatic years, and you are stuck with the results long after the emergency is over, as that field generates its own response, creates its own reality as is the nature of potential. Fields are kept active by participation—the positive or negative aspect of that participation is irrelevant. For instance, even events apparently remote from automobiles are changed by automobiles, making them indispensable. Every new factory, invention, fuel, late-model supercharged highway menace incorporating them;

every road, by-pass, super-highway, traffic light, and traffic police-man trying to control it all, strengthens the category: automobile. Small wonder a savant sooner or later appears who links with such a "morphogenetic field."[21] These fields of potential shape us as we shape them—whether we are aware of it or not.

CHAPTER 3

Mind and Matter

*Mind and matter are two aspects of one whole and no
more separable than are form and content.*

PHYSICISTS DAVID BOHM AND DAVID PEAT

Such a viewpoint of an underlying "whole," as our two physicists
propose, is quite ancient: Kashmir Shaivism, a psychology-cosmology
perfected over a thousand years ago, spells out in fine detail this dynamic of mind and matter and its evolution.[1] The viewpoint is sci-
entifically quite new, however, and the source of much contention. In
a recent article in *The Scientific American,* Abner Shimony wrote
about a major enigma of current science called "non-locality."[2]
Brought about by laboratory tests of "Bell's Theorem," repeated for
nearly twenty years now, non-locality continually upsets classical
academic thought.[3]

In brief, under certain conditions one particle of energy can influence measurements of another particle of energy at so remote a distance there is no possible way for a "message" to be sent from one
to the other. In the same way, if we set up the proper conditions, two
people in remote parts of the world can exchange information as
such, when we know there is no way for a "message" to be sent. If
mind and matter are two aspects of one whole, however, then the
"whole" to which Bohm and Peat refer is the "cosmic soup" itself,

the nature of which should solve the enigmas of Bell's Theorem, the remote viewer, and our savant equally. The nature of that "whole" cannot, however, be a substance, thing, place, person, or god but, of necessity, only a function, a process. Since both physical matter and savant can be spun out of it, this process must unfold according to the nature of our interaction with it, our frame of reference, which then becomes our experience of the process. And that is the real and final nature of the function itself. Seeing, for instance, can be a creative act. The creative process is a dynamic that responds according to our participation with it. What we see is what we get—we can get whatever we can see, and we can learn to see in new ways. This chapter will explore the relation between what goes on in our heads and our experience of the happenings "out-there," as preliminary to proposals for new forms of seeing.

A neural field is a group of up to a million or so linked neurons operating on the same frequency. A field in scientific terms is a state of potential. Physicists refer to wave-fields, groupings of resonant frequencies, that give rise to particle groupings such as atoms, molecules, stars and moons, mice, men, and brains. If mind and matter are aspects of a whole, then the two fields must at some point converge. That convergence, I propose, occurs as neural fields of our brain translate such groupings of potential according to resonance. When the frequencies between neuron and potential-wave match, or can adjust and come into sync without too much trouble, that potential actualizes. That actualization is our experience. We have a near-infinite number of neural fields available and no end of potential states to draw on.

What a scientist experiences, in the laboratory, nuclear reactor, cyclotron, or wherever, always reduces to a "peak of activity in a population of neurons," projected "out-there" since that is the way the brain works. If scientists analyze physical matter minutely enough, sooner or later they will come full circle and be looking at their own internal processes by default, without realizing it. So it just may be that quantum physics, our current yardstick for almost everything, is *also*, and possibly no more than, an expression of the translations going on in those neural fields. And this may be why a correspondence between quantum physics and consciousness is so popular a subject today. Perhaps the mind has finally turned on and is looking at itself.

Most of us know that the particles of matter making up our physical world apparently arise from wave-fields and that we experience the particles ("localized" and actual) but not the wave-fields ("non-localized" and only potential). Sooner or later, I propose, everyone will know that the neurons in his or her brain are the translating devices between this potential-wave and actualized-particle. Scientists use such figurative terms as an energy wave "collapsing" into a particle when we participate in that wave. This participation goes on all the time, whether we know it or not. That particle's "collapse" is our particular perceptual experience. Our experienced world results from a play of wave-neuron-particles, to use this current "quantum" frame of reference.

If their frequencies match, the waves that give rise to particles can overlap or mesh in a kind of coupling. The particles produced from this mesh are "bonded," held together as a complex display, giving us physical forms such as rocks and microbes, you and me. However, the wave-potential, that mesh, is not a perceptible part of the form that results from it any more than are the microwaves broadcast from a television studio perceptible in the show we watch. To perceive the wave is to experience its display of particles. Our act of perception translates wave into particle; our neural fields and their receiving senses are the means of that translation.

For many years now scientists have wrestled with the problem of "non-locality" found in the results of Bell's Theorem—the fact that the wave aspect of the wave-particle complement doesn't "exist" as does its particle. Particles of energy held together in a "closed" system (a mesh of resonant wave-fields) can be split off from that closed system and sent in opposite directions. No matter how much they are separated, they maintain the precise relationship determined by that closed system. Suppose for instance, we have a group of molecules, which, observed through the microscope, are seen to form a perfect hexagon. Suppose we then broke the figure up, sent those molecules off in every direction, out to telescopic depths of the universe, and found that they still maintained their hexagonal relation, now enlarged astronomically. We would know that the relational force of their bond, the original closed system giving that shape, was not affected by time-space. This would be an example of a "non-local" energy, since it is operating outside of and not subject to any of the energies of our everyday world.

In tests of Bell's Theorem, scientists do just that. They break up an atomic-molecular structure and send its bonded particles in opposite directions. An interferometer changes the angle of spin or polarity of the particles going in one direction and measurements made of the untouched group, going in the opposite direction, show an instantaneous realignment of their polarities to mirror the state of their bonded pair. The two groups maintain the same relationship found in the original sub-microscopic state, even after the particles are separated by large "macroscopic" distances. Suppose again, in an even wilder for instance, that on marrying, my wife and I find we mirror each others actions, the perfect meshing of persons. We travel in opposite directions, one to Timbuktu, the other to Kalamazoo and find, to our amazement, that we still mirror each other's movements though widely separated. When she stands on her head, I find myself standing on my head. Telepathy as explanation would be ruled out by the instantaneous mirroring as would be any and all sending devices known, including light itself. Thus we would say our relation was non-local.

Of major importance in the proofs of Bell's Theorem is that the "history" of one group of particles, its experience in the broad world, determines or enters into the history of the second group, no matter the distance. The influence is instantaneous. No signal can travel faster than light so there is no way the first group could signal the second about the change of polarity. Computer projections show that the two groups would instantly mirror each other though they were separated by an entire universe, untold billions of light-years apart.

Abner Shimony, writing on "The Reality of the Quantum World" discusses how the "bizarre nature of quantum action" challenges all previous notions. Atoms were considered discrete entities that formed into molecular groups through attractions between the atoms themselves, like magnets and filings. When atoms were found to be made of infinitely small particles of energy, the same attraction was assumed. Matter was assumed to act on matter through exchanges of energy, similar to striking a ball with a bat. Attempts to explain the results of Bell's Theorem by such classical notions lead to what Einstein scoffed at as "spooky" actions at a distance, about like swinging the bat in St. Louis to hit a ball thrown in Detroit.[4] What has been found, however, is that the bonding force between particles is the wave function that gives rise to those particles.

———

A brief lay-person's explanation will provide the metaphors needed to pursue the nature of the "whole" of our mind-reality. Particles (and the universe built of them) being essentially light and variations on light, are subject to the speed of light as their ultimate limit of movement.[5] On the other hand, the wave-fields from which they manifest are of a different state entirely, not "movement" of light but a frequency from which light itself springs—not in time-space, but the source of time-space. They are, in a word, non-localized, whereas the particles they display are localized. A particular mesh of resonant waves gives a "closed state" of equally related particles. The closed system can display those particles at different quarters of the universe as easily as in the sub-microscopic level of ordinary "quantum" action, since the point of origin, that closed state of potential energy, is not in time-space—not in the universe that results from its displays of particles. Particle and wave are two different, though absolutely interdependent states, as distinct as waking and dreaming. You cannot have one without the other, and you cannot have both at the same time, which is the nature of any complement.

Equally important is that even though the states are so different, what happens in time-space affects the wave-state giving rise to it, just as our being awake affects our dreaming and vice-versa. So in the testing of Bell's Theorem, changing the condition of one particle group changes its wave-field, and the changed wave-field, by default, instantly affects and changes its other displayed group of particles. Wave and particle are a complementary dynamic, and dynamics are a two-way affair, interchanging and interacting. There is no time lapse since the field from which the two displays are made is not in time; time is its effect. What happens in the physical world of form and time impacts the non-temporal state giving rise to that world. What is loosed on earth is loosed in heaven, but that loosing changes the structures of heaven: Each instant change of state effects in turn each further display (billions of times per second according to quantum physics). Relationship is a "non-temporal spatial" frequency shaping matter and all the events in a matter-world, but those events can also create and shape new fields.

Before continuing, I should point out that I think an error concerning Bell's Theorem is rapidly evolving, as writers refer to Bell's Theorem as "proving that all particles of matter are connected," which is not the case. The particles showing such influence are particles of a closed system—bonded particles. Were one able to snag a wild particle out of the air and knock its polarity asunder while checking the polarity of another wild particle snagged at a remote place, no influence would be found. Particles are not all joined or connected. Great seas of random particles pour forth in places in this universe, as nature operates by her own profusions, creating chaoses that will give rise to orders of their own. The conditions wherein Bell's Theorem can be tested require bonded wave-fields that give rise to bonded particles. Then, and only then, we find a bond not subject to time-space conditions. This is at least one significance of the theorem's tests. Russel Targ sets up a condition wherein someone in Russia attempts to guess something happening in San Francisco four hours later, and the attempt pays off. Were no conditions set up, nothing would happen. To jump from the payoff and assume that "all our thoughts are really one, that our separateness is just delusion," is nonsense. There are levels on which thoughts can, under very special conditions, interchange, and there are levels where they cannot. Particles are not all bonded; that would be just as great a chaos as no particles being bonded. Particles bond to create certain formal structures. That all arise from a singular source is another matter, for then we are led to discover that the source is not in the same state as its product, and that is a different ball game altogether.

A major proposal on which I base this book, one that seems to me strikingly self-evident, answers many puzzles concerning our brain and experience. The proposal, which I take as axiomatic from this point forward, is this: For our experience, neural fields of our brain are the median between wave-field and particle displayed. For us, a particle displays as we perceive it. Our perception is the particle-event "out-there" in our environment, exactly as nature designed. Our environment is the result of this "structural-coupling" between mind and its potential. That the resulting structure of our reality is an internal "self-organizing" system gives no basis at all, however, for assuming we "create" that world as it is to itself. Tree and stone in my backyard, bat in our church belfry: Each is its own display, each its own dynamic drawing on, spinning out of, feeding back into the cosmic soup. As Ilya Prigogine observed, "Whatever we call reality, it is revealed to us only through the active construction in which we participate."[6] The issue is not just a reality, but what is revealed to us.

Scientists prove the wave effect by setting up laboratory experiences in which a wave effect is detectable to our sensory-perceptual apparatus, that we might perceive as a particle-experience an otherwise imperceptible "wave" effect. Ilya Prigogine, writing on scientific experiment verifying theory, says,

> What must be done is to manipulate physical reality, to "stage" it in such a way that it conforms as closely as possible to a theoretical description. The phenomenon studied must be prepared and isolated until it approximates some ideal situation that may be physically unattainable but that conforms to the conceptual scheme adopted.[7]

A clear insight into the workings of our mind and reality has been offered for decades now by physicist David Bohm (if not a sage, as close to one as the scientific community can offer). In 1957, he published a work called *Causality and Chance in Modern Physics*, which according to many should have won for him a Nobel Prize. His point of view established in that work led to his theory of the "holomovement," in which he describes the force giving rise to our reality as a conscious intelligence that can be expressed as matter or energy. He carries the well-worn paradox of the wave-particle dynamic into one of universal proportions, which he terms the "implicate and explicate" orders of energy. The following is my description-application of Bohm's model, mixed liberally with my limited understanding of quantum physics, to help us unravel the mystery of our cosmic soup.

Bohm proposes an "implicate order" of energy as a formative power, which has "implied" within it all our physical experience. Experience is "explication," making explicit that which is implicit, so our perceived world is the "explicate order," the expression of the implicate order. To illustrate this, suppose that I use a hidden projector to display lights on a screen. If we want to see the light show we look at the screen (explicate-order) and its display, not the projector (implicate-order). The light show is our time-space world, the screen is our own "screen of mind." We participate in the display of lights and continually change them. We think *we* change them by pushing the bits of light about on the screen, but change takes place only through re-arrangements within the projector itself.

The projector is our brain, of course, and the screen our mind, but, in our "quantum-world" frame of reference, this projector does not exist as do those lights it displays. The projector is "non-localized," that is, not there on that screen-of-mind wherein the light show takes place, though it must, of necessity, be a complementary part of the whole process. The implicate order exists through setting apart from itself particles "of itself" such as energy, light, matter, emotions, thoughts, which we call the explicate order. The history of those particles (what happens as they interact) affects in turn the implicate order projecting them. Without a projector giving the light of our conscious experience, our material world could not be. Without the screen on which to project, the projector would be useless. A dynamic is a mutual two-way flow of information-energy. Implicate order and explication are a dynamic in that their energies exist only in their exchange from one state to the other, that is, their complementarity.

According to Bohm, the implicate order, in turn, is the product of a vastly more powerful "superquantum potential." This he calls a "supra-implicate" order, which "represents information that 'guides' or organizes the self-active movement of the field."[8] The supra-implicate order is causal and determines the nature of the implicate order, which is its median, the link between causality and the resulting explicate order. An interacting three-fold hierarchy of energy systems unfolds: an explicate, giving rise to our lived experience; an implicate order, giving rise to our personal consciousness; and the supra-implicate, a causal order giving rise to and guiding the implicate order. I propose that a direct, indeed dramatic relation exists between these orders of energy and our threefold brain system, as we shall see shortly. In every way we *are* these three orders.

Going back to our previous analogy of a projector and screen, we can say the supra-implicate order is the very source of the projector—creating, powering, and running it. Since it is all conceivable power, an unlimited number of universes could be spun out of the supra-implicate order through its lower forms of expression. To go from physical matter into the implicate order we leave a world of things and move into a more powerful frequency realm of organizing wave-fields and form-potentials. To move into completely undifferentiated potential, an inconceivable power, we leave form-potential behind and enter a pure energy (free of any trace of the lower orders of its own expression).[9]

So the supra-implicate is all-power conceivable, the implicate is all-power manifesting, and the explicate is the contracted end-result so manifested. Each level of energy is discontinuous, like the proverbial "quantum leap," yet each leads into the other. All these energy levels interact and are simultaneous, at any one point of the holomovement the totality is displayed. Any point within the whole hierarchy of energies is always dead-center. The final point from which all springs is "consciousness without an object," a void, an absolute unknown.

So the supra-causal energy is itself increasingly subtle. The word *subtle*, from the Latin word meaning "finely woven," is used by physicists to describe frequencies beyond direct physical detection; the more subtle an energy or finer its vibrations, the greater its potential power. Visualize the "peaks and troughs" of the quantum wave getting closer and closer together, faster and ever more powerful. A threshold is reached when the potential wave reduces to so fine a vibration that, further reduced, the interval between peak and trough disappears. Then no wave-pulse exists and all movement stops. This non-moving state of energy we call pure consciousness, and it is "the realm of insight-intelligence," to use a later phrase of David Bohm's, the still-point from which the holomovement springs.

Earlier in this century, physicist Max Planck proposed a limit to the possible fineness or subtleness to which the quantum-wave could hypothetically be reduced, and he came up with a figure reading 6.626×10^{-34} joule-second, so minute a part of a centimeter's length that it is hardly imaginable. Yet, if we compute the quantum potential of a single cubic centimeter of pure vacuum—absolute nothingness—that is, find how many units of energy it would hold using Planck's Constant as our gauge, we would find that it held all the energy that could ever be, more than in all the universes stretching out from us. Nothingness (void, vacuum, non-locality, silence) holds everything within it in potential form, a seeming departure from common sense and part of the bizarre nature of quantum reality.

This "constant" of Planck's (represented by the symbol h) has been a critical part of quantum theory throughout our century and is found in nearly every computation opening new fields of technology or experiment. We would have few of our new technical trinkets such as televisions, lasers, computers, star-war initiatives, and such were it not for that h (or an equivalent mathematical metric). Assuming that Planck's Constant and Bohm's origin of the supra-implicate order are the same, we come up with creative energy that springs from a single point to give rise to all realities through a three-part creative action: (1) the supra-implicate order—an initial pulsation (Planck's Constant) gives rise to pure, undifferentiated potential; (2) the implicate order—the supra-implicate order unfolds myriad frequency displays, which it guides; and (3) the explicate order—the implicate order gives rise to an explicate-display, the physical order itself. Although we assume all relations are on the surface, physical level, as dictated by common sense, in fact (as the figure found on p. 36 demonstrates) all relationship is from within-out.

Again recalling our analogy of light projected on a screen, if we could shift our vision and trace any point of that light to its source, we would arrive not at a different source for each light but at the single projector. The projector is a "unity" that gives rise to an infinite diversity. According to David Bohm, the vast universe stretching out from us at every hand is but a "mere ripple on the surface" of the creative power inherent within the supra-quantum state. Creative energy is an unbroken holomovement resonating from a single source, though it is expressed as fields springing forth endlessly, giving rise to infinite expressions. Because of the indivisible nature of this energy, any of its "displays" (such as you and me) is at some point the totality of its order of energy, and, of logical necessity, one with the unity of the whole; William Blake expressed this in his line "to see the world in a grain of sand. . . ."

Eastern philosophers have claimed that each of us contains the whole of creation within us. Thus in Kashmir Shaivism, that ancient psychology-cosmology mentioned earlier, we find a striking parallel to quantum physics and Bohm's holomovement.[10] In Kashmir Shaivism the metaphors are not mathematical but stem from a "human metric." This theory states that all creation springs from a singular pulse of vibratory energy called a Spanda, which is the initial creative pulsation expressed by a non-moving point of consciousness termed The Self. The Self simply witnesses the moving creative energy springing forth from the Spanda. An ever larger series of interweaving vibrations unfold, which eventually articulate as matter, a final irreducible state of contracted but stable energy. This creative power (the Kundalini Shakti in Sanskrit) radiates from that Spanda, the initial pulse of infinite energy, down to the gross finite world. For each of us that world is our very body; the creative Shakti resides in each of us as a subtle energy wave stretching from the base of the spine to the top of the head at the fontanels. All of creation takes place therein.

Embedded as matter, the most contracted form of energy, that Shakti-power is a wave-frequency that, were its peak-trough measured, would be only some 1/100 the thickness of a human hair. Rising up from physical energy to the subtle and causal expressions, this Shakti becomes ever more subtle and powerful until finally, at the Spanda—the source itself at the fontanels at the top of our skulls—the energy wave would measure but 1/100 millionth the thickness of a human hair. Further reduction is not possible since the wave contracts totally, peak and trough merge, and movement stops. At that point, the place of the witnessing Self, that energy is infinite, holding all power within it.

Spanda and witness are an indivisible whole according to Shaivism, so the entire unfolding from Spanda to matter takes place inside each of us equally, our body is the field of the play itself; we are each a diverse form of this unity, while, as a necessary corollary, we are the unity itself. Diversity in unity is the game consciousness plays, the play of the universe. Thus the famous Sanskrit statement: *Tat Tvam Asi*, "thou art That"—that Self, that ultimate unity. The whole, being indivisible, is within us and we are within it, aware of it or not.

Putting Bohm, Planck, and Shaivite scholar together we can "visualize the unvisualizable" in a model which shows that all relationship and all action arises "vertically" through these dynamics, not laterally within any one level, as we assume.

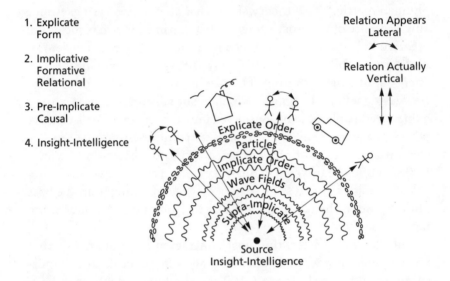

1. Explicate
   Form

2. Implicative
   Formative
   Relational

3. Pre-Implicate
   Causal

4. Insight-Intelligence

Relation Appears
Lateral

Relation Actually
Vertical

Explicate Order
Particles

Implicate Order

Wave Fields

Supra-Implicate

Source
Insight-Intelligence

Whether one elects a mathematical metric such as Max Planck's 6.626×10^{-34} joule-second, or the more human "metric" of "1/100 millionth of the thickness of a human hair" may be no more than a matter of intellectual aesthetic. The underlying function is the same. Whether we elect to measure the length of our house in meters, which requires some instrumentation, or "feet," which one can more or less pace off by walking, doesn't change the nature of our house. Choose your metaphoric mode, however, and you choose the nature of your lived experience. Go the route of Planck's Constant if you wish to explore the infinite complexities possible within the implicate-explicate dynamic. Go the route of the Spanda and be led into the realm of insight-intelligence, a journey into silence and the unknown. Either way, the function is the same. The way chosen determines the nature of the function that unfolds. The frame of reference through which we attempt to understand function determines the nature of what that function is for us. That is the nature of function; why only function is "truth"; and why Bohm's "whole" from which matter and mind spring is not a place, person, thing, or god, but that singular function of unity in diversity—the dynamic from which all springs and which we are.

CHAPTER 4

Fields of Intelligence

Mind is knowledge . . . knowledge [is] identical with the
object of knowledge. [Knowing this is liberation.]

GURU GITA

The universal soup-source on which we draw is many things: the generative force giving rise to such things as brain-minds; the potential for brain-minds to act on; the force of that action, which expresses that potential; and the response to the expressions so made. The more complex a brain structure and complete its development, the greater the portion of the soup it can access and experience. A portion of this soup-source powers the worm in our flower bed through the few neural ganglia needed to do his worm-thing, or bird on the wing to experience its world of delight. The source is both personal and universal; the process in my head draws on the same source as you and all other forms.

Our lived experience grows out of and feeds back into the source, which changes continually, accommodating to our responses as we must then accommodate to our source's corresponding change. A wise man stated, some two millennia ago, "What you loose on earth is loosed in heaven, and what is loosed in heaven is loosed on earth." "Heaven" is a metaphor for the cosmic soup, the frequency realm on which our brain draws for our lived experience; "earth" is that lived experience itself. Heaven and earth mirror each other yet are distinct, perfect complements as described in Humberto Maturana and Francisco Varela's "structural-coupling" between mind and environment.

This dynamic of complementarity underlies all creation, whether seen as structural-coupling, reaping-sowing, or quantum wave-particle. Inorganic forms such as stones cannot participate in the dynamics giving rise to them. Random collisions of atoms and molecules will eventually wear them away, their particles incorporating into other forms, participating in evolution in a slow random way. Organic life enters into the dynamic of that wave-particle and speeds things up, at the cost of a stone's stability. The more complex that organic life is—starting with organic chemical molecules, moving on to microbes, and ending with such as you and me—the more complex are the wave-fields involved and the interactions possible between wave and particle. Unlike a stone, we humans can enter into and play with the dynamics creating us, but this open possibility is gained at the cost of permanence and stability.

Viruses and bacteria can interact with their environment, which is the parameter of that interaction—a small world. With multicellular creatures nature added a nervous system: special cells linked together to control and coordinate the collection of cells that allows them to interpret a wider range of potential fields, experience a greater environment, and participate in the broader universe that results. The tiny hydra in our fish pond have the simplest nervous system known, occasional neurons connected by slender neural-threads scattered amid the two layers of cells that make up their bodies.[1] Yet in creating that rudimentary nervous system evolution took a major leap that paved our way. That little hydra can participate and act on its own behalf, and in so doing displays more intelligence than single-celled creatures.

All creatures respond for their own well being through an intelligent causal force that guides and directs them. Our central nervous system is an awesomely complex series of overlays and re-organizations of the hydra's simple system. Our brain encompasses myriad fields, specific constellates of neurons that can translate any number of fields of wave-potential into "particle form" or particularized

39

experience, mixing these in an infinite number of ways. And no line can be drawn between a wave-field of potential and the corresponding neural field of brain that translates this potential into our experience; our neural fields are only partly temporal-spatial. Just as the particular frequency picked up by our television receiver determines what we experience on the screen, the wave-fields or frequencies to which our neural structures of brain are tuned determine the nature of what we perceive as our physical, intellectual, and emotional reality, the reality of our thought and awareness.

The "history" or expression of our individual experience feeds back into the general fields giving rise to that experience. Instant by instant we reap what we sow, individually and collectively. We can experience fields and create new ones, loosing on earth and heaven and back again, often to our regret, since the whole dynamic works out within us. Emotional experience tends to constellate as a field, within which is a continual branching of sub-fields of varying but similar emotions; the emotion we experience arises from a common pool, the one we generate by our response to that common pool feeds back in to it and other people pick up aspects of it. Intellectual experience creates "archetypal" fields of potential such as mathematics, music, religions, and so on. Each field is a "unity" in that its potential holds all experience of a like order that manifests as the field's ongoing variable-diversity; this diversity interacts with that unified field from which it arises, changing that field's potential without changing its nature. (Søren Kierkegaard, considering the absolute unchanging nature of God cried, "Even the fall of a sparrow moves Thee, but nothing changes Thee.") Thus fields of potential are always of the same nature or general potential, yet continually shifting according to the history of their expressions, giving an open-ended, fluid, evolutionary creation.

Our three different states of experience—intellectual, emotional, and physical—are self-evident. All of us experience being lost in thought, caught up in an emotion, or reveling in the senses. Although these three states cross-index and overlap, they spin out of their own frequencies. That these states require and indeed have within us their own neural structures, development and integration of which constitutes our whole "developmental" stage from birth to maturity, is made evident through research into the brain, which we will explore in the following chapter.[2] The various lines of influence being brought forth here will interweave more tightly as we go along, giving a definition of ourselves that is sobering, breathtaking, and challenging.

CHAPTER 5

Triune Brain:
The Mind of Three Minds

When simple cells join . . . they exhibit organizing forces
in new directions which were impossible by any of the
individual cells.

LUTHER BURBANK

All new Fields embrace lower-level morphic units that
[already] existed. . . . New patterns . . . contain the old
within them.

RUPERT SHELDRAKE

When the higher flows into the lower it transforms the
nature of the lower into that of the higher.

MEISTER ECKHART

We have three distinctly different neural structures within what we
once thought was a singular brain. Paul MacLean and his medical
associates at the National Institute of Health's laboratory of brain
evolution and behavior derived this description of neural systems
through a synthesis of research from their own and other major centers, such as those headed by Karl Pribram and Wilder Penfield.[1] These
three structures in our skulls represent the major neural systems

42

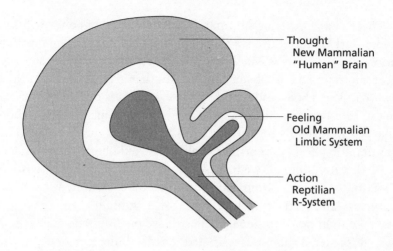

Thought
New Mammalian
"Human" Brain

Feeling
Old Mammalian
Limbic System

Action
Reptilian
R-System

developed throughout evolutionary history, through which we inherit all accomplishments that preceded and led to us, plus, may I add, a quantum-leap of additional potential we have not yet developed.

MacLean calls these three structures the reptilian, old mammalian, and new mammalian brains, in order of evolutionary appearance and placement in us. Our experiences of thought, feeling, and action, as well as sleep, dreams, and wakefulness, all associate with this three-fold division. Karl Pribram suggests the term *core brain* rather than reptilian, since this extensive system presents us with our physical world. The second brain, he points out, represents this presentation to us, while we reflect in our human fashion on this presentation and representation through our third, highest structure. I will use MacLean's more colorful terminology, however, since he so clearly characterizes behaviors inherent within the separate systems.

This triune system demonstrates how nature builds her new and more complex structures on the foundations of previous structures, as when a simple cell is incorporated into a multi-cellular creature, opening up a new drift of evolutionary potential. Each of our three structures has its unique duties, characteristics, and behaviors and can, to some extent, act "laterally"—within its own structure and according to its unique specialties. The three are designed to act vertically as well, as an integrated unit.

These characteristics summarize the evolution of behavior itself, and exactly parallel the stages of child development. The reptilian brain, or R-system as MacLean calls it, encompasses our sensory-motor system and all physical processes that give us our wake state awareness in a body and world.[2] This R-system is our means for acting in that body-world, and it "stores" our various learnings about that world made by higher cortical systems and turned over to the "automatic pilot." Our primary behavior would be primitive indeed were this R-system all we had. We would push relentlessly, without emotion or reason, for physical survival: food, shelter, sex (species survival), and territory. Our visual world would be limited to contrasts of light and dark, enabling us to see outlines and edges of objects immediately about us with little spatial dimension or depth, and we would interpret that limited environment in a simple twofold manner of "aversion-attraction."

Incorporated into service of our two higher brains, this R-system gives us our explicate order. Nestled above it is our emotional, or "old-mammalian" brain. This structure, with help from the temporal lobes and possibly other parts of the newest cortex, is called our emotional brain or limbic system (from *limb*, meaning "to wrap around"). It wraps around the reptilian brain and gives us a far more resilient, adaptable, and powerful intelligence, along with a wider and richer universe. Further, all the crude instincts of the reptilian system are transformed into more flexible and intelligent forms of behavior when incorporated into this higher system. That simple reptilian aversion-attraction response, for instance, is elevated to a complex of "feeling-tones" that spin out a vast web of like-dislike, good-bad, angry-happy, sorrow-joy, love-hate polarities. These direct that primitive reptilian servant according to a constantly shifting aesthetic, an insatiable desire for pleasurable sensory-reports, anxiety over unpleasant reports, chronic resentments of previous painful experiences, and so on. Here too is an intuitive intelligence to move for the well-being of the self, offspring, and species.

This emotional brain, or limbic system, maintains all relationships such as our immune system and our body's capacity for healing itself. Here lies the seat of all emotional bonds, from that of mother-infant, child-family, child-society, the foundational pair-bond of male-female, and so on. It is involved in dreaming, visions of our inner world, subtle-intuitive experiences, and even the daydreams and fantasies spinning out of its upper neighbor, the neocortex. This middle emotional system ties the three brains into a unit, or directs the attention of any one to the other as needed. It can incorporate the lower intelligence into the service of the highest or vice-versa, it can lock our intellect into the service of the lowest defense system in an emergency—real or imagined.[3]

The third and highest member, our neocortex or new brain, is five times bigger than its two lower neighbors combined and provides intellect, creative thinking, computing, and, if developed, sympathy, empathy, compassion, love. Here we reflect on reports from those two lower neighbors concerning our life in the world and our emotional responses to that world. Here we scheme, figure ways to try and predict and control our environment of world and people; brood on our mortality and galloping morbidity; spin out poems of other climes and days; experience worlds within or beyond; hammer out restrictive laws for the behavior of others; invent religions and philosophies, pondering the destinies of man.

Just as no limbic system can exist without the reptilian foundation, no neocortex could operate without both "animal brains," limbic and R-systems, as support. This highest brain can, if developed, access causality itself; through that potential we can radically alter those lower orders, alter the very nature of the environment given by our two primary systems. This neocortex is divided into separate hemispheres, each with its specialties. It directly builds its own corresponding neural patterns of all the "hard-wired" learnings of its two lower neighbors. The snake's responses are laid out ahead of time in its simple neural system; it needs no guidance from Mamma snake to respond to its world. As such laid-out responses in our R-system are made, they directly feed into our neocortex, which builds parallel neural structures of what would otherwise be automatic stimulus-response mechanisms. This allows us to guide and direct such simple systems, modulate them, and use them for higher purposes, and imprinting such patterns uses only a small portion of our enormous new brain. Through this three-way, or "triune-brain" connection, those more primary instincts and intelligences take on a profoundly different character and have, as well, the intellect of our highest brain at their disposal in emergencies. Through operational development, which we will discuss later, our highest "causal brain" can also act on its patterning of those two lower systems and change them to varying extents, even, as Mircea Eliade put it "intervening in the ontological constructs of our universe."

Although the three systems function as an integral unit, we can tune our channels to some extent and concentrate attention and energy on one at a time, or use any one of them on behalf of the other. For example, when we get caught up in the R-system's territoriality or survival concerns, we might then use our new brain's intellect and our limbic system's emotions to narrow our focus and concentrate on that self-defense. Of course, we can use these lower systems on behalf of the higher, as well, as in creative thought or invention.

Our lower order intelligences become refined when incorporated into service of our neocortex. Our R-system is the seat of sexuality, for instance, but what we humans do with that basic instinct is different from blacksnake's (or should be). Our high, neocortical system transforms this crude reproductive impulse into Tristan and Isolde or Romeo and Juliet. As Burbank observed, the simple system incorporated into the more complex opens new vistas of possibility. Same instinct, different setting.

The R-system is involved in language usage, as seen when the in-utero infant moves a muscle to each phoneme the mother speaks. We use this primary system to speak and write or observe others speaking and writing. Equally, our basic brain has its own form of imagery, which, crude as it is, when overlaid by its higher neighbors and their evolutionary expansions on vision, plus the shaping force of language, gives us our rich view of an endless universe.

Within our reptilian brain lies a "reticular formation," a gateway through which our senses funnel and roughly coordinate before being dispersed to the two higher structures. When our biorhythms of sleep-wake close this gate, our outer world disappears and our awareness shifts to an inner world; we go from wake to dream. Open the gate and our physical world reappears; the higher brains shift gears from sleep-dream to tend, fill in, and respond to the environmental reports coming in. Our personal awareness is both recipient of these reports and a "roving point" that can shift back and forth between our three brains, utilizing their lateral or vertical capacities.

Very little of our new brain is needed to augment and give power to the ancient territorial, sexual, and survival (flight-fight) instincts of our primary R-system. It may be that only a small portion of our neocortex resonates with the lower systems or is even available for concentration on them. If we get stuck in a defensive posture and focus the higher system on the needs of the lower, the bulk of that higher system must simply idle along until the coast is clear. If the emergency (or rage) persists, as in chronic anxiety or paranoia, that highest system can actually atrophy since so little of it is needed by or adaptable to serving our lower system. Thus we find highly anxious, insecure children at risk intellectually, and paranoid adults operating on minimals of intellectual power, subject to serious errors of judgment.

Even though our neocortex can act directly on sensory reports, and of course influence all sensory action, these actions are funneled through the emotional or limbic brain for general cataloging, memory, learning, relating. Our emotional brain acts with our neocortex in all internal imagery and creative vision. During the day most of this capacity overlays to transform the crude imagery of the R-system to give us our wide, rich world. The dreamlike emotional-limbic system also gives body and substance to creative thinking. Our limbic system must transfer the causal creations of our new brain to the physical system for translation into our everyday world. In the same way the more abstract information from our environment must be translated to that highest brain, and such translation occurs through the limbic system. Much of this translation takes place as imagery, a major way in which the three structures integrate.

The emotional-limbic brain develops the nuances of language, which precede the infant's actual use of words. The syntactical relating of sounds into meaningful groupings is an emotional or relational function. Were it not for our sensory-motor brain we could not speak or write. Were it not for our limbic system we could not communicate. Were it not for our highest evolutionary brain, we could not think as we do.

The two older brains used to be considered mere vestigial leftovers, as tonsils or appendix were. All real brain work was thought to take place in the neocortex. Contemporary research indicates the opposite:

47

Most of our lived experience comes from the work of our two primitive brains—our R-system providing our world-environment; our limbic system giving our sense of relatedness, memory, and individual ego. Only peripheral "computational" benefits seem added by our huge new brain—at a superficial glance.

Our two "animal brains" are immeasurably superior to the same organic structures in lower creatures. By evolution's intent the higher is designed to incorporate the lower into its service; this intent transforms the lower genetically, from the beginning, whether that higher system is developed or not. The reptilian system we are born with is light years beyond that in a reptile, even should we (theoretically) never develop either of the upper structures. So, even were we to operate primarily out of our two older brains and not develop much of our newest at all (as many authorities now claim), we still get more out of those shared primary systems than is possible for any other creature.

This growing belief that we use, at best, no more than 10 percent of our highest brain is contested by many neuro-scientists, and there is little way to test for it. Our mistake is in considering "use" rather than development. There are strong indications that we seriously under-develop our neocortex and hardly touch its potential, though we use all of it by default, simply because the brain functions as an integrated unit.

John Lorber, a British neuro-scientist, found during a preliminary survey, over 150 people with virtually no neocortex at all.[4] They had all suffered hydrocephalic disease (water on the brain) since birth. Brain scans with our new devices showed normal basal and limbic structures, but only about 5 percent or so of the normal amount of human neocortex. For all intents and purposes, their heads were 80 percent full of water (or, more precisely, cerebral-spinal fluid). Disturbingly enough, these "brainless people" had I.Q.'s ranging up to 120, many held advanced educational degrees and important professional positions and seemed perfectly normal, bolstering the claim that we modern humans apparently get along quite well using only a fraction of our new brain's capacity. The hydrocephalics may function as well as we do, since we are using no more new brain than they are, though they are using and developing all of theirs, while we develop and use only a minimum of ours. Whatever the proportion, we seem to come out about even.

Some use Lorber's examples as proof that our brain operates as a hologram, and thus can operate out of only a small portion. This is countered on many levels. For example, a lesion on one tiny brain area can eliminate a whole block of experience, action, vision, language, or other cognitive process, which can't be compensated for by other areas. Strokes annihilate the capacities of one side of the body for hundreds of thousands of people each year. Sectioning the two hemispheres by cutting the corpus callosum (which joins them) seriously disrupts operations. And loss of certain key parts of the limbic system is catastrophic to overall operations. Our brain contains many specialized areas whose "lateral action" can't be taken over by other parts. Surely a "holographic action" takes place, in that our brain draws on holographic or morphogenetic fields complementary with fields of the brain, but our brain is not a piece of a larger hologram, it *is* the holographic process, the function lies within us. Karl Pribram refers to the brain operating through *patch* or *pocket* holograms, a powerful description of neural fields.

It seems to me overwhelmingly evident, and I present as axiomatic such a proposal from this point forward, that our three brains translate for our experience the three orders of energy described by David Bohm. Surely the three operate vertically, as an up-down unit, in giving us our matrix, the explicate order or physical reality, presented by our reptilian system. Our two higher systems are hardly limited to assisting in this creation, however, or just responding to that creation. Both hold within their own lateral processes our experience of, and development within, the subtle and causal potentials of the implicate and supra-implicate orders. This simple recognition of parallel processes offered by our higher structures brings everything into new focus, and clearly shows the intent behind evolution. Whether or not these higher, parallel processes are developed, however, depends, as usual, on the model imperative. That is, they must be given the appropriate stimulus and supportive environment. Acknowledging, as it does, only the explicate or physical realm as valid, the scientific frame of reference, accepted as our world-self view as it has been, denies such stimuli and prevents such a supportive environment. This brings about a split of intellect from intelligence, eliminates a majority of the functions possible to be developed by the higher evolutionary structures, and leads to anxiety, despair, and rage, as do all devolutionary moves.

At any rate, I propose, in summary, that our reptilian system registers physical experience but has no access to the formative fields giving rise to such experience. Our limbic brain, on the other hand, can access those formative implicate fields of relationship and greatly expand on or alter the patterning of our physical body-world. It can't, however, access those causal fields that underlie everything; this is the job of the neocortex, which employs or interacts with the primary frequencies that cause the show. Through our access to these causal fields and the various hybrids between pure causation and implicate ordering, we can analyze any image or experiential formation taking place, intuitively sense the form-fields before they concretize, and intervene in our reality over a wide range.

When you grasp the significance of our triune system, our daily life begins to make more sense and many aspects of current scientific research take on new meaning. Robert Cloninger, for instance, has recently published his discovery of three brain chemical systems: one for novelty seeking, one for reward maintenance, and one for harm avoidance;[5] the same three major categories of our behavior as described by Paul MacLean. Those brain chemicals, however, are particular names given forms of energy playing on fields of energy within us, nature's modus-operandi, her means of communication, transference, movement. Shaivite sages claimed that the initial Spanda gave rise to a vast sea of vibrations, the final grossest expression of which is a particle, the most contracted form of energy. Constellates of particles, though only "displays" of frequencies, then provide boundaries for the infinite variations possible to that basic frequency itself. It is all a "measuring out" of a self-contained play. From that unique but essentially simple process a universe springs forth, at base a frequency-vibration, at length, experienced as our world. We perceive that vibratory universe through our threefold brain system and its limitless, flexible neural fields. The first, the R-system perceives the particle structures resulting from the actions of the other two. The second, the limbic system, can perceive the shaping fields giving rise to the particles. The feedback of the R-system's sensory-experience into this implicate realm completes the dynamic and opens a vast world. The third, the neocortex—our intellectual system—can perceive the causal force behind the shaping fields of the limbic system, along with the emotional-relational experiences within them, which enlarges that universe and opens limitless potentials.

The triune brain displays our universe, created within, projected without, and we enter into that creation, identify with it, lose ourselves to it, and become subject to it. Both fascinated and terrified, we plunge through it looking, till strength fails us, for some point of peace of mind or permanence. Since by its nature the vibratory universe unfolds in keeping with our movement, we find only ever-unfolding fields of particles and movement. We perceive this as chaos or order depending on our state of mind, while the silent point of origin we seek, the Spanda and our Self silently witnessing it all, lies, of course, only within.[6]

CHAPTER 6

Images of Wake and Dream

Man's perceptions are not bounded by organs of
perception; he perceives far more than sense
(tho' ever so acute) can discover.

WILLIAM BLAKE

Sense, as William Blake refers to it here, is physical sense. We surely have other senses: one, in fact, for each of the neural systems outlined in our previous chapter. Each of our three systems has, for instance, its own distinct form of imaging; the images of wake differ from those of dream. The highest brain has inherent within it the most unique of all images: three-dimensional, brilliantly colored, constantly changing geometric forms that can numinously and awesomely fill our visual field. As reported by people under exceptional circumstances—drugs, deep hypnosis, the hypnagogic periods between wake and sleep, meditation, or religious experiences—researchers have listed eight categories of these forms, though their numbers are surely legion.[1] They are universal patterns in that they are inherent within the nature of our brains, and, I propose, they are causal in that vision arises from them as language arises from an inherent "pool" of phonemes.

These universal forms include a snowflake, spider-web, and honeycomb pattern; parallel lines overlaying in grid-form with small spheres moving along each line; radial fan-like lines; checkerboard shapes, and so on. They are fields of compatible-variables in that they are in constant motion and change, yet always clearly the same generic pattern. For example, no two snowflakes (out of the untold quadrillions that must have fallen) are ever alike, yet any single one is instantly recognizable by its category: snowflake.

These forms involve, and/or arise from, the frequency-realm from which our visual world is created; neural fields within our brain draw on and combine the infinite varieties of shapes available through these pattern-fields. David Hubel finds crude bits of lines, arcs of curves, angles, and so on, in the more primitive areas of our visual system.[2] Higher cortical structures apparently build on these geometric fragments to give us our rich, visual world.

Ordinarily we can see these patterns as themselves only inwardly, though they may break in on our ordinary wake-state. A friend who has practiced meditation for years reports that these images superimpose his ordinary vision, fading slowly, when he is coming out of meditation. Once, while listening to my meditation teacher, a vibratory buzz filled my head and I saw her in a flat projection through a clear hexagonal grid, which then dissolved and left my vision intact. Neurologist Oliver Sacks gives a stunning, roughly similar account of losing his left visual field during a migraine attack, causing complete blindness to the left half of his visual field, which breakdown he refers to as "scotoma."[3] When the nurse would come into his room she would move across the right half of his visual world and disappear exactly in the middle, reappearing as she moved to the right side again. As his recovery began, traceries of light began to flash into his left field, which then filled with perfectly fitting transparent hexagons forming a grid through which that missing left half of his world appeared. That hexagonal world was flat and shallow, however, without dimension or movement. When his nurse came into the room she moved in her usual fluid way through his right field to appear on the left half as a sequence of discontinuous non-moving flat figures in varying positions occupying different parts of the grid, thus "moving" across it as a series of still, one-dimensional pictures. After a half-hour or so of this bizarre effect, the grid slowly dissolved and his left visual world took on full depth and fluidity.

In some way our brain "superimposes" these geometric fields to construct its imagery. The visual systems of all creatures do the same, though only an evolutionary system as advanced as ours can see the fields as fields (and even then only under special circumstances); our highest, neocortical structures can directly access these geometric fields as themselves. These frequencies are causal, they underlie the creation of all visual reality, and our neocortex is, as I have proposed, our causal brain. Accessing them directly, however, is rather like the savant accessing a mathematical or calendrical field, not ordinarily part of the creative function, but "leaks" in the system.

Patterns similar to our inner geometric fields can be elicited from such material as sand, powder, viscous liquids, and other mediums by subjecting these substances to sound waves.[4] When bringing water to a boil, at a certain temperature hexagon-type formations of molecules occur.[5] When vibrations interact with gross materials, or particle aggregates, geometric patterns emerge. Two things are required, vibration and boundaries. Vibration as itself has no boundary; boundaries are provided by physical mediums and physical mediums may well be provided by interference of waves with each other. Our brain is fluid and in constant vibration; our eyes vibrate at many billions of cycles per second; all muscles of the body vibrate at a low frequency even in deep sleep; the stapedius bone of our inner ear is in constant fine vibratory movement, all this points up the vibratory nature of our experience.

The structure of imagery shifts with our states of consciousness. Dream images can be brilliant, clear, beautiful, and joyful or hideous and terrifying. They are seriously real at the time yet by common consensus unreal. Even our wake-state images are considered real only if shared with others. Wake-state images require full arousal of our R-system, are generally available to all or most of our senses, and take place in a definite, continuous locale. Dream-images occur when our R-system is shut down and our outer world gone—ordinarily. They are usually only visual, private, fluid, random, a-logical, and non-local.

All imagery, however, regardless of its nature, is constructed in the same way, and logically placed by the brain. This logic is subject to disruption or error, however, and dream images can break into and become a part of our wake-state, as in the hallucinations of fever dreams, delirium tremens, or drug-induced states. Dream images can take on solid dimensions in our ordinary world. They can impact our senses just as our wake-state images do and get "filled in" with full sensory materials as day-time images are. Then our neat categories of real and unreal get fuzzy at the edges and, should such persist, men in white coats will come and take us away.

My wife had fever dreams once. Her temperature soared to 105° and she perceived little gray moths swarming over her, itchy, crawly, and repulsive. She begged me to help her brush them away, but, alas, my brushing of the unseen-to-me moths was of no avail (though I dutifully tried). The episode was an integral part of her memory of the illness, as perceptually "real" as anything else, although in retrospect she recognized it as a hallucination. The opposite happens in a form of dreaming called night terrors: Even though we are awakened by someone and open our eyes we don't wake up to the outer world, as in ordinary dreaming. Rather, the inner world of dreaming continues, and our wake-state outer images tend to be incorporated into and become ingredients of our mad nightmare world.[6] As a child I had such dreams and as my mother or some sibling would try to awaken me their faces and voices would become part of the dream, intensifying it.

Similar is "false-awakening," a strange state in which we think we have awakened from sleep, seem to get up and go about our affairs, only to find ourselves still semi-asleep in bed (as when in our need to urinate we think time and again we are getting up to do so). Our brain incorporates such actions into our dream-state, perhaps trying to complete its cycle of dream-sleep. Often this twilight zone has a malevolent tinge to it, and our familiar surroundings seem strange and threatening.[7]

In sleep-dream research, experimental subjects who wear red goggles during the day dream in red that night.[8] And, just as our wake-state world influences our dream-world, what goes on during the emotional period of REM sleep enters into the shape of our wake-state world. Much homework goes on at night, relating the day's events to the general reference-maps and memory that our system constantly calls on in putting together our daytime reality.[9] For, as we shall see, our ordinary reality is, like our dream-world, a "construction" the brain must make, and reality-construction calls on our totality of experience.

Our eye muscles move rapidly when we dream, so we call this period rapid-eye-movement, or REM, sleep. All higher mammals need sufficient REM sleep to survive. The emotional, limbic-brain in-volved in dreaming needs time to relate the materials of our day's log-ical events to those reference maps on which their construction depends. So dreaming is part of our general housekeeping, and dream deprivation leads from fatigue to derangement and death if prolonged. Whether lower mammals dream or not isn't known (perhaps can't be), but it seems they must have their quota of REM sleep as we do, because all mammalian brains are constructed on the same basic pat-tern and have somewhat the same needs. I believe my dog dreams— she will start panting, whimpering, legs running in the air, and may even wake herself up with a howl of terror, only to look around sheepishly, as though surprised to find herself safely at home and a bit ashamed of making such an idiot of herself.

Delirium tremens is caused by (or related to) severe alcoholism. Alcohol apparently damages the ordinary "gating" (reticular forma-tion) that keeps our sleep-dream and wake-state worlds separate, as well as affecting the body's biorhythms that time the ordinary swing from wake to sleep. These breakdowns prevent the alcoholic from becoming fully asleep or fully awake; neither a proper housekeeping nor an alert wake-state is possible, and confusion follows. The brain's need for REM repair accumulates, and, with the gating dysfunctional, dream imagery begins to break in on wake-state imagery. Pink ele-phants and boa constrictors appear to crawl out of keyholes, or other hallucinations occur, and feel real to the victim. The R-system duti-fully refers the dream-imagery to the brain's reference maps that fill in the dream images with the same supportive sensory information any environmental stimuli receives (just as with my wife's fever-dream moths).

The Australian Aborigine lived in a state they called Dream Time, a perfect balance between implicate and explicate orders. (A few still do.[10]) Their worldview was quite different from ours, leading to dif-ferent capacities, perceptions, and ways of reasoning. The Kalahari !Kung also employ a state of consciousness different from ours, and can do things most of us in the West can't, such as heal serious wounds, sit in the middle of roaring fires, and other unlikely things.[11] Carlos Casteneda's many volumes about his mentor, don Juan, hinge around a dream-state wherein our ordinary logic does not hold. The state is held by its own logical set, its "rule," which is also the way to get to that state (as is the case with fully developed yogis). The result is a non-temporal-spatial reality that gives a valid lived experience. Since this is an effect created from a subtle-causal dynamic it is a higher evolutionary achievement than our subtle-physical one. Apparently it hasn't been developed by enough people over a long enough period of time, and so is unstable, easily overwhelmed by the far more stable behaviors locked into our R-system with its ancient habituated, rock-like grounding. Perhaps this is why Westerners, having developed a high strain of intellect identified with the R-system, so quickly destroyed the Aborigine of Australia and other cultures.

In my earlier books I cited Charles Tart's research in mutual hypnosis, a phenomenon I now see in a new light: Two of Tart's graduate assistants, a young man and woman, were skilled in giving large-scale tests for hypnotic susceptibility and proved, as well, to be good hypnotic subjects themselves (a rare combination).[12] Tart trained the woman to put the man under hypnosis and the man to put her under in turn. Tart stayed in close touch with both of them to give each the suggestions needed for the experiment, observe, and be ready to intercede if problems arose.

To be put under hypnosis, a person must be willing and able to suspend ordinary selective criteria about reality and possibility and to surrender such criteria selectiveness to the hypnotist. This involves a certain flexibility in one's "gating" mechanism between physical and subtle, or wake and dream (as found in imaginative, creative children, for instance). When the woman put the man under hypnosis, she became his criteria of what is possible. Her commands became the source of his R-system's "world response," which then drew freely on his ordinary "reference maps" and the fluid potential of his dream-state to create a hybrid of both wake and dream materials. When she, in turn, commanded him to put her into a like state, he became *her* criteria of what is possible. Thus they enter a state of suspended reality, each having given over their world-construction to the other, each subject to, and awaiting direction or stimulus from the other.

Tart then had to intervene in the impasse, as designed, and instruct the young woman to use suggestions (conventional "guided-imagery") to deepen the young man's hypnotic state, after which he is instructed to deepen her state in the same way. Thus they lead each other into a mutually shared hypnotic experience. In one instance the man suggested the woman "see" and go into a tunnel, a metaphor for going into deeper trance states, leaving the world far behind. (The power of this internal imaging in reality organization will become clear in our chapter on child's play.) When the tunnel was stabilized in her imagery, Tart instructed her to use the same visualization to deepen the young man's state. When she did this, the pair suddenly found themselves together in an "actual" tunnel, which they perceived just as they would any ordinary event. They spoke in the tunnel and held hands to bolster their faltering courage. Another graduate assistant, an excellent hypnotic subject herself, had slipped into the laboratory to observe the proceedings, fell into hypnosis herself, and found herself in the tunnel with the other two. They sensed her presence and resented it as an intrusion into their thing. She picked up their resentment and retreated to a far part of the tunnel, where she watched them unobserved. The couple finally terminated the venture spontaneously because of their mounting anxiety and perplexity over the perceived realness of the tunnel world.

When the pair found themselves together in their tunnel, they stopped speaking or responding in the laboratory, and Tart was left out of the proceedings. With no way to make an objective report he had them independently write out a full report on coming back to the wake-state, which then became the standard procedure. On another occasion, the man used the image of a golden rope-ladder, which the woman could climb to the highest hypnotic state. When she reported herself at that high point, he suggested she find herself on a beautiful beach, and, from that position, put him into the same state. On gaining the same hypnotic height the pair found themselves together on a magnificent beach, with a champagne ocean, crystal rocks, and heavenly choirs singing overhead. The experience was both majestic and, again, fully tactile: They could taste, touch, smell, and hear as they could in everyday life. All such experiences were stable; phenomena did not shift, as such things do in dreams. (Either party could later go into self-induced hypnosis and find that beach intact, exactly as they had left it, something that can't be done with self-induced hypnotic dreams or ordinary visual-imagery.) On one occasion, they turned toward each other unexpectedly, occupied the same physical space, and their personal identities merged, each perceived his or her self as their combined personalities. This was unnerving. The man insisted on leaving the state and counting-down to normal. Tart conducted a series of these ventures; the woman eventually became quite at ease in her creative world-making while the experiments unnerved the man so severely he withdrew from the research. He could no longer grant himself consensus about what was real; the "non-ordinary reality" mutually created and shared had exactly the same tactile-sensory quality as their everyday experience.

The Poseidon Group is an organization of people who have learned to lucid dream, a kind of conscious, deliberate dreaming in which one is aware of the state and can enter into, participate in, and even direct the flow of events. The members enter into a shared group dream by agreeing to gather at a specific time in a commonly recognized meeting place (such as a school bus). Each makes the preparations that encourage lucid dreaming (it is hardly a cut and dry procedure) and, at the agreed-upon time, concentrates on the common image (schoolbus), and indeed find each other in that target-sight. They exchange quotes, rhymes, short sayings with each other, return to their ordinary state and write down the shared bit of information and the name of the person involved. Strangers from across the country take part in the events; accurate information exchange reportedly does take place, even between people far apart geographically. (Again, remote viewing comes to mind.)

These lucid dreamers meet in the implicate order, in effect, and carry out dialogue. The implicate order is non-localized and, at best, quasi-temporal. Ordinarily the implicate order translates through our R-system as our physical world. Our direct translation of the implicate order as itself is through our emotional-cognitive system and parts of the neocortex; it requires shutting down all R-system reports. Ordinarily, our only direct perception of the implicate order is through our undeveloped dream-state. Developed, however, that state offers an open-ended potential. We can enter it directly, and it translates according to our suggestions or our intent.

The scientist in his laboratory, locked into his mechanical-electronic devices that alone establish his parameters of legitimacy in a "testable, repeatable reality," insists that "none but organic perceptions" are true; anything more is delusion and an embarrassment.

59

And within his established parameters he speaks the truth since the truth is function, a process that we experience as we participate with it. As William Blake pointed out anything capable of being imagined is an image of truth, a dramatically different viewpoint than that Cartesian-Newtonian idea sweeping the world of his time. Descartes denied that man's mind played any part in creation at all, a notion that leads, Blake claimed, to the "deadness of the stone" as the only real, an apt description of our classical scientific paradigm.[13]

No matter where imagery is finally placed, the inner or outer world, or in between, image-production is singular and draws selectively on every aspect of our brain, body, and mind. In the coming chapters we will explore these processes but remember that our exploration changes things and enters into the nature of what is then discovered. "When the soul wishes to experience something," Meister Eckhart said, "she simply throws out an image, and enters into it." This throwing out is utterly simple as given us, awesomely complex when analyzed.

CHAPTER 7

Sight

Between the physical processes which are released in
the terminal organ of the nervous conductors in the
central brain and the image which thereupon appears
to the perceiving subject, there gapes a hiatus, an abyss
which no realistic conception of the world can span. It is
the transition from the world of being to the world of
the appearing image or of consciousness.

HERMANN WEYL

When French writer, philosopher, and professor, Jacques Lusseyran
was eight years old, his eyes were completely destroyed in an accident at his school.[1] When the boy's bandages were removed, his parents informed him that he had entered into a new kind of life, and
that he must keep them informed of every discovery he would make
in his new world. Children live in an open-acceptancy at that age, and
within two weeks the first great event took place, his reports were ecstatic: The light he thought he had lost came flooding back in. But,
and this was the far greater discovery, the light was within him. "All
my life," he reported, "I have seen only the light reflected off of
things. Now I can see light as it is directly." The light within, brilliant, awesome, and numinous, was a state as well as an experience,
the light without pale by comparison.

Then color came back, in a pristine, direct radiance of intense clarity unknown before; green was pure green, rather than the varied but
weaker reflections of it off objects. Soon he could perceive the general presence of objects by a combination of his overall body-sensing

and the subtle differences within the state of light itself. While he still couldn't run and play with the other children, he never again bumped into objects and hurt himself as did most newly blind.

He found, further, that at the slightest hint of anger, irritation, sadness, or self-pity, the light within him dimmed. If he persisted in a negative thought, the light went out. Only then was he truly blind, which was terrifying. He quickly learned, from sheer necessity and direct biofeedback, to rule out negative thought. My meditation teacher once said, "No thought would dare enter my head unless invited." Would we be so mentally lazy and indulgent were we to lose our sight at every negative thought?

Anna Mae Pennica was born blind from congenital cataracts. At age sixty-two one eye was operated on, the cataract removed, and a missing link in her visual system established.[2] Ordinarily this operation is not successful with congenitally blind adults, because seeing is the end-product of a long and complex construction designed to begin at birth. Such a powerful sense suddenly flooding one's perceptual system disrupts the compensations nature has made. Seldom can adults endure the sensory chaos and long re-learning involved. They unwittingly shut the new sense out through a form of hysterical blindness.[3] Anna Mae, however, saw immediately, and made medical history. The world, she reported, is "just about as I imagined it would be."

She could immediately identify colors correctly as well, but in reverse order to Lusseyran. She was astonished at the myriad shades of green, for instance, having seen just straight "pure green." More uniquely, Anna Mae could immediately read and write, a clue to the fact that her visual world was "just about as I had always imagined it would be." Every day of her childhood, her mother had guided Anna Mae's hand in "making our letters" on a blackboard. In the same way she was taught spelling and writing. And everyday her mother said, "When someday you learn to see, you will be able to read and write."

A child can entertain any and all propositions as equally valid, up to about age eleven, and by then Anna Mae was well prepared for her eventual gift of sight a half-century later. Imagination is the ability to create images not present to the sensory system. Anna Mae had never experienced an outer image but she had created a world-image within. Without that operation, this could never have been discovered. Research people now claim that congenitally blind people think in images, but without a way to attach our visual descriptions to their experience, we have no way of knowing the nature of the images involved.

Carl Jung spoke of the child living in the unconscious of the parent. The parent's implicit beliefs and expectations are decisive factors in the formation of the child's world-self-view, even when not spoken or expressed in any way. Anna Mae's mother's continual affirmation that she would see someday gave her the right conditions to fulfill that possibility. That expectation gave the formative structure around which sensory input could be organized, provided by her mother's guidance in making those letters, spelling words, and naming objects. Lusseyran's parents gave him a creative cuing that enabled him to see his "light within," which more than compensated for his physical blindness.

Two centuries ago, William Blake claimed that he did not see with his eyes but looked through them as a pane of glass; we should learn to see creatively, he said, using active rather than passive vision. About thirty years ago the scientific community found that our eyes cannot convey light to our brain. The retina does not "collect light waves" and send them to visual receptors in our brain. Vision is a construction of the brain that we see with the help of our eyes when it refers to the outer world.

Light is a measurable wavelength, with visible light but a minor segment of the spectrum available. This light can't be transferred from retina to brain, so where does the light we actually see come from?

A physicist friend pointed out that "We don't see light, we perceive something we know as vision. Light as waves or corpuscles is not something our brain can handle directly." I found this revealing on the one hand and at odds with the concept of "visible light" on the other. Is light as wave or corpuscle just "laboratory light"? I am reminded of physicist Menas Kafatos's definition of wave-function as only a metaphoric device, "a mathematical . . . [idealization] . . . which expresses the relationship between the quantum system, which is inaccessible to an observer, and the measuring device, which conforms to classical physics."[4] Perhaps light as corpuscle or wave is our "mathematical idealization." When light *is* analyzed in the laboratory, the only result is the scientist's visual "reading" of the laboratory devices, his visual experience of those particular manipulations he has made in conformity with a particular idea he wants to test or prove.

Research people do what they can to explain vision, coming up with diagrams of retinal cells, cones, rods, bipolar cells, ganglions, optic nerves, lateral geniculate bodies, primary visual cortexes, and "higher cortical regions" to show how, within that rich body of complex names, visual information is transferred, through synapses, chemical neurotransmitters, ion exchanges, and so on. But within that rich body of information about information and its transference we find nothing about light, vision, or seeing. Visual action is happening—information is conveyed across the synapse by ion exchange and along the axon by neurotransmitter and so on—but in all that information involving the retina-brain dynamic there is no explanation of vision, nor the experience of seeing.

David Hubel's Nobel Prize–winning work on vision has been done on monkeys and cats who have been anesthetized and had their skulls removed, micro-electrodes placed in various neural cells, and their eyes taped open so that electronic devices can flash lights on them in various shapes and forms.[5] The electrode responses from those neural cells with an electrode in them are then recorded and interpreted. Over the years, the various parts of monkey brains that respond to various bits and pieces of these laboratory flashes have been painstakingly mapped out. Although there is some variation, certain large-scale regularities are found concerning the "edges" where contrasts between light and dark elicit a neural response according to the electrode in that neuron. The electrode's response is recorded and read by the research people, who "see" what the recordings mean. The recording's "meaning" accords with the nature of the experiment itself; the researcher's "seeing" is their interpretation and understanding. The only light observed is in the eye of the beholder, not the creature beheld. The monkeys or cats are not conscious—there is no light in their life at that time (and probably never again).

David Hubel finds that one visual field may process one particular part of a line or an arc; other neural fields will process the minute variations of that line or arc in its direction, or each fractional degree of that arc. The related fields may be in remotely different areas of the brain, but these somehow connect to, for instance, complete a circle. Still other fields will process information concerning the contrast between areas of light and no light; a light spot against a black background; a black spot on a white background; and the sorts of things applicable to or available to laboratory research with its necessarily linear processing.

Visual objects are apparently built up from the infinite combinations possible to these visual fields. All this activity congregates at a central nexus called the lateral geniculate nucleus (LGN), the crossover network connecting our right and left visual fields. People used to think all visual information came from the eyes and congregated at this LGN, but Maturana and Varela found that 80 percent of the information exchange at the LGN comes from the many parts of the brain known to be involved in vision, while only 20 percent comes from the eyes. And, as they make clear, the brain is sending the information congregating at the LGN on to the eye and receiving feedback from the eye in turn (as found in all the dynamics of brain function).[6]

David Hubel finds that different parts of the brain are involved in detecting the movement of images and the edges of forms and shapes. (Recall Oliver Sacks's scotoma experience described on p. 53.) Color is handled by more recent evolutionary areas. Maturana and Varela point out that we will "see" an orange as orange-colored even in a wave-spectrum of light that doesn't contain or allow orange color— according to the rules of optics and "laboratory light."[7] A recent study shows that one area of the brain recognizes faces while a different area recognizes the expression of faces, such as happy, sad, angry, and so on;[8] another area connects names with faces.

So color, form, and movement are each processed by different brain structures, and where the "picture" actually forms or is perceived is unknown. Some lower creatures respond to only one color, as in the case of bumblebees and the color purple. The bumblebee, however, probably doesn't "see" purple but responds to that wave-length of light because its neural system is set to that frequency, which flows with honey. And his progeny prosper. That color is the wave-length of light or general frequency certain clover and pollen-bearing flowers reflect, but the frequency that gives rise to that clover as a living form also contains that frequency *for* color to any neural system that can translate it.

The parameters of the bumblebee's universe may be determined by the wave-frequency of purple, not time-space dimensions as in ours. Vision appears to be quite economical in lower creatures, since vision doesn't take place in the eye, but in the eye's dynamic with the brain behind it. While some of these brains seem scant to us, each is adequate for that creature's needs within nature's overall balance. We marvel over the long-range vision of an eagle, who can spot a mouse from enormous distances, but that eagle might not register unmouse things in the same way. Distance in this selective capacity, whether five miles or five inches, is relative to those creature's needs, and nature provides a selective neural structure to meet those needs. (Crows, ethologists claim, can tell whether or not a man has a gun from quite a distance.)

Recently a gentleman was brought to a hospital where he died within twenty-four hours. In that time he displayed an uncanny eagle eye. He could make out the tiniest of objects at a great distance, the proverbial flea on a dog a block away. An autopsy showed severe lesions in a part of the brain directly related to vision.[9] His eyes still saw according to what the brain was doing, and the brain did as his eyes saw, but the logic of operations was faulty. His localizing had gone awry, and become selective like an eagle's.

Nature perfected the eye quite early in her game. Our eyes are remarkably similar to rabbits', cats', and monkeys',[10] yet research indicates that each species sees both shared and different segments of whatever is available, since there are serious differences in their brain's evolutionary capacity. The bumblebee is hard wired to translate a specific frequency and hone in on it. That specific frequency is part of a larger field of frequencies from which *we* can translate an environment in full color and smell including bumblebee and flower. The implicate field is the same, but we have different neural fields with which to translate, leading to different selectivities and different realities.

Have you ever had a brilliant, technicolor dream or a hypnagogic experience, when, just as you are drifting off to sleep (or waking slowly) vivid forms or images flash before you, generally reflecting some significant adventure of the day? Where do the bright colors and brilliant light come from? Try this experiment. If you wear glasses, take them off; if you wear contacts, take them out. Press the heels of your palms hard as you dare against your closed eyelids, even to the point of discomfort. Try not to move your eye muscles and simply wait and watch. The display is about the same in all of us, although it pales in comparison with real visions. The flashes of light, the geometric patterns and shapes, the sprinkling of blue dots unfold in regular sequences. Nerves, cones, and rods are involved, but are not the source, just as a television set is involved in our reception of the play being performed, but is not the source of that play (nor is the electricity running the set, or the wave-fields carrying the information from station to set).

The other morning in my meditation I found myself in a breathtaking landscape with a coppery sky and a long range of magnificent hills. The hills had gullies and vegetation, all of which cast shadows. I was fascinated that the light was from a single source, and, though that source was undetectable, the shadowing from every object, including the shady side of a far hill, was in perfect perspective to it. In another meditation I thought morning light had broken (though dawn was a good hour away) and that I was looking through the window at an intricate play of colorless, crystalline, three-dimensional geometric forms, changing in kaleidoscopic fashion. None of this was my doing; I was witnessing what my creative power was creating for me. Such visions are seldom of actual places or things.

Hallucination as a term tells us nothing. The eye sees what the brain does, but the brain must, also, do as the eye sees, the "structural coupling" found in all life. Since all systems are built on dynamics, the brain must respond to its own output as fed back to it from the eye. Recall again that 80 percent of the information fed into the LGN comes from the myriad parts of the brain involved in vision, and the 20 percent coming from the eye is in response to information sent to the eye from that very LGN. Such feedback completes the circuitry, concretizes, stabilizes, verifies, and amplifies the brain's self-organizing functions, precisely as with sound, as we shall see in the next chapter.

Research people claim that images are a primary part of thought. We think through imagery. Even congenitally blind people think in images. Congenitally blind teenagers were recently found to have more accurate internal imaging than seeing teenagers, as well as a more creative and constructive imagination.[11] The eye sees in response to what the brain is doing and the brain responds to what the eyes are seeing only if the eyes are working. The brains of our blind teenagers are doing their part but a vital link in the dynamic is missing. Richard Restak speaks of "bypassing the eye" to pick up the visual process "further upstream," that is, skipping the lower visual structures and directly intercepting the more advanced ones.[12] Surely the blind person fills in with other sensory-cues, as Restak suggests, and out of it comes an internal "seeing" and understanding.

Research people speak of the reference maps on which the brain draws in its constructions. From studies in optical illusions they conclude that the brain is, in effect, continually guessing and filling in gaps. Senses cross-index within us to amplify and verify our imagery. As Restak points out, the very young child responds tactilely to an object it is grasping for even before contact with that object is observable.[13] Just as the LGN is sending both information to the eye and receiving it from the eye's complementary feedback loop, the brain "refers to its maps" in response to the nature of what it is translating and sends this information on to its tactile senses in order to receive from them the necessary feedback to complete the circuitry and concretize the event.

Image making is a singular function, involving almost all of our brain-mind. If the image is abstract and non-local, our neocortex will be involved. If it is dynamic, moving, nonrational, and emotional, our limbic brain is primarily involved. If it is an outer image shared with others, stable and available to our senses, the R-system, the eyes, and all the sensory maps to which the brain refers will be involved. The image-making function is the same for inner and outer images, but the eyes are involved only in outer imagery (and movement in dreaming).

The implicate visual fields contain everything, but we draw on them selectively, according to our capacity, upbringing, need, and intent, an orderly selectiveness subject to disruption, as in the man who displayed an eagle eye shortly before dying.[14] Recall that our kitten raised in an artificial world of only vertical stripes can't perceive horizontal forms and will stumble into them. Our world is a construction of knowledge and each act of knowledge brings forth a world.

Knowledge and the object of knowledge are one and the same. "And in this new world (of darkness) you are entering, you must tell us everything you discover." And Jacques discovered the light within, by which all outer seeing takes place. "And someday, when you learn to see, you will be able to read and write." And fifty years later Anna Mae saw, and could immediately read and write. Consider the scope of the self-fulfilling prophecies given children, during those infinitely open years when the constructions of knowledge bringing forth a world are at their peak: What were the prophecies made for you? I know some made for me, and I shudder. And I recognize many I unwittingly made for my own children, and I weep.

CHAPTER 8

Sound

Back in the early 1970s a chap I know was tricked into taking one of those popular mind-altering drugs while at a party. He had a terrifying time, later reporting that he experienced each cell of his body as a separate three-dimensional geometric form radiating brilliant light and sound, each cell's frequency differing from all others, creating a horrendous cacophony that lasted for hours. The interesting thing here is that his friends claim to have heard remarkable sounds when they came within a foot or so of him. Recall that geometric patterns give rise to imagery; sound waves acting on various substances will create geometric patterns, changing according to the frequencies.

As we progress in this chapter, remember that those friends shared the drug victim's sounds only when within about a foot of him, but perceived nothing of his visual experiences. As with our eyes, our ears hear in response to what the brain is doing and vice-versa, though sound is also spatial. Our drug victim sensed the sound and sight as a paired sensation and, indeed, every neural field primarily involved in hearing has a secondary field involved in vision and vice-versa. When we dream our eyes move. We used to think this was to follow the movement of the dream images but every movement of our eye muscles shifts the auditory fields of our brain.[1] Shifting the auditory fields shifts our visual imagery. Spatial location and movement of images are part of the sight-sound dynamic within us. Our auditory function is directly involved in the construction of our three-dimensional world-space, the three dimensional objects filling that space, and movement of those objects in the resulting space. (Recall Oliver Sacks' recovery from scotoma in which objects were flat, dimensionless, and moved in a series of stills throughout his left visual field.)

Body balance and muscular coordination involve the vestibular rotation functions of the inner ear, a balancing act that places us at the center of our lived sound-space. French physician Alfred Tomatis found the labyrinthine nucleus of the inner ear's cochlea system a principle congregating point for all our senses.[2] Every neural process passes through or relates to this inner-ear complex. The ear is neurologically involved with the optic nerve (the second cranial nerve), the oculomotor (third cranial nerve), and the various cranial nerves involved in movement. All channel through the vestibular labyrinth of the cochlea, deep in the inner ear. Eye, head, and neck mobility have traditionally been associated with the optic nerve, but Tomatis found these functional structures "under the control of the acoustic nerve . . . a major mechanism of reception and integration of perception."[3]

The first embryonic cells are sound-sensitive, and by four-and-a-half months in the womb the auditory system is virtually complete. The temporal lobe, a major cortical area for sound activity, has myelinated by birth. The cochlea nerve plays a major role in sound and myelinates early in utero. Henry Truby and an international team in Stockholm found that "babies in the womb were not only hearing, but apparently learning speech and 'practicing' the fine neuro-muscular movements of the vocal tract that are used in crying and vocalizing after birth."[4] The separation cry a newborn makes if parted from its mother is the most ancient and primary sound made by all mammals, and some people think it may have played a role in speech development.

The mother's heartbeat is a major stimulus in embryonic and fetal development—both the sound and the steady movement it produces. In 1947, Lester Sontag found that sound affects the fetal infant's heartbeat and initiates body movements in the infant.[5] Recall that from the seventh month in utero, precise body movements synchronize with the phonemes of the mother's speech. By twenty-eight weeks after

71

birth the infant's response to sound is stabilized. "Hearing," as David Chamberlain explains, "has a very high priority."[6]

Alfred Tomatis found the entire skin area of the body involved in hearing; every cell registers sound waves, sending its reports on to higher centers for processing.[7] Experiments in blindfolded sensing of colors suggests that the brain can interpret a hybrid form of seeing through these vibratory skin reports.

Our ears are the final focal point for hearing as our eyes are for seeing. We don't hear through our ears, but with their help. All sound impacts us and can nourish or debilitate. Lightning striking a telephone line can kill people through "auditory shock" though neither lightning nor an audible sound is transmitted. Sound is frequency and the brain functions as frequencies—frequencies can either clash or interact. I recently tried a newly invented device that shines a tiny strobe light into each eye while a synchronized auditory beat is played to each ear through earphones. Immediately my visual field exploded into a riot of colors and geometric shapes, a panorama brought about through the combined activation of different auditory fields by the changing sonic beeps and visual variations from the strobe light.

Richard Restak reports that in cats the cells in the superior colliculus, a primary visual receptor, respond to auditory stimulation as well as visual. Tones, sweeps of sound, and even noise will activate these cells. Eighty percent of the cells in the deep layers of the superior colliculus that "maximally respond to light" respond to sound and touch. Stimulation of the inferior colliculus, which is a waystation of the auditory path, brings about movement of the eyes and parts of the external ear.[8]

Roderick Power, at the School of Behavioral Sciences in New South Wales, has found that sight and sound are the major senses. The tactile senses, taste, touch, and smell, are secondary and may depend on clues furnished by those major senses. What we smell and feel can be influenced by what we see more than the other way around.[9] In infants, visual information regarding size correlates to touch and feeling before there is any observable physical contact.[10] The visual stimulus activates the sensory reference maps, causing the brain to guess and fill in gaps. The final tactile contact completes the visual circuitry, concretizes it, and feeds that concretized perception back into the sensory process, stimulating the ongoing perceptions. All functions are dynamics.

Dyslexia offers clues to the inner-ear's relationship with vision. Many dyslexics don't see the letters of words lying flat on the page but floating freely in space above it. Having no stable placement on a fixed background, letters are as likely to rearrange, reverse, or transpose as not. English osteopathic physicians noticed that dyslexics reported temporary improvement on taking a motion sickness remedy (a drug that effects the inner ear). So they twirled, tossed, and tumbled the afflicted individuals in various ways to get the vestibular structures and inner ear parts free and fluid. Because there is a direct connection between the temporo-mandibular joint and the vestibular rotation process of the inner ear—which is involved in our sense of body balance and spatial orientation—osteopaths developed a technique called "cranial osteopathy," manipulating the skull plates and mandibular joints of the jaw until these are flexible. Through a combination of such techniques they make the inner ear functional and so are able to cure dyslexics, since the inner ear is involved in spatial organization and the placement of objects in that space.

Alfred Tomatis found that the tiny stapedius muscle deep in the inner ear is always vibrating. This structure regulates sound perception, he surmises, by controlling the stapes (the innermost bone of the ear) and high frequency audition.[11] The neurologist Oliver Sacks notes that all muscles, including those of the extremities, are in a constant state of low vibratory motion—too fine to be easily detected. Our living system is a vibratory set of frequencies, from the sub-atomic to the gross frequencies such as muscular tonus.

In laboratories in Israel, France, and England, scientists have inserted tiny microphones deep into the inner ears of various people and found in each the same unvarying frequency of sound: a fundamental hum-like tone and a series of overtones ranging between two and three octaves above middle C on a piano.[12] If you get very quiet and pay attention, you will hear this as a whistle-like "ringing of the ears" common to all of us. This steady frequency is not a sound picked up by the brain but one broadcast by it, produced somehow in that inner cochlea region.[13] Tinnitus is an ailment in which this broadcast gets out of balance, its "volume turned up" so high it drowns out the sounds we ordinarily hear. Severe tinnitus can be heard by other people if they stand within a foot or so of the victim. (Recall that people could hear sounds from within a foot of the drug victim described at the beginning of this chapter.) This foot extending away from us is the range of our brain's broadcast and constitutes a subtle sphere that is critically important in early infancy (a point to which we shall return in the next section).

Other frequencies coming from those various cranial nerves feed through the cochlea area where the steady frequency is broadcast and interact in typical wave fashion with this steady frequency. Interference patterns result that create frequency modulations in the steady state. Three wave forms are then present: the steady frequency, a variable wave, and the resultant modulations. With three wave forms, according to basic physics, you can create a three-dimensional holographic effect of height, breadth, and depth. As you recall, Tomatis called the acoustic nerve the "major mechanism of reception and integration of perception." Through this intricate dynamic within the inner ear and our sensory reception, our brain apparently creates our spatial experience with ourselves in the center.

Space is a "volume of sound"; a great cave, empty hall, or mountaintop is its own distinctive sound. Eastern psychology speaks of the silence found within all sounds, and, of course, pure vacuum is absolute silence. Close your eyes for a minute and tune into the sound within your own head. (Outer sounds don't have to interfere, but a quiet place helps.) Note that you are centered in a space that resonates out from you. Mentally feel out the parameters of your body or the space within your skull. If your mind is quiet, your body relaxed and you are focussed only on your inner sound-space, no body boundary exists. Your sound-space is your body-space and within this space everything you will ever experience takes place.

You will hear in your space the clear, high ringing of your "steady-state" broadcast. The more attention you pay it, the greater its clarity (not volume). Sounds heard as out there (or perhaps gut-rumblings within) are variables interacting with and adding to the modulations going on in that steady-state frequency. Ordinary sounds that catch our attention are the end result of modulations "broadcast out," received by our senses, and processed as our perception. What is

74

perceived is the modulation itself. The "outer" heard sound is our physical reception of our own broadcast.

A primary "causal" frequency or energy gives rise to both this steady-frequency sound within us and the variable frequencies modulating it.[14] These varying frequencies are furnished by the myriad neural fields translating the potential variables. Those potential variables are, again, held within the primary frequency. The variables being translated furnish instant by instant "information" concerning the current sensory productions. These translations feed into the labyrinth of the inner ear as the variables creating modulations in the steady frequency produced there. These modulations broadcast out about a foot and arc back into our body's physical receptors. Sent from all parts of the body to the R-system, coordinated and sent on as sensory reports acted on by the whole brain, the broadcast received becomes part of the ongoing broadcast. Thus we have the ongoing dynamic from the brain's myriad looped feedback systems that give rise to our perceptual world.

Brain operations funnel through the cochlea to give us our perception of a spatial world. A car horn honking, for instance, is a variable wave, translated by its appropriate neural field and sent on to the inner ear. There it enters into the spatial information the steady-state broadcast furnishes and participates in the modulations taking place, which gives that horn its location in space. Thus the horn variable both enters into the creation of its space and determines its place within that resulting space.

Location is relationship; to locate something is to relate it to other things. Where the sound is placed in our space is in relation to ourself and other sounds. The sound of rain on the roof, or an airplane approaching and receding as I sit here writing, comes from waves locating by interrelating with other waves with me as the center. Our limbic brain resonates with waves just as the R-system does with particles. With the help of the neocortex our limbic system can translate waves directly, before their "display as particles" is picked up by the R-system. The implicate-explicate energy dynamic is the same as the R-system and limbic-system dynamic and is the reason they are so closely knit. The limbic system picks up the R-system's report and feeds it back into the fields from which the information arises, as well as to the rest of the neocortex. The totality of the response is sent to the cochlea where the steady-state broadcast is modulated in a continuing dynamic loop. The report from our body gives tangibility to our felt-space just as the feedback from the eye concretizes an otherwise incomplete visual system.

Tomatis finds that hearing and touch are closely related; bass sounds are closer to touch than treble ones.[15] We interpret the primary tactile vibration being broadcast as touch through one sense and/or as sound through another. Perhaps touch-starved children turn to extremes of loud rock music not so much for their listening pleasure as for the pleasure of physical impact-stimulus.

In a reptile's limited experience, physical vibrations, which we can interpret as sound or touch, play a major role. A snake can be charmed by vibration as I can by sound. A snake sticks out its tongue to help pick up vibrations because its tongue is far more sensitive to vibrations than its scaly skin. The snake has a wider sensory-spatial world than an amoeba, but less than a mammal, since the mammal has a limbic brain that can translate directly from the relational wave-fields. The color of a flower is a vibratory experience to bumblebee and vibrations are the tactile world of snake, while our limbic brain gives limitless dimensions to our sound-space.

By my participation in my world I place myself in the world that forms around my point of placement. This sounds circular, and it is: the structural-coupling of mind and its environment. We used to think that we heard the direction from which sound came by the slight difference between the reception of our two ears. We hear stereophonically and spatially however, not just because we have two ears but because of the effect created by this threefold frequency system consisting of the steady-state broadcast, it's variable, and it's modulation.

Hugo Zuccarelli, an Italian physiologist in London, made a rough electronic equivalent of our inner broadcast, overlaid ordinary sounds and music on this synthetic steady state, and produced a threefold modulation he called "holophonic sound."[16] This intriguing substitute must be heard through earphones, the sound directly transmitted into the ears. (Exterior stereo speakers introduce general waves and feedback loops.) To get the fullest effect of holophonic sound, one should hear it, particularly the first time, in the dark, to eliminate competition and "corrections" from the other senses.

Briefly, when holophonic sound is broadcast from earphones directly into the ear, it is not heard "in the head" as with stereophonic earphones, nor is it perceived as coming from the earphones. We hear the sound "out-there" in the very direction, and at the same distance away from us, that the original recorded sound was from the microphone picking it up. If the sound source moved around the microphone at a distance of three feet, we hear the sound moving around us three feet away. Holophonic sound furnishes the brain with a synthetic substitute for its own spatial organization and interjects into the brain's dynamic of spatial production a variable that replicates the completed process; in effect, it bypasses the modulations of the steady-state broadcast and its variable by direct input of not just the modulation itself, but the sensory system's reception of that broadcast. Holophonic sound intervenes in the final link in the feedback loop of the sound dynamic that gives us our spatial world. Thus the brain interprets the sound not from its actual source, the earphones, but as though it were from the proper distance the original sound was from the microphone recording it. These manipulated frequencies fool the auditory system as an optical illusion fools the visual system.

Even though I had read on the subject and knew something of what to expect, my initial holophonic experience, listening in the dark, was surprising. The sound of a powerful automobile roaring straight at the microphone, until it was indeed directly atop it, prompted my ancient survival instincts to get out of the way. One of the episodes recorded on this demonstration tape was of a woman walking around the microphone whispering sweet nothings into it.[17] Most people (men?) on hearing this, particularly in a dark room, smell perfume, feel the warmth of that body speaking, and many even feel her breath wafting gently. A friend in New York City was given the tape with the suggestion he listen to it in the dark. He locked his doors, turned off his lights, and started the tape, only to leap to his feet, certain some woman had broken into his apartment and was walking around him whispering in his ear.

The brain fills in its long-range cues from sight and/or sound, according to close-range sensory reference maps. In a darkened room the holophonic recording of a match being struck elicits a smell of sulfur and a flare of light to many listeners. Suffice to say that the world we know is given its dimension and location through the threefold effect of our brain's own interpretations of our steady state broadcast, the variables introduced, and the third effect of the two in combination. This is the means by which all spatial effects we experience are produced—our visual-tactile objects, the three-dimensional shape of those objects, and their movements and interactions within our spatial world. All this, in turn, involves "peaks of activity among populations of neurons" and the vital feedback from the brain's sensory extensions of body.

The dolphin brain is primarily auditory; dolphins communicate through a complex of sounds sent back and forth. Almost surely their communication is not "language" but the totality of an experience, the multi-level sounds sent, received, and perceived in the same fashion originally perceived by the communicating creature. What is communicated is a direct replication of perception as itself. We communicate through words, which, in turn, stimulate an inner imaginary, visual approximation of the intended message. I believe the dolphin doesn't tell *about* an event but gives the experience of the event itself as itself.

Researchers at Cornell University report that homing pigeons can detect sounds with frequencies of less than one cycle per second, infrasound too low for our ears, waves believed to travel great distances without significant reduction in their strength. William Keeton proposes that "birds flying over Ithaca, New York, may be able to hear ocean breakers crashing on New England shores hundreds of miles away."[18]

All this is described in safely external terms but offers a clear example of how nature programs neural systems to draw from the implicate fields in as wide a variety of ways as is needed by the creature involved. Whether hundreds of miles or hundredths of a centimeter is relative within the frequency-field on which brains draw. The non-localized can localize in an infinite variety of spaces—according to the nature of the brain translating the potential into actuality.

Congenitally blind two-year-olds can move away from their mothers and encounter an object, go back to their mothers, go out in a completely different direction to encounter another object, return to their mothers, and then out in a third direction for an object encounter and return. The toddlers can then, with unerring accuracy and without hesitation, go straight from object to object without going back to the reference point of the mother. Blind-folded three-year-olds can do the same.[19] Lacking visual cuing, the spatial organization is confirmed and verified by the sensory-motor act as a whole. Sensory-motor action can operate not so much independently of cuing as out of its own cues.

These two chapters have given a rough sketch of the self-organizing nature of our brain, showing our sensory web to be our universe with ourselves at its center. Recognizing that this is true for each of our fellow travelers we can appreciate Maturana and Varela's urging us to guard against the "temptation of certainty" in regard to other people's perceptions. Another person's "certainty," no matter how objectionable to us, is the sum of their "structural-coupling," as their system constructs its worldview. We are urged to recognize that the world everyone sees is not *the* world, "but a world which we bring forth with others"; a world that will be different "only if we live differently."[20]

CHAPTER 9

States of Mind: Body to Match

Esoteric traditions refer to three states of consciousness—physical, subtle, and causal—and three "bodies" or ways for perceiving or being in those states.[1] These match our triune structure of the brain with its three states of consciousness—wake, dream, and sleep; David Bohm's explicate, implicate, and supra-implicate orders of energy; and other trinitarian metaphors. Universal causal fields, drawn on by all forms, translate through our highest brain; the relational fields are expressed through our subtle limbic system; and the localized experience of our body-world through our R-system. We live in that R-system as overlaid by our two higher brains, identify with it, and rightly find it rich and fascinating. We have available, however, higher evolutionary states connected with our limbic and neo-cortical structures as their own "domains," parallel processes offering perceptual experiences in their own right. The subtle realm, for instance, is complementary to our physical world; we are very much "in" it at all times, though unaware of its nature, just as, involved in a "particle world" we are unaware of the wave-field complements of it.

Rudolph Steiner believed our species-wide evolution was to move from physical into "etheric" or subtle realms.[2] Our species may have tried time and again to do this, as we find in the Australian Aborigine and Kalahari !Kung. Our personal evolution need not stop at these way-stations however, fascinating as they are. Evolution's end for us as individuals lies far beyond the "etheric."

Events occur continually that can be fully explained only by recognizing the nature of our subtle system and its complementarity with the physical. For instance, hard-core drug addicts treated with methadone have given us striking insights into the interaction of subtle and causal systems. Methadone is an "analog" of morphine, the endorphin that inhibits the neural transmission of pain and trauma. As a substitute of other opiates, methadone supposedly relieves the patient of withdrawal symptoms. The studies by Dr. Richard Lippin and his medical group regarding this drug's effectiveness reveal side-effects far more controversial than the drug.[3]

Briefly, one patient on high doses of methadone had a negative skin test for TB. A year later, Lippin withdrew him from methadone, and immediately the patient developed a strong positive skin reaction at the site of the original TB test. Another patient on methadone suffered a fairly severe leg injury but felt no pain and suffered no apparent ill effects. Several months later the doctor withdrew the methadone treatments, at which point a large bruise appeared at the site of the injury, and the patient underwent severe pain. Where, Lippin asked, was the positive TB skin reaction, with its rash and swelling, all those months in the one patient; where was the pain, the bruise, the physical trauma in the other patient?

The reverse of this is phantom limb pain, a phenomenon that accompanies most amputations. Here an injury is still felt directly "in the limb" long after the limb is gone.[4] A further reversal is a variation of "scotoma" reported by Oliver Sacks, which occurs when an injured limb is plaster-casted and immobilized for long periods.[5] The nerves of the limb atrophy, and, as a result, the patients lose connection with that limb, can't recognize it as part of their body, can't send it any signals and receive none from it. The limb is for all purposes dead to that person though alive on some cellular level. Sacks regained awareness of and some control over his long "lost" leg in a period of traumatic confusion, which must be read to be appreciated. When his subtle system began to again process reports from that part of its physical complement, his whole orientation was thrown awry. His leg would feel twelve feet away, or appear to him to be two inches long and then a gigantic ten feet.[6]

All events arise from a mirroring between subtle-potential and physical-actuality, and the mirroring can be distorted or broken. In phantom limb pain, for instance, the subtle "wave-form" body is left stuck with its last reports of pain from its corresponding "particle-form" limb; the emotional report remains in its wave-form sensory receptors with nowhere to go. Neural fields, "sensory maps," and other organic systems continue to report since neural fields are as much subtle as physical.

Hypnotists touch a hypnotized subject with a stick, tell them it's a hot poker and they experience a burn and raise a blister. Hypnotic suggestion depends on "concrete" language formed in childhood, where the word for a thing and the thing-as-itself are a single neural pattern. This language is retained by the right hemisphere of the brain, which, recall, has closer connections with the limbic system than the left, and can thus act on those limbic–R-system interactions giving rise to our physical experience. The left hemisphere, with its abstract logic and semantic language can, through the right hemisphere's direct connection with the limbic–R-systems, act on the named things in our primary world structuring and change the dynamics between cause and effect bringing about our physical experience. In post-hypnotic suggestion the hypnotist tells the subject they will experience the burn an hour later and they do. Following Lippin's line of questioning, we can ask, where was the blister during that hour? The dynamic between our time-bound physical and non-temporal subtle-system can be delayed or broken, the effect remaining in its non-temporal state.

Recall Charles Tart's experiments in mutual hypnosis where a person suspends ordinary R-system reports and allows someone else's verbal suggestions to substitute for them. Suggestions given concretize in the subject's perception in a reverse order of daily life. The higher cortical system acts on the two "body-world" systems, creating a reality from "higher upstream." Norms of a shared, common-sense wake-state world can be suspended as well. Those neural fields that are the intermediary between non-localized potential and our localized experience can intervene in the dynamics of reality that brain-body bring about.

Just as imagination is the ability to create images not present to the sensory system, phenomena not "present to the senses" can be created by our self-organizing structure, particularly private experiences such as in Tart's experiments or general hypnosis. When the creation is only within our own self-system, no universal fields have to be involved. My meditation experiences are often extraordinary but simple creative acts spontaneously taking place with me as witness. To be shared with others, the dynamic must extend into the causal level shared with all. Anything can be experienced personally since all the potential fields to draw on are always "there," and we can perceive far more than our physical senses offer.

Once my meditation teacher told me to spend half my time in morning meditation sitting in the conventional cross-legged position, the other half lying flat on my back. The next morning, I dutifully sat as usual and then stretched out flat. Without warning or any of the usual transitions into an altered state, I felt myself rise out of my physical body and for a long period simply "lay" some six inches above it, my emotions, self-awareness, and senses intact so far as I could tell. I could hear my physical body breathing and feel my body heat coming up from beneath me; I was weightless, couldn't move about, had no blissful experiences, found the state uneventful, and wondered why I didn't travel to other realms as my friend Robert Monroe did. This happened for five straight mornings, however, and I finally got the message my teacher had intended for me: I knew that my self-sense was not limited to this body, and my subtle body was a very real experience, independent of context. My teacher later explained that one couldn't move into other realms in that subtle body until it was integrated into the "causal body." Only the causal system, he said, has the power to move our awareness beyond the physical.

The phrase *out of the body*, I realized, is a misnomer; we but shift between the states inherent within our three structures of brain. Occasionally medical patients under total anesthesia watch their own operation from nearby and later give a full report of the proceedings. To stand "outside the body" and witness it, we detach our awareness from our ordinary subtle-physical dynamic, and observe that physical system from our higher subtle-causal dynamic. Recall that image making is a singular action placed according to the state involved. We are not restricted in our loci for viewing, even of ourselves.

Just as we draw on fields of intelligence common to us all, our senses draw on common sensory fields. My meditation teacher once spoke of each of our senses as "its own universe." Each sense both draws on its own "universe" or category and feeds each experience back into that respective field in the usual dynamic. Recall that Jacques Lusseyran, whose eyes had been destroyed, first experienced light simply as light itself. Then all the colors came back, each in its own singular and pure form. The basis of our consensual world lies in a commonly shared visual field, olfactory field, tactile field, taste field, and so on, just as our mental world draws on shared fields of intelligence. We all draw on the same field of light Lusseyran experienced, but we experience it as its "pale reflections off objects."

Again, no distinction can be made between a neural field and that universal potential the field is resonant with, though potential fields are outside the physical time-space they bring about. In the same way such "mental fields" as mathematics, music, language, and so on, are beyond as well as in the time-space they create. Thus, assemble a large number of minds to interpret an aggregate of vibratory fields, and all such minds share the same reality—more or less. And all potential fields reflect their usage just as the particles of energy in tests of Bell's Theorem influence their own fields of genesis. Mathematics, as a field of intelligence, is probably stronger today than in Egyptian times thanks to a pageantry of mathematical genius in the last few centuries; the music field is stronger as a result of our six centuries of European composed music and its genius composers. Each successful display of a field increases that field's potential for display and makes access to the field more available. As Jesus said, "To him who has [power,] more will be given" (Mk. 4:25, RSV).

Each sensory field is made up of compatible variables that create sub-fields, as we find in fields of intelligence or language. White light contains all the colors; each color is an independent state in its own right and has a potential for infinite variations. Consider our sense of motion, for instance. Nothing exists except through motion, of course, but motion as a felt experience is its own category within the general sensory field. We connect motion with specific physical events, but a moment's reflection shows motion to be its own field effect as well. People occasionally have "inner ear trouble" that brings loss of balance and orientation. They are often terrified as they sense themselves falling without direction. Minor problems in our inner ear can be major traumas since our "coupling" with the environment and our placement in it takes place there.

Following a long automobile or train trip we may continue to feel the movement for some time after. Recall David Hubel's work: Movement of images requires a different operation in our heads than just imagery itself. Observe a waterfall for a few minutes, then glance off to the side of the falls, and objects seem to move in the opposite direction from the water flow, an optical illusion of movement. When I first experienced Robert Monroe's "hemi-sync" system in 1976 I found myself doing "barrel rolls in space" while I knew my body was safely ensconced on its pad. The movement felt in such cases is identical to ordinary movement. We say it is our "subtle body" sensing movement, but that is the same sensing system operating within our physical body all the time. That subtle-physical dynamic is the dynamic between "implicate and explicate," and the subtle body is the one that continues to suffer in phantom limb pain. Since the implicate is not in time-space, the subtle "sensing body" may sustain the pain of a limb even after that limb is removed.

Subtle movements often occur in lucid dreaming and meditation experiences. Fear of falling often blocks people from "flying" in lucid dreams, according to Jayne Gackenbach and Jane Bosveld, who claim that most lucid dreamers must develop a new sense of balance and overcome vertigo in that dream state in order to "learn to fly."[7] In meditation I occasionally hear two or three distinct roars followed by a feeling of falling, fast, most often into "other domains," a purposeful, straightforward maneuver that carries me through landscape after landscape, often brilliant, sometimes dark and obscure. If I try to stop the movement and investigate a particular scene, I lose the state.

Years before I began meditating I went into anaphylactic shock one day from a massive injection of penicillin, to which I was seriously allergic, and all my vital functions quit. I dimly remember falling to the floor but clearly remember falling through endless spaces thereafter. Particularly vivid was falling through a sound-realm I took to be the buzzing of billions of bees, a buzzing so enormous I thought they were brass-bees, for surely only metallic ones could make such noise. Years later I read in yogic literature of just

85

such a sound realm described as the buzzing of myriad bees, encountered in the after-death state.

All sensations of falling seem the same, whether in meditation, ordinary physical-world tumbles (as in my parachute training for the Army Air Corps nearly a half-century ago), or death. In the same way, every sense can be traced back to its field. Yogic literature refers to the *Nada*—the primal sound from which all creation springs, often heard in meditation. I have experienced my own version of this, the epitome of massive orchestras, choruses, pianos, filling my universe with oceans of glorious sound. The phenomenon is tactile with every nuance equally light and sound, my body both sounding device and receiver; I am the sound, composer, performer, and audience.

Biologist Rupert Sheldrake describes "morpho-genetic" fields that shape physical form, fields lying across time-space.[8] Similar is the ancient Vedic theory of samskara, formative fields inherited from our predecessors and created continually by our present actions.[9] Our personal ego reflects our major samskara and is where our various minor ones are toted about. Every action or even thought sets up feedback between our action and the fields from which we draw our experience. Samskaras are not localized but give rise to localization; they are residues of previous actions that can act on our present situation rather as extended "phantom limb pains." Any chance stimuli can activate samskaras and they unfold as part of our general world. Every category of "structural-coupling" between mind and environment operates out of or sets up such a field effect. Enough participation by enough people over enough time can stabilize any field effect by shifting it from personal to social to species-wide and finally universal—from our physical-subtle interactions into subtle-causal structures, but this takes a tremendous amount of parallel or similar effort on a wide social level.

Once set in motion, all causal-implicate forces tend to self-perpetuate. Our lives spin out of an infinitely interweaving web of such implicate-causal forces, many of which we may bring with us at birth. Recent studies have been made of scores of identical twins separated at birth and adopted into different and widely separated families.[10] The twins experience remarkably similar patterns of behavior, decision-making processes, and life events, marrying at the same age partners of the same name and type, naming their children the same names, following the same professions, and so on, quite unaware of each other. All this points up the power of a "hereditary" factor that can in no way be accounted for by chromosomes or DNA.

Sages claim that every day we experience the results of causes we set into motion years ago. Just as Lippin's methadone patient may well have forgotten that a year ago the site of his present rash was the site of a TB test, we may not recognize that today's allergy or ulcer, fear, anger, illness, or apparent random bad luck is the result of something set in motion some time back, an event that just hangs around in the quasi-temporal subtle realm until some stimulus triggers it into motion. Time may be only indirectly a factor in the subtle realm but is always tending. "The mills of the gods grind slowly" and not always with a logic we understand.

New York University's Robert Becker studies electro-magnetic fields and claims that our body is a conglomerate of them, as is the body of our world.[11] I had heard of energy fields around people, which I dismissed as occultic until my wife went into labor with our daughter. I started at one point to put my arms around her in a protective, supportive way, and found, to my surprise, a moving field of energy about a foot out from her body, as vibrant and palpable as though material. My wife was quite aware of this field as both her personal power and the parameters of her private sacrosanct world. She needed to be left alone and indeed I drew back from the field as from a charged wire. She was quite in control of the situation.

One morning in meditation I experienced a "sphere of energy" resonating out of myself in vibratory waves extending about a foot, arcing over and back into me. I perceived that this energy was my own consciousness "broadcast" out and coming back as my physical reception of what was being sent—my felt-perception feeding back into and becoming part of the arcing "broadcast." All of this I knew to be the moving, vibrant power of creation itself. I could feel the power with my body and embraced its outer arc with my arms. I experienced it as an overwhelming love holding me in a cocoon-like vortex that constituted my universe. I knew that all creation unfolded within this cocoon. The screen of the world out-there was the screen of my own mind and was out-there by virtue of this on-going dynamic. I knew that it was this cocoon of power to which Eckhart referred when he said the soul "throws out images to enter into." What is being "thrown out" is our universe itself.

My meditation teacher once said that our life force extends out about one foot from us and therein lies our universe. Our breathing envelope is our life envelope; our breath, prana, and light itself is a single power. Our perception of this cocoon of consciousness is our concretization of it. Sages and sorcerers speak of seeing us as globes of luminosity, the light of consciousness. Everything in our history is "written there" my teacher told me, and our lived experience emerges out of this to be shared in a common domain. This common domain is common because of our shared universal fields. We forget that our experience of our own body is only our sum of perceptions concerning it, which is no different than the perceptions of our large body, the world. Our subtle energy arcs back in on us, our sensory-system receives this impact and sends this perceptual experience back into the system. This completes the dynamic circuit and becomes part of the on-going "arcing-out" of formative power. When we interact with this subtle-causal realm through our movements and thoughts, the whole play of consciousness resonates accordingly. Ordinarily we can't perceive the essence of this creative play, only its results, which leaves us living after the fact, trying to catch up, but never quite here in the now.

CHAPTER 10

Who Remembers?

The late Wilder Penfield, an early and most original brain surgeon, sawed off the skulls of some 1,500 patients in his long career and probed their brains with electrodes.[1] The brain has no feeling, and, other than a local anesthetic to remove the skull, Penfield's patients were fully awake as he searched for tumors and other troublemakers. His operations were leisurely affairs, for he took advantage of the rare chance to probe the neurons of a live, fully conscious brain and talk with that brain's owner about what was happening.

Occasionally Penfield's electrode probing activated a cell, and this brought about vivid recollections from the patient's past—from commonplace childhood events to the precise playing of pieces of music. The patients all claimed to experience these memories as present-moment, fully real "sensory" events, equal in every way to their experience of the operating room and Penfield, with whom they conversed. "But how can you be in two completely different places?" Penfield would ask, to which the person could only answer that they didn't know how, they simply were. "But who is looking at the other scene, experiencing this other, remembered reality?" Penfield would ask. "I am" the patient would answer. "But you are looking at and talking with me," Penfield would say, and around they would go, the paradox unresolved. So long as Penfield kept the electrode charged, the recalled event or tune would play itself out from beginning to end and then stop. If the current was cut off in the middle, the episode stopped. When the current was resumed, the event or tune started over, from the beginning again, not where it left off. Once completed, the episode would replay if the current was shut off and back on. Penfield found these memory cells in the temporal lobe, which is involved in dreaming, sound, and spatial constructions.

Researchers have recently proposed several different kinds of memory, each with its own procedure. We know that a single cell doesn't "hold" a specific memory; as many neural fields are involved in memory events as in ordinary perception. A single cell produced the Penfield events, however, which indicates a form of "target-cell" action.[2] Here, a single cell organizes a wide range of fields for a highly specific construction. This same cell and the fields it organizes, can also function as parts of other networks when sparked by other field interactions. Any neural field can lend its actions to any other field through the complex of connections (as a phoneme lends itself to an endless variety of words). Out of this comes further evidence that our construction of reality is an internal affair—"peaks of activity in populations of neurons." Since two such structures can play simultaneously, each as real as the other, the constructions can hardly be a direct reaction of neurons to a preset world acting on us.

Key organizational cells like this may underlie our personal history on which all our memory and learning draw. No more than a million or so target cells of this sort could provide a playback of every instant of our life. (Among the 100 billion available neurons, that would require no more than about .000,001 of 1 percent.) Drawing on such target cells is something our brain doesn't ordinarily do. It draws on broad, diffuse "memory fields" for our general memory. Recall that the savant can only draw on a single field with a precise effect; we can draw on many fields but with less precise results. Most of us, when we try to remember, get a vague, general impression at best. If we could access such a target cell voluntarily, we would get a full sensory replay of the original event.

David Chamberlain presents excellent evidence for pre-birth and birth memory and suggests that memory is probably not "in" the brain at all.[3] Researchers agree, he says, that memory is not one but many different systems, "not always unified . . . functioning as 'modules' independently and in series . . . working both automatically and at will, limited and perhaps inaccurate." In altered states of consciousness, however, memory is sometimes remarkably reliable and clearly beyond previously accepted limits; what Chamberlain described as the "expanding boundaries of memory." Recent research indicates that memories can "extend completely beyond the neurological substrate which is supposed to contain them or make them possible."[4]

Perhaps, however, we need to simply extend our notions of a "neurological substrate" and recognize that neural fields are quasi-temporal. The brain's fragile cellular structure is in time-space, visible, and subject to dissection, but its operations, states of consciousness and resulting perceptions are both in and beyond time-space. George Franklin asked, "Where is a memory when it is not being re-membered?"[5] Memory "storage" refers to storage of a conscious experience, and how would consciousness "store" itself? How can any movement be stored, other than in and as those dynamic fields of potential that are the stuff of consciousness itself?

For years, Ernest Hilgard of Stanford University has investigated an enigmatic aspect of personality that he calls the "hidden observer."[6] No matter what our conscious state is, whether we are sleeping, anesthetized, under hypnosis, or drugged, we have another aspect of self that is always alert and aware of everything going on and that responds intelligently. When conditions are right this "hidden observer" will respond to requests, even with physical movements if asked, even while the person is asleep or anesthetized. Perhaps this accounts for post-hypnotic suggestion. The hidden observer may be connected with our causal system, "observing" the actions of the subtle-physical systems. The hidden observer displays an unemotional, detached intelligence, more powerful and cohesive than our ego-self. Perhaps this is that which "breathes" the archer in Zen, moving the body without employing the muscular system, which only a subtle-causal energy can do.

It seems to me that we are one with this hidden observer until about age seven, at which point our intellect begins to form and a split takes place. The pre-logical child is focussed on the dreamlike world of play, with no clear distinction between self and experience. Perhaps the maturation process divides us from our subtle, dreamlike part so that we can (or must, perhaps) identify with our social world and develop our analytical, objective intellect. The price of this "loss of contact" may lend to that alienation and sense of aloneness so

91

poignant in the adolescent. Such a split is surely not intended as permanent, and re-union with our hidden observer may be a major part
of true maturation.

The sages claim that we are not the "doers." We represent only a
small percentage of the total conscious machinery of our brain-mind.
Much intelligent decision making and action takes place within us
which we are never aware of or only become aware of after the fact.
We can rationalize and try to claim this supportive intelligence as our
own, but as long as our ego-self is undeveloped and immature, we are,
like the betrayed spouse, the "last to know," which makes our notions of action more like lame reactions.

A recent account by a Texas woman indicates a combination of
hidden observer and target-cell memory that, while obviously very
rare, could play a profound role in our lives if we knew how to open
ourselves to it.[7] On the day this woman's husband left her, while
she was at her office working, the details of their twenty-year relationship began "passing through" her head. The review was complete,
in proper sequence, and centered exclusively on their relationship
and the misunderstandings and errors on both sides that had ruined
it. The experience went on for hours, the memories "began and ended
as if a tape had started and stopped. . . . I felt incredulous, overwhelmed, awed. . . . It was fascinating and breathtaking. Yet as I experienced this I was aware . . . of the heat of the noonday, of walking
in the bright sun by the swimming pool." She was, however, only
vaguely aware of where she was as she continued her duties. Again,
as with Penfield's patients, two parallel realities played to one witness.

The experience wiped away her anger and hurt, gave her a more
powerful self-awareness and brought a new level of understanding
into her life, with a greater sense of awareness and self-worth. This
understanding emerged in her "permeated with a totally uncondi-
tional love. . . . To know that such love could be a part of me was
stunning, even thrilling. The complete understanding and complete
love were part of each other." We may ask why, if such intelligence,
love, and guidance, are within us, do they manifest so rarely? On reflection we might note that this intelligence usually manifests itself
only when we are in a state of crisis. Perhaps if we gave it anywhere
near as much attention as we do our ordinary attempts to outwit

our daily world, we would learn to tune in to and heed it. This, after all, is the claim made by all the great spiritual paths.

Since all perceivable dynamics translate through our body-brain-mind system, we all have access to the source from which those events spring. As William Blake said, "Everything possible to be believed is an image of truth,"[8] a capacity that involves us, in actual creativity, for better or worse. This possibility generally leads to disaster though, since we employ it blindly and, out of ignorance, let ourselves be led by an intellect isolated from a deeper intelligence. Though all of us experience this intelligence, on some level, it is usually unrecognized or ignored.

One of the most frequent phenomenon I experience while in meditation or at odd moments-out-of-mind, is a wave that engulfs me momentarily, bringing a fleeting shift of awareness—a brief opening of an ancient, "familiar otherness" directly connected with my sixth year of life. I regularly got up at dawn as a child, for this wave of awareness seemed to manifest more strongly then, and I didn't want to miss it. I used to wonder if this "wave" were not rather the state of memory itself—not memory as content, but memory as function, a field like Lusseyran's light as compared to specific light. When this wave engulfs me, I instantly identify with and recognize it; "it" is more familiar than my named-self. When I was very young it would linger, but as I grew older it was gone even as it arrived, leaving me only with the memory-of-a-memory and an immeasurable backwash of intense longing. Perhaps this is a "flashing-forth" of the hidden observer, the one who remembers, and the one I have forgotten.

———

We hear about wholeness, the "holographic" universe, the unity of all things, holistic education, the whole brain, and so on. Unity, however, does not deny diversity nor does diversity mean a loss of unity. Complementarity between unity and diversity is how experience unfolds. A new pseudo-scientific philosophy has arisen that speaks of the separation of things, even of particle from wave, as only an illusion; even apparent divisions of locality are considered not authentic. Picking up on Eastern philosophy they call everything "Maya," the "veil of illusion." "None of this is real," they say. One such philosopher stated that when a person becomes "enlightened," the universe disappears and one realizes it has never actually been; it was just a figment of the imagination, a joke on ourselves.

David Bohm points out that the Latin word for reality is *res*, meaning "thing." This world is a *res*, a thing, a realness. The great sages speak of the living earth as our larger body, a miracle of creation to be respected and loved, upheld by dharma or right action. *Maya*, the Sanksrit word bandied about so often, refers to that which is measurable; its fullest meaning is "to unfold out in measurable units." Sages have for millennia claimed that our world is unfolded out in measurable form from an enfolded vibratory, formless potential. A particle is constructed out of wave-form possibilities, an "explicate order" displays from an "implicate order" in Bohm's terms. Or the world of Maya leaps forth from the mind of God if you like. Metaphors are cheap and expendable, but the eternal function remains the same regardless of what we call it (though our metaphors establish the frames of reference for our experience of that function).

The word *illusion* comes from the Latin *illudere*, which means "inner play." The word *play* is from the Latin *plicare*, which means "folded in measurable units or acts." Our world is a great creative play that unfolds out in measurable, discrete units or acts from an enfolded potential. The creative aspect of God dances before her consort, the silent, witnessing self. She unfolds her Maya, her universes before him. Without the witness, creation is lifeless and barren; without the creation's Maya the witness is null and void. Maya and witness are the perfect complement, neither is possible without the other. They are mutually exclusive, yet interdependent—one indivisible intelligence. Kashmir Shaivism based its theory of evolution on the metaphor of the eternal love of the Primordial Shiva, the witness, and his consort Shakti, the creative process, each in simultaneous eternal union and separation; from this ecstatic vibrancy springs all. This creative action is referred to as Lila, the "play of consciousness," a self-contained play unfolding out from itself.

So our intuition of an underlying wholeness shouldn't imply melting into a homogeneous mass. Our need as individuals is for appropriate relationship, a challenge of far greater magnitude and difficulty than dissolving into a homogenized unity. Maturana and Varela write, "If we want to coexist with the other person, we must see that

94

his certainty—however undesirable it may seem to us—is as legitimate and valid as our own because, like our own, that certainty expresses his conservation of structural-coupling in a domain of existence. . . ."[9] We share the same domain, but the coupling can never be quite the same, wherein lies the diversity that gives unity its life.

Existence is from the Latin *existere*, meaning "to be set apart." Without separation there can be no diversity, no creation, no experience, no love, longing, and subsequent union. What we long for in each other is a perfect relationship. Out of perfect relationship comes the unity we seek, a unity that exists only within us. Finding that point of unity within, love and compassion for all creation, expressions of our own selves, is boundless.

As living creatures, we are all Maya. As witnessing selves we are all that witness. We have identified of necessity with Maya since conception. Our maturation lies not in denying Maya but in identifying with the witness in order to love and protect Maya as our own being. Even this is no final point, however; evolution's end pulls us beyond separation, beyond all name and form, as Meister Eckhart put it, beyond all structures of knowledge, and all emotions known therein. Even the sublime union between the separated self and its source is but another point of departure into the unknown. My meditation teacher summed it up by saying: "We don't go back to unity, we move beyond diversity."

PART two

DEVELOPING OUR KNOWLEDGE OF THE WORLD

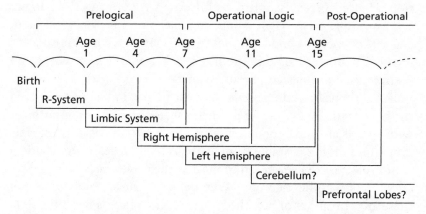

Brain Growth Spurts and Shifts of Concentration of Development

Brain "growth spurts" take place in utero, at birth, and at the beginnings of each stage of child development—ages one, four, and six.[1] The focus of development shifts at each stage, starting, quite logically, with evolution's oldest system, the reptilian, and moving up through her later additions. Each part of the triune system has its own block of intelligences and behaviors inherent within it, and the growth-spurts, mostly axon-dendrite masses, provide the new neural fields needed to develop each block of potential.

So the growth spurt at birth prepares the infant for development of the R-system and its intelligences. Around age one, if that R-system has been stimulated and exercised enough, nature shifts attention to development of the limbic brain as well, requiring another brain-growth spurt. The eighteen-month-old toddler, with a skull only one-third the size of an adult's, has as many of those critical axon and dendrite connectors and neural fields as an adult brain. An enormous construction job takes place in those first four years; "structures of knowledge" of self, world, relationships, and language must be built, and nature provides ample neural fields for the project. By age four, some 80 percent of this primary worldview is complete and myelinated. Then nature shifts her developmental agenda into the neocortex's right hemisphere for a threefold focus. Another

99

growth spurt provides the needed neural fields, through increases in support cells and the connectors between neurons.

By around age six this fundamental world-self-language system is complete, and nature turns to the development of her latest addition, the neocortex, ushering us into the world of intellect, logic, and reasoning. An average adult neuron has some one thousand axon-dendrite connectors branching out from it, through which it can connect with upward of ten thousand other neurons directly and indirectly. (Some special-purpose neurons connect with upward of a hundred thousand others.) Our six-year-old brain has five to seven times the ratio of axons and dendrites it had at eighteen months or will have as an adult, though it is still only two-thirds of adult size. If neuron number is stable from birth, as some researchers claim, a neuron at age six or seven can connect with an average of sixty to seventy thousand other neurons.[2] Whether new neurons are also part of these growth-spurts or not, the six-year-old still has a potential field capacity vastly greater than it had earlier or will have later. Estimates of neurons in our brain range to as many as a hundred billion (perhaps a trillion if the granular cells of the cerebellum are included). Obviously an infinite number of possible neural fields and an unlimited possibility for translating potential into actuality is inherent within that six-year-old's head. Our forthcoming analysis of concrete operational thinking, which begins around that age, will show why nature makes such an enormous preparation for it.

At age eleven, however, instead of a brain growth spurt, nature releases a chemical in the young brain that dissolves all undeveloped neural fields. Myelin, recall, forms around axons when a neural field is employed sufficiently, helps make field operations rapid and energy-efficient, and, of most significance here, is impervious to these cleanup chemicals released periodically. Only those neural patterns stimulated and sufficiently developed are left at age eleven. These become our permanent "structures of knowledge," and any neural field not myelinated is removed from the scene. This economizes on energy but, more importantly, "cleans house" in preparation for the new intelligences that unfold at age eleven, which we will discuss in a later chapter.

Nature can be quite extravagant in materials *for* development, but quite economical once development takes place. At age eleven, when that house-cleaning chemical is released, we would expect some loss, a trimming down for the new action ahead. Such a neural cleanup also takes place right before birth. At age eleven, however, 80 percent of the neural mass of the brain disappears, and we end up with the same "brain weight" we had at eighteen months. I know of no other case where nature ends with the same capacity with which she began. There seem to be no further growth spurts after age eleven,* and it seems strange that we enter adulthood with the same brain potential that we had as toddlers. This may not be nature's fault, however; she seems to provide far more potential than our environment provides models or nurturing. Use it or lose it is nature's dictate, and in this case I think we lose more than is necessary. Indications are that most of this loss involves the neocortex, since we know the two "animal brains" are largely myelinated by age four and complete by around age six. In the coming chapters we will explore both what might be intended through these huge growth spurts at four and six and what happens to prevent our putting them to work.

We share 98 percent of all our genetic materials with the higher apes, giving us but a 2 percent additional genetic "weight" over our cousins. From that slight addition comes a light-year leap of ability, however, and perhaps only a small addition of developed fields at age eleven would give a likewise disproportionate increase in capacity over our present state; perhaps just enough to make a difference between true intelligence and a misguided intellect.

* it is now realized that the prefrontal cortex, the executive, or fourth brain, has a second growth spurt lasting three to four years and which begins around the age of eighteen

CHAPTER 11

Heart-Mind Bonding

In the 1940s Lester Sontag reported that the mother's heartbeat affected the infant in utero.[1] In the 1960s, some researchers recorded a heartbeat and played it in hospital nurseries for newborns, which reduced infant crying by 40 to 50 percent. This led not to in-depth investigation into the reasons for reduced crying, but to the invention and patenting of a "Rockabye Teddybear," which broadcast an audible heartbeat for home use in cribs and bassinets. Such are the vicissitudes of a commercialized, pseudo-science.

Research on the heart is now where brain research was decades ago, but already our concepts concerning it are seriously challenged. Recently, a famous heart surgeon was reported to have said that we must give up the idea of an artificial heart, since we have found the organ to be far more than just a pumping station.[2] Our heart apparently plays a major if fragile role in our overall consciousness. Transmitters, which play such a critical role in neural behavior, have now been found in the heart and are connected in some way with the brain. Actions in the heart precede the actions of both body and brain. A key dynamic between heart and brain is centered in the limbic system. Years ago John and Beatrice Lacey, doing research for the National Institute of Mental Health, reported that our brain sends a running report of our environmental situation to the heart, and the heart exhorts the brain to make a proper response.[3] We know now that the heart does more than exhort, it controls and governs brain action through hormonal, transmitter, and possibly finer quantum-energies of communication.

The atrium area of the heart produces a hormone that dramatically affects every major organ of the body and the operations of our limbic system.[4] Called ANF, this hormone impacts and determines the actions of the thalamus and its dynamic with the pituitary gland, the so-called master gland that regulates the endocrine hormones. ANF is involved in the immune system and the body's healing response; it impacts the hypothalamus and pineal gland, regulating production and action of melatonin; and it plays a key role in our emotional states, memory, and learning.

A heart cell plays a dual role: It contracts and expands rhythmically to pump blood and communicates with its fellow cells. If you isolate a cell from the heart, keep it alive and examine it through a microscope, you will see it lose its synchronous rhythm and begin to fibrillate until it dies. If you put another isolated heart cell on that microscopic slide it will also fibrillate. If you move the two cells within a certain proximity, however, they synchronize and beat in unison. They don't have to touch; they can communicate across a spatial barrier. As Shimony would say, there is no passion at a distance here, non-locality is involved. Our heart, made up of many billions of such cells operating in unison, is under the guidance of a higher, non-localized intelligence.

Here, then, is the source of that intelligence which keeps our diversity of body parts in functional wholeness, that "wisdom of the body" to which W. B. Cannon referred: a vital, yet primitive, cellular, chemical-hormonal kind of heart-intelligence that, through the limbic structure, maintains the integration and proper balance of the three parts of our triune brain and all body functions.[5] The reason the heart can govern these physical processes is, I propose, because it translates from its own non-localized "field of intelligence" just as the brain does.

Those heart cells communicate through their mutually non-localized base of relationship, a field of intelligence that is a larger, more universal, non-physical "heart"—creative consciousness as itself.

Two closely bonded people often share information across time-space, to which we attach occultic labels of various sorts, while all the time it is only our true biology, the logic of our life system, the language of the heart. And, just as our physical heart maintains our body, the non-localized intelligence governing the heart in turn maintains synchrony with a universal "consciousness at large." So we have both a physical heart and a higher "universal heart," and our access to the latter is, as in all development, dramatically contingent on the development of the former. Just as the intelligences drawn on by the brain lead to specific abilities, the heart draws on the supra-implicate order and the realm of insight-intelligence. These higher orders don't articulate as specifics, but as a general movement for the well-being and balance of the overall operations of the brain-mind-body.

The three major stages of life are heart-centered in this sense: (1) the development of a heart-mind synchrony, needed for physical life, and observed in the various "Piagetian" stages; (2) a later "post-adolescent" development, which synchronizes the developed physical self and the creative process; and (3) a final "highest heart," which moves us beyond all physical-emotional systems. Two poles of experience lie within us, our unique, individual self generating through the brain; and a universal, impersonal intelligence generating through the heart. The success of human life depends on the development of this heart-mind dialogue; in this complementary dynamic each profoundly effects the other and both are developmental. Since nature's model imperative always holds, even a supreme intelligence must undergo development within us if we are to access and benefit from it. Unfortunately, no academic concept or nurturing model-environment is provided for a "heart's intelligence," making our ignorance of it a dismal and crippling fact.

Though the intelligence of the heart is a "higher" order of energy, it reflects the history of its own "display." People getting heart-transplants often dramatically reflect certain behaviors of the late donor. This organic effect is not the case with the later states of the heart. Just as the behaviors of the R-system and limbic structure are not found in the highest intelligences of the neocortex as itself, the higher orders of intelligence unfolding in later heart development are not influenced by the lower orders they then incorporate.

My meditation teacher once said, "You must develop your intellect to its highest possible extent, in order that it be a proper instrument for the intelligence of the heart; but, only the intelligence of the heart can develop intellect to its highest level." This describes what evolution is about, and what our personal evolution must be, an issue that we will clarify as we examine development itself. But again, remember that the intelligence of the heart must itself be developed, and it does so through the conventional methods nature employs, according to the nature of the models provided. Given the appropriate environment, that intelligence will flower; without it the heart will function on a straight cellular, hormonal level maintaining life only on a "reptilian-mammalian level."

Saints and sages have always claimed that the true seat of the mind is in the heart. In 1932 an American Indian medicine man told Carl Jung that white men, with their wrinkled faces and constant anger, were insane and killed so wantonly because they thought in their heads. Whole people, he explained, think in their hearts. We smile indulgently at these "primitive" and quaint words. Our medicine man was only half right, however. Intellect, the very essence of Western man, is head thinking, for sure, but evolution has concentrated a lot of energy in such action and will never cease to push for the true maturation of that power, dangerous as it is in its half-developed stage. Intelligence is the ability to function for our well-being, a capacity, not a content. Just as a multi-cellular organism has incorporated the single cell into its higher evolutionary possibility, intelligence is designed to incorporate intellect into its service. To do this, that intellect must first be developed. The intelligence of the heart must not only be developed as itself, it must in turn have something to "operate on," something to respond to. Without a brain system to function in synchrony with, the universal intelligence of the heart is still-born.

Since all intelligences are coded to unfold within nature's timetable, intellect opens on target whether an intelligence of the heart has developed or not (just as sexuality unfolds at puberty whether we are ready for it or not). And therein lies the problem. The dynamic of the heart and brain is the dynamic of intelligence and intellect, the principle dynamic on which our life is based. If we develop intellect and fail to develop intelligence we are then subject to a novelty-seeking mind that operates without regard to our own or others' well-being. Anything is possible to us, but what is appropriate?

This example will illustrate the simple dynamic between our physical heart and the two elementary brains. Here comes your unpleasant

106

supervisor. The hormone ANF responds, impacts the thalamus and hippocampal areas, which fire a message to the pituitary, which in turn alerts the adrenals, and we go into a "flight-fight" state. Corticosteroids tighten up the muscles, speed up the lungs and heart, and alert the general R-system. Even just thinking of that supervisor brings on a minor hostile alert, maintaining tension, draining us, and setting the stage for ulcers, immune-system breakdown, allergies, and any number of other reactions. From the simplest disagreement with our spouse over breakfast to a final murderous rage, a spectrum of negativity centers around these physical heart-limbic dynamics.

When threatened, our triune system lines up from top-down. On behalf of what we interpret as a threat to our survival (of ego-image or actual body), our ancient R-system integrates into its defenses both the limbic system's emotions and our highest brain's intellect, reasoning, analytical logic, and so on. This heavy machinery sets about to justify to ourselves any violence called for by those most non-logical reptilian-mammalian survival emotions: Intellect and its analytical expertise, unimpaired by the positive-negative emotions incorporating it, may well be called on to make our now justifiable violence thorough and efficient. Using intellect defensively we function in an anti-evolutionary mode: Our neocortical system serves our lowest and most primitive structures. The open universe available to us through that highest system closes down at that point to the tight confines of our ancient R-system. Our already selective brain selects more rigidly than ever, discarding all signals except those strengthening that primitive defense system. Our world itself is a threat and we become like William Blake's "armed crustaceans eternally on the alert."

The exact opposite can take place, too. Here comes your long-absent lover. Your heart leaps, ANF alerts the highest structures within the limbic system, where bonds of love, nurturing, and care form. Adrenals may be called on here, too, since they bring excitement and assist in flooding you with euphoria. Poetry springs to your tongue and you feel one with the universe, until, twenty seconds later, your lover informs you that he or she has found another lover, at which point the open universe crashes down into a tight knot of anger and pain. The flow of your life flips as the highest intelligence locks into service of the lowest, and dark thoughts of revenge hatch in your violated ego-mind. Such are the vagaries of this animal-heart as it responds as genetically programmed to govern our biological relationships, moving us toward the pleasant, away from the unpleasant.

Three major stages of heart development should take place, through which we can be lifted beyond such constraints. The first opens at birth and follows the usual childhood stages of development, giving the world of emotions outlined above; the other opens at mid-adolescence, a "post-operational" development we know very little about, which enables us to develop an awareness incorporating those animal emotions into a higher and fully human state; and a third, unfolding later in life, relates us to the realm of insight-intelligence and moves us beyond biology.

In all cases nature's "model-imperative" and a nurturing environment are the keys to success or failure. As in all development, if the foundational intelligence isn't developed, the higher structures can't be. As primitive as that heart-limbic connection sounds, its firm establishment is critical beyond measure. The mother is the first teacher of the heart, and a bonding between mother and infant must be established at birth, the critical period. The mother must then awaken the undeveloped intelligence of the infant and be the constant model for the ongoing development, until that child's intelligence has been self-actualized and no longer needs such nurturing. As Paul MacLean makes clear, nature could add those higher cortical structures only through assuring such a prolonged period of helplessness and corresponding care. The biological function giving us physical life is precisely the biological intelligence of the heart. If we awaken and develop the one, we get the other because they are in dynamic. The intelligence of the heart is not some sweet sentiment but a primary biological necessity and the foundation of all bonding. Bonding itself develops in clear stages: mother-infant, infant-family, family-society, and a final male-female "pair-bonding" on which life is based. This series of biological links is the primary job of the first level of heart intelligence, and far more powerful stages lie in wait, contingent on the successful completion of this first major stage.

We are witnessing in our late twentieth century the loss of the bonding force that holds family and society together, and that holds the three layers of the brain in their synchronous power. The following chapters examine why failure to establish the infant-mother heart bond leads to a loss of intelligence, love, care, and nurturing, leaving only a gross defensive reptilian world. This is not just self-betrayal but a betrayal of the reason for life itself, leading to the negative side of evolution's end.

CHAPTER 12

Mother-Child Bonding

The Big News with the evolution of mammals is
the progressive attention and care that they
give to their young. . .

PAUL MACLEAN

A few days after conception a tiny clump of pulsating cells forms in the embryo; the beginnings of a heart. Alfred Tomatis claims that the first group of embryonic cells is sound-sensitive. Since any development depends on a proper stimulus from the environment, the purpose of sound-sensitive cells could be to pick up the stimulus of the mother's heartbeat, needed to generate production of the embryo's own heart. At any rate, the mother's heartbeat, breathing, and general movements keep the uterine infant in a continual, gentle movement and sound, which fosters neural development over a broad level. There are brain growth spurts and developmental stages in utero. Neural structures form for specific uterine needs and are removed before birth in a general brain house cleaning. The mother's emotional state is shared hormonally by her infant, and any repetitive pattern, such as singing a certain song, will imprint along with her voice; remember, language learning begins in the seventh month in utero.[1] Nature provides many ways to assure that the infant establishes a frame of reference in utero to which it can relate the unknown experiences in store for it after birth.

Nature's model-imperative, evident even in utero, grows ever more important as development continues, and the mother is the major model as well as caretaker. Her role is absolutely critical at childbirth, the focus of this chapter. First, recall the reticular formation, that congregating point of body-senses where a rough gestalt of environmental messages is sent to the rest of the brain for weaving a worldview and responding to it. This reticular system can't be completed in utero because most of the senses that comprise it aren't developed until after birth.

Right before birth the infant's body releases adrenal hormones that set into motion a chain of events. First, these hormones alert the infant's body and mobilize it for the challenge ahead. Second, they translate back through the umbilical cord and alert the mother's body, which goes into its own program of response; and, third, they bring about a brain growth spurt providing new neural fields for the adaptations and learnings that lie ahead. These powerful birth hormones will continue to flow and keep the system at maximum alert until birth is completed. Should birth-completion fail to take place, and hormone production continue for too long, a "critical mass" level of hormones accumulates and the infant goes into shock, ranging from mild to severe enough as to cause death. Statistically, this critical level is reached within about forty-five minutes should it continue unabated; so nature's agenda is a cascade of overlapping procedures designed to assure that the birth is completed in ample time and the birth hormone production ceased before danger sets in.[2] This birth completion involves the bonding between mother and infant immediately following the actual passage from utero.

Throughout history, the mother has placed her newborn to her left breast, its home base during the "in-arms" period of the first several months. (Ancient clay figurines of mothers and infants show the infant in that position.) Fathers also spontaneously hold newborns to the left.[3] This simple position unlocks a cascade of overlapping functions designed to assure cessation of hormone production and successful adaptation to the new environment. Originally called "attachment behavior" by John Bowlby, and later, "bonding" by John Kennell and Marshal Klaus, the pattern of this primary genetic program unfolds perfectly through the simple act of "skin-to-skin" contact between mother and newborn at that left position.[4] This contact assures the activation of all the senses that couldn't be awakened in utero and provides a confirmation of those senses that were. This completes the reticular formation, which then functions fully and shuts down the birth-stress hormone production. With the reticular formation functioning, the newborn can translate signals from the new environment and respond to them, which means learning begins immediately.

If such stimuli are not given, the infant's senses remain dormant and the established senses are not confirmed in their new setting. The reticular formation is then incomplete, and the infant can't coordinate sensory information even when sensory experience takes place; birth itself is incomplete, so the adrenal-hormone production continues.[5] Adrenal overload and shock ensues, a shock which, while disastrous to future development, is rather a kindness on nature's part, like releasing opiates in the brain to relieve trauma.

Home base at left-breast takes care of everything. Recall that playing a recorded heartbeat in nurseries reduces crying by 40 to 50 percent. Proximity with the mother's heartbeat is the number one priority in bonding and the major signal shutting off the stress hormones. The infant's five senses are stimulated automatically from that left-breast position. The newborn has one genetically encoded visual circuit: the ability to recognize and respond to a human face at a distance of six to twelve inches immediately on leaving the womb.[6] A face is the only object the newborn can recognize, and immediate proximity is critical. The hard-wired visual circuits respond to that stimulus and the entire visual process goes into operation.[7] Vision will be functional within a matter of minutes, including short- and long-range focus and parallax (muscular synchrony of the eyes), giving the newborn the ability to track moving objects. Within minutes the infant smiles in response to any face presented, a response critical to bonding. The stimulus of a face must be provided throughout the in-arms period, particularly in the early months when the infant spends about 80 percent of his or her "visual time" locked in on that hard-wired stimulus. Such "face constancy" leads to "object constancy," which forms in the infant somewhere around the eighth month after birth. (*Object constancy* was Piaget's term for formation of a stable visual world and indicates that the visual system has myelinated.)

That universal left-breast position places the infant in direct proximity with mother's nipple and within minutes nursing begins. Nursing activates the sense of taste, helping to complete the reticular formation. Again we have structural-coupling: An environmental stimulus activates its corresponding ability within. Nobel Prize winner, Nikos Tinbergen, and his team of English ethologists, found that our newborn is designed by nature to feed between forty-five and sixty times a day, a conclusion based on actual averages and on an analysis of mother's milk and the nature of infant metabolism. Human milk is the "poorest" of all mammalian milk, lowest in fats and proteins, and human metabolism is designed only for such nutrition, making feeding about every twenty minutes necessary. The higher percentage of fats and proteins found in cows' or goats' milk or in any of the many synthetic infant "formulas" on the market, require far more time and energy to digest, so that only occasional feedings are required, leading to far less contact between infant and caretaker. Nature can, if needed, produce extremely rich milk, making only occasional feedings necessary. Rabbit milk, for example, has so much fat and protein that one feeding a day is sufficient, freeing mamma for the long hours of foraging needed. The rapid metabolism of human milk, low in fat and protein, is designed primarily to assure continual contact between mother and infant. Paul MacLean pointed out that only through a prolonged period of nurturing can higher cortical systems be developed.[8]

Touch is even more critical. All mammals lick their newborns vigorously, off and on, for the first twenty-four to forty-eight hours after birth, not to "clean the infant up" but to activate the body's sensory nerve endings.[9] These nerve endings, which are involved in motor movements, spatial orientation, and visual perspective as well as touch, can't be activated in utero because they are insulated. The skin is protected from its watery environment by a fatty substance called *vernix casseus.* Should these nerve endings not be activated in the infant after birth, the reticular formation will not be fully operative, leading to impaired muscular movements, curtailed sensory intake, and a variety of emotional disturbances and learning deficits.

113

If we keep a totally touch-deprived animal infant alive arbitrarily, its development will be slow if at all, since its ability to organize sensory input into coherent information is seriously impaired. Researchers separated newborn lambs from their mothers at birth and re-introduced them twenty-four hours later.[10] The mother generally can't recognize her newborn if separated that long, but, ready to lactate, will sometimes adopt and nurse a stray infant (as in mother dogs nursing kittens, cats nursing newborn puppies, and other such anomalies). If our mother sheep can be persuaded to "adopt" her own newborn after that twenty-four-hour separation and nurture it, that newborn will survive. But it will grow into a seriously dysfunctional sheep, unable to separate from its mother and function on its own; unable to play, either by itself or with other lambs (the significance of play will be discussed later); unable to communicate with or participate with the flock at maturity; and unable to breed. Though kept alive, bonding fails, and with it general intelligence. Species-survival is put at risk since that lamb can't reproduce. Mother cats vigorously lick their kittens, concentrating on the soft underbelly. Researchers have taped this area over, preventing its stimulation, and these kittens develop no sensory-motor responses and cannot survive.[11] So mammals have this automatic instinct for nurturing the newborn's skin in this way, and infants are born expecting it. (Eskimo and Aborigine mothers vigorously licked their newborns as our mammalian cousins do.)

The newborn can recognize his or her own mother's smell as soon as the amniotic fluid drains from the nasal passages. Picking up this smell is another strand in the completion of the senses. Also, having responded physically in utero to each phoneme spoken by the mother, the infant is thoroughly imprinted to her speech, and most mothers speak (in a surprisingly similar way) to their newborns right away, confirming the imprinted language bonds. So within a few minutes after birth, under ideal conditions, a cascade of supportive, confirmative information activates every sense, instinct, and intelligence needed for the radical change of environment; the vital reticular formation is complete and functioning. All of this has been dutifully signalled to the heart, which organizes the triune brain into synchronous response and locks the news about the new environment into the infant's permanent memory, a memory that will influence all its future interaction with that environment.

The six- to twelve-inch distance from a face that activates the infant's visual system, and correspondingly its reticular formation, also places it in direct proximity to its mother's heart. Consider that a single heart cell can, given the proper spatial proximity, communicate with another cell, even across a physical barrier. Thus, in the same way, the heart, made up of many billions of such cells operating in synchrony, can communicate with another heart given the appropriate proximity. Nature's imperative is, again, that no intelligence unfolds without a stimulus from a developed form of that intelligence. All evidence indicates that the mother's developed heart stimulates the infant's newborn heart, thereby activating a dialogue between the infant's brain-mind and heart. Then the newborn knows all is well and that birth has been successfully completed. The R-system, with its primitive survival instincts, serves the higher systems, a balance that is brought about by the heart activating the limbic system, which coordinates integration. Thus intelligent learning begins at birth.

Besides sending a major bonding signal to the infant's system and shutting down the adrenal hormone production, this heart to heart communication activates corresponding intelligences in the mother as well. On holding her infant in the left-breast position with its corresponding heart contact, a major block of dormant intelligences is activated in the mother, causing precise shifts of brain function and permanent behavior changes.[12] Ancient mammalian nurturing intelligences and latent intuitions are awakened in her (possibly related to the cyngulate gyrus area in the upper regions of the limbic system, according to MacLean).[13] The mother then knows exactly what to do and can communicate with her infant on an intuitive level. The mother's own defensive birth postures can relax to higher cortical structures. Nature's agenda is a dynamic in which the infant stimulates a new block of intelligences in the mother, which then enable her to respond appropriately and nurture her infant.

These birth intelligences awakened in the mother are not learned nor can they be taught. They are an archetypal and primal knowing, a complete wisdom that opens spontaneously if the mother is given the proper structural-coupling with her infant. As John Kennell and Marshall Klaus say: "a great love affair is being born"—an affair that is nature's assurance that the infant will receive what it needs—the longest nurturing demanded by any species, since the greatest intelligence is at stake.

Behavioral changes in the bonded mother include a new sense of personal power, physical strength, and an intuitive knowledge of her infant's needs. She acts out of that vast intelligence through which our species has survived for untold eons. This is the intelligence of the heart, a non-verbal, ancient knowing. She has, in bonding to her infant, bonded to her own heart and has come into her own power, unlocking the insights on which our species has depended for millennia. She has joined and so perpetuates the continuum of human intelligence that sustains our species. She has become the mother, not just of that child, but of our kind. And we do poorly indeed without her.

With her "species survival instincts" fully operative, a mother will breast-feed her infant on demand for an average of two to three years. Nursing initiates strong contractions in the mother's uterus, pulling it back into its original shape. Nature also provides intense feedback from breast-feeding: rewards of a strongly sensual and loving nature. A nursing mother's ordinary sexual responses will be sharply curtailed as all her energy will go into this critical in-arms period of infant-toddler development—a major, overwhelming relationship leaving little energy for other pursuits. A mother's love is probably as strong an emotional bond as afforded in human life. The infant's intelligence will be nurtured and a natural spacing of children will be provided, so that each child can be given its proper start in life.

Research indicates that breast-fed infants are more intelligent than bottle-fed infants.[14] (Since 97 percent of our population is bottle-fed, this bit of research may cause rightful indignation and denial in nearly everyone.) The issue is not merely physical nourishment, but the constant face contact, heart contact, and overall stimuli the breast-fed infant receives. Far more neural fields are activated and stabilized as the mother carries her infant about. This gives the infant a variety of visual environments, and continual overall sensory stimuli. No deadly "separation anxiety" or "psychological abandonment," so disruptive to development, occurs.

Bonded mothers talk to their infants more, and bonded infants are generally far more verbal than unbonded, bottle-fed ones.[15] They achieve object constancy (the first major shift of locus and brain development) far earlier than unbonded ones, and every aspect of intelligence is enhanced both in earliest infancy and throughout life.[16] French physician Michelle Odent claims that the infant's immune system is shaped for life by the relationship established at birth.[17] Colostrum, the first milk produced by the mother's breast, is thought to pass on to the newborn the entire set of immunities gained by the mother in her lifetime. Surely the constant "heart contacts" that breast-feeding assures plays an equal and possibly more powerful role. At any rate, the home-birthed and bonded child has a six-to-one better chance of survival than the hospital infant, and so has the mother.[18]

With the need for face and skin contact so critical, nature provides a umbilical cord some eighteen to twenty inches long; an infant can be placed at that critical six to twelve inches from the mother's face while remaining connected to the still functioning, life-giving placenta. Thirty percent of the infant's blood remains in the placenta during this adjustment period, providing all the oxygen necessary to the child. Ample time is given for the amniotic fluid to drain from the newborn's nostrils and trachea before he or she attempts to breathe alone.

The infant's subtle sphere, that critical radius of potential-response dynamic, is around twelve inches maximum. The subtle sphere must be "invaded," in effect, if the newborn is to register any stimulus. There is no problem with this in utero, and there won't be after birth if bonding takes place. The infant must be kept within the mother's (or permanent caretaker's) own subtle-sphere for a sufficient amount of time. Within that sphere the infant is fully functional and alive; outside of it his heart signals "abandoned" and the infant becomes anxious and stressed. When Carl Jung commented that the infant-child lives in the "shadow" of the parent, he touched on a vast issue. No outer world in our sense has yet formed. Newborns are, in effect, still in their subtle world and almost completely identified with the mother's body. When the mother's subtle sphere overlaps the infant's, a major communication takes place. This subtle communication might be below the level of awareness of the mother, but it is the *only* level of awareness fully active in the infant. This vital "heart level" is far more than sentiment, or just physical. The subtle realm is the infant's actual world-environment. Newborns have no active potential fields yet for picking up long-range information. So they must have immediate, short-range stimuli. This is a major reason for the need of constant caretaker contact and prolonged breast-feeding. The foundation of intuitive knowings shared by infant and mother, so obvious in pre-literate societies and leading to the power of true intuition and insight in children and adults, is established at this time. Infants held at arm's length for bottle feeding, or kept too much in cribs, carriages, strollers, or playpens are at biological risk of stunted physical and emotional development.

Bonding is a dynamic in which the mother learns moment by moment from her infant just as the infant learns from her. She will mature and experience fulfillment as the mother of the species. Regardless of what happens later in the child's life, this security enables her or him to cope. Since this first great movement into the unknown has established the precedent of entering into it, exploring it, learning from it, and moving through it, the child then becomes a person who is at home in a universe of movement and change; someone who is in creative dynamic with that life force which is our own consciousness; someone who stands firm in the strength of our matrix, our whole living earth.

CHAPTER 13

Bond Breaking

Birth, as we have seen, is an ancient mammalian function; its procedures, well worked out by nature, are encoded in our equally ancient mammalian brain. All mammals, when ready to deliver, seek out a safe, hidden place for birth. At the first sign of interference, some unknown noise or intrusion, this innate mammalian intelligence stops the birth process, and the mother waits until threat has passed; or, she may even look for a safer, more private birthing spot, since during birth she is at her most vulnerable. The optimum length for birthing seems to be about twenty minutes. This is possible only for women in optimal emotional and physical shape who are informed about the birth process, in touch with their own bodies, and, above all, given maximum nurturing, support, and protection from interference or anxiety (as rare a combination as a twenty-minute delivery). Each interference or anxiety, regardless of reason, adds time to the birth.

The average expectant mother in the United States is ignorant of the birth process, having never witnessed it, and may never have held a baby, especially a newborn. In our society sex is a major economic commodity and cultural obsession, with pregnancy an error and threat. Our mothers are conditioned to believe that birth is an unbearably painful and dangerous ordeal needing maximum professional assistance. She is told by her obstetrician not to worry, that he will take care of everything. After nine months of such expectations (perhaps along with taking drugs, alcohol, or chronic smoking) this mother is whisked to a hospital where she is kept isolated in a strange setting. Efficient and often over-worked nurses give her sedatives lest some impromptu action upset their routines. Then she is given drugs to induce labor or speed up a labor that has become stalled and confused. Her child will be born, statistically, between 9 A.M. and 3 P.M., convenient hours for hospitals, obstetricians, and staff. (Nature tends toward night or early morning, perhaps because newborns are sensitive to light.)

Though changing somewhat in upper- and middle-class births today, for the last half century our mothers have been strapped into knee stirrups and restrainers, flat on their backs (the one position known to make birth most difficult and unknown in history until recent times); wheeled into brightly lit operating rooms; and surrounded by masked strangers employing a variety of electronic devices to monitor the chemically induced operation. To guard against emergencies, various monitoring instruments are placed in or around the mother's uterus to "make sure all is well." Various emergency bells ring should some electronic gadget fail to register its quota of statistics (vital for possible later use in courtrooms in case of malpractice suit). Such major invasions send both mother and infant into paroxysms of anxiety that, in turn, send to those monitoring instruments a host of misleading signals. These signals prompt a further round of invasive measures by the operating team. The splayed-out private parts of the mother—glaring in the bright lights like a laboratory frog awaiting dissection—elicit dramatic pronouncements from the staff, such as, "I don't believe she is dilating," "we may have to cut," "the fetal heart beat is too slow." (Actually, fewer than .05 percent of natural births have complications, most of which can be met by a well-informed midwife, as they have been throughout our species' history.) So, employing forceps or whatever device is deemed necessary, the infant is extracted. In 30 percent of American births this is done by cutting the mother open and lifting the infant out, a major surgical procedure called a caesarean or C-section. Considered the "only civilized way to have children," as some obstetricians now state, this practice is far more lucrative than a normal birth and is growing by leaps and bounds. The higher the mother's income, the higher the chance that a caesarean section will be performed.[1] (Upward of 50 percent of all births in wealthy areas of the United

States are caesarean.) A massive medical study, sponsored by the Department of Health, Education, and Welfare, reported that perhaps only 1 to 3 percent of these operations could be justified.[2]

Nearly a third of the infant's blood and oxygen remains in the placenta for five to ten minutes after birth. The long umbilical cord provides the infant access to the breast with his oxygen source from mother intact and allows for a calm and leisurely discovery of breathing once the amniotic fluid and mucous drain from the nasal passages.[3] Our medicine men, however, have routinely cut the umbilical cord the moment the infant is out of the womb, putting the newborn instantly into oxygen deprivation, a major fear in all mammals; the infant gasps for breath before the mucous and amniotic fluid have drained from the nasal passages, gags on this fluid, and is dutifully held by the heels and pounded on the upper back to expel a supposed mucous-plug and take that first breath. "Spank the baby" has become an archetypal symbol of the life and death drama the surgeon-star plays in his well-masked role.

Research by Dr. Abraham Towbin, at Boston University's hospital, showed this resuscitation measure to be the source of some 80 percent of the sudden infant deaths autopsied.[4] Sudden infant death syndrome (SIDS) occurs between the sixth and eighth week after birth for "no known reasons" according to medical people. Eighty percent of sudden crib death victims are black infants (sickle cell anemia or poor prenatal care, we're told). When black newborns can't breathe, they are smacked harder to get their air going. "Spank the black baby" is a more vigorous affair than "spank the white baby," as an in-depth study beginning at a major hospital in New York City and carried throughout the country showed. Eighty percent of the SIDS victims specially autopsied by Dr. Towbin showed death was caused by bleeding of the upper spinal cord, *inside the vertebrae;* this is undetectable in an ordinary autopsy. The bleeding, in the upper back area where the infant is pounded to get the breath going, slowly builds a clot that presses against the major nerve plexus controlling the action of heart and lungs until finally both actions quietly break down. In 1977 I was sent a thick medical study, begun in New York and then carried throughout the country, that showed an underlying hostility by hospital staff toward poor black mothers and babies, who receive far more callous, impersonal, hasty, and minimal care than more affluent white mothers. This uncaring bordered, the report claimed, on sheer brutality, particularly toward the growing ranks of young, black teenage welfare cases. Whatever the psychology, 80 percent of SIDS cases occur in the minority poor.

But, black or white, in every case of a prematurely cut umbilical cord, some oxygen deprivation occurs, even when resuscitation isn't needed.[5] Oxygen deprivation is a major cause of brain damage in newborns, and an estimated 20 to 40 percent of resuscitation cases, where an infant fails to breathe spontaneously and artificial means must be used to induce breathing, end in brain damage.[6]

In the last chapter we learned how the awakening of the senses through the mother's touch and the infant's proximity to her heart completes the reticular formation, giving the child the ability to co-ordinate sensory intake and motor response; we also learned that newborns can recognize their own mothers' smell. For the last half century, however, 97 percent of our infants have smelled only disin-fectants, anesthetics, and the other harsh chemicals presumed needed, since a natural passage of immunities from mother to infant is prevented. Newborns can recognize their own mothers' voice, to which they have imprinted in utero, but 97 percent of our infants hear only the hum of machinery and strange voices for a brief time before the silence of the nursery. Newborns can also recognize their own mothers' taste, but breast-feeding, already disparaged by the medical community, disappeared for 97 percent of all American in-fants born after World War II.

Recall that if a face is presented at a distance of six to twelve inches, the newborn's entire visual system is activated; and soon af-terward the infant smiles when a face is presented. For 97 percent of the infants born in the last five decades, no face is seen at all, just masks and bright lights, which are quite painful to brand-new eyes. Those sensitive eyes are forced open and a harsh, irritating chemical is dropped in; the baby is then washed, wrapped, and dispatched to the nursery cubicle where he or she experiences two states unknown in utero—silence and stillness—which the infant has no genetic en-coding for handling. Cut off from the mother's nurturing and with none of the encoded expectancies met, the newborn's adrenals con-tinue to release steroids in the face of maximum fear and abandon-ment. The infant screams for a brief time, and then silence falls.

122

The separation cry is the most primal sound of mammalian life. Human infants practice the many muscular actions involved in this action in utero.[7] Nature's agenda is that this cry, generally stilled on reunion with the mother, not be prolonged past a certain point. If that reunion with the mother fails to take place, genetic encoding dictates that the infant get very quiet and still. (I have observed this sequence in animal infants separated from their mothers in the woods.) In our distant past, prolonged separation cries indicated abandonment and attracted predators to the scene.[8] The final survival maneuver nature provided for the abandoned infant is silence—while the adrenals continue to pump until the infant goes into shock and loses consciousness, nature's mercy. The predators have come—and gone.

For most of this half century, the response of smiling at the presentation of a face does not appear in the infant for an average of ten weeks, the length of time it takes nature to compensate for the missing signals and stimuli—should the infant survive the trauma at all.[9] Years ago Muriel Beadle wrote of the puzzling fact that babies seem born in a state of high excitement, which reverts immediately to extreme distress.[10] A wide range of studies show that learning begins in utero, and in a drug-free birth the newborn is conscious, aware, and sensitive.[11] The reason for the shift from high excitement to extreme stress is hardly obscure.

Ninety-seven percent of our infant population since World War II has been bottle-fed. Decades ago the medical community analyzed mother's milk and found it lacking in every way: poor in fats, proteins, all the good things of life. They disparaged so primitive a process as breast-feeding and introduced substitute milks with high protein and fat content. Babies were immediately rolly-polly fat, not the rather lean things seen before. But rarely is a face presented six to twelve inches from the bottle-fed infant. No heart-beat is picked up; no stimulus of the skin is felt. (In the 1950s we were even advised to use bottle-holders, so the infants might be fed in the crib lest holding of any sort reward crying and spoil them.)

It takes an average of 45 minutes for the shock of separation to bring on conscious withdrawal in the newborn. It takes an average of ten weeks before the minimal handling, casual physical stimulus, and occasional eye contact many bottle-fed infants receive can begin to compensate for the loss and for a tentative consciousness to reappear.

It takes almost three months before the visual system gets enough stimulus to begin functioning again and before the infant smiles. So all our developmental textbooks and authorities starting with Freud refer to the human as being born some three months premature, with three post-uterine months needed before consciousness finally begins to function, when, in fact, it is our own barbaric birth practices that cause this delay.[12]

We have an even greater surprise in store for males, however, for before leaving the hospital they are routinely circumcised without anesthetics, as they have been for these past fifty years. "They don't feel a thing" we are informed; they "cry a bit and go right to sleep" is the verbatim doctrine quoted for decades by surgeons queried about the practice. Nevertheless an elaborate restrainer device (the Circum-strainer is the cute brand-name for one on the market) holds the infant down for the operation since he struggles fiercely, if all-too briefly, when the cutting takes place. Recently some surgeons allowed an EEG (brain-wave recorder) to be attached to infants while the operation took place. The brain wave patterns show serious disturbance as the infants scream; they do not then "just go to sleep"; they go into shock. The brain-wave patterns show no resemblance to ordinary infant sleep-patterns after that, and don't again for several days. [13]

Dentists don't work on teeth without anesthetic, and the barbaric practice of circumcision bestowed wholesale on American males plays its part in the current massive and growing epidemic of violence and sexual dysfunctions of every kind. Yet even this trauma could be compensated for. The really major disaster of history is the separation of mother and infant at birth. This experience of abandonment is the most devastating event of life, which leaves us emotionally and psychologically crippled.

Meanwhile the mother often experiences her reaction to this abandonment as "postpartum blues," a depression considered a medical enigma; she, too, is cut off from the bonding that was supposed to happen. For a while she will weep, but the weeping gives way to anger, hardness, an armor covering a gaping wound that is never healed, that most women aren't even aware of, since it is projected onto the general environment and too often taken out on the hapless infant-child.

Cultural childbirth, intellectual interferences with that which is spontaneous and natural to women, has eroded this bonding process for centuries. Nothing in our entire history, however (or else we would have had no history) comes close to the disaster of twentieth-century medical childbirth, which has destroyed our genetically encoded bonds point for point and brought about massive damage, probably past the point of repair. I have no more than touched on some of the macabre, grisly details of our "modern" enlightened practices here: Young interns have told me how, under direct orders from their supervisors, when delivering the ghetto mother under a strict timetable that can't await a normal after-birth, they were instructed to seize the umbilical cord and jerk the placenta loose as soon as the cord was cut, unaware of the massive hemorrhaging often taking place—another department's concern. Others have told me of the unique staph viruses bred only in hospitals and to which we do not develop immunities. Meanwhile, the United States' astonishingly high infant mortality rate accompanies an equally astonishing price tag. Ours is the most expensive delivery-system in the world, a multibillion dollar a year industry, yet nineteen other industrialized nations have better birth survival rates than we have.

No good comes from discussing any of this. An enormous literature has appeared over the years to no avail. These obscene practices have become not just acceptable but the model for childbirth. Our current generations are the unbonded victims shaped by the system, terrified of the thought of birth outside the medical umbrella, willing to pay any price to avoid personal responsibility for what is considered a dreadful experience. As my New Zealand physician friend, Stephen Taylor, put it, this is really a basic war of man against woman. In the male intellect's long battle with the intelligence of the heart, the real trump card was found in catching the woman when she is most vulnerable and stripping her of her power. Now, it seems we *have* her—and are surely had. Beneath it all grows great anger: children angry at their parents; men angry at women because they didn't get what they needed from women at life's most critical point and still fail to get it; women angry at men for robbing them of their power and, identifying with their oppressors, rejecting motherhood and men in the process. This has caused a rising tide of incompetence and inability to nurture and care for offspring. The genetically encoded intuitions for nurturing have been shattered, and the re-sults are cloaked by ever-so-practical rationalizations. The largest growing work force of the 1980s were the mothers of children under age three. Day care, an unknown phenomenon until recent years, is a major growth industry. Seventy percent of all children under age four were in day care by 1985, and the major concerns of the nation are how to get them all into day care—and who will pay for it.

Our species has survived throughout its history by women caring for women in childbirth, yet midwifery in the United States has been virtually illegal for the last half century. Male surgeons are in charge and many of the female obstetricians follow their system and are lit-tle better. Home birth under any circumstances is safer and more suc-cessful than hospital birth, by a six-to-one ratio.[14] That is, the death rate is six times higher in hospitals than at home, regardless of con-ditions. Male doctors' intellect has interfered with women's intelli-gence and in effect, destroyed a major segment of their lives. Medical childbirth is one of the most destructive force to issue from the mind of man and a most destructive force on earth today. And, as so often in history's ironies, we bow down and worship that which is destroy-ing us. We "honor our doctor as our god" (as one medical man's sign admonished), and offer up in propitiation our mothers.

In 1979 the government of California funded the first scientific study ever made of the root causes of crime and violence. Their first report three years later stated that the first and foremost cause of the epidemic increase of violence in America was the violence done to infants and mothers at birth.[15] It is the primary cause of our ex-plosive rise of suicide, drug abuse, family collapse, abandonment and abuse of infants and children, deterioration of schooling, and so-cial disintegration in general. Only television, to be discussed later, comes close in destructive force.

One final observation has to do with the black community in America. In the pre–World War II South, from where I originated, the black community delivered its children through its own net-work of midwives. The major characteristic of these black commu-nities was their solidarity. They took care of their own and were in effect, one extended family—which is the key ingredient of any true society. They took care of each other not just out of the grim neces-sities for survival but spontaneously out of the bonding function their home birth assured. I have watched the destruction of the poorer black community's "extended family" power, which was its strength through centuries of oppression, through the simple act of shifting its birthing from midwifery to hospital charity wards, where new mothers receive atrocious treatment. And now many of these mothers are unwed teenagers with virtually no family, no support system, no education, no knowledge of birthing or mothering, to say nothing of the influence of drugs, alcohol, and AIDS. The situation worsens at an alarming rate.

Many of these teenagers want babies; they reportedly get pregnant purposely to have someone to love who will love them too, a natural instinct, and they think motherhood will give them some self-esteem in a world that often scorns them. They have no idea what is in store for them, however, for by the time they get out of hospital, they are at war with the infants they dreamed of as sources of love. Black mothers were a model at one time, as Mary Ainsworth and Marcelle Geber found in old Uganda.[16] This is no longer the rule here in America.

Several hundred infants a year, of every race, are murdered outright by their parents in New York City alone. Our national average of infant murder is in the thousands, the average age of the victims from two weeks to two years. One million children a year, from every race, creed, and financial level, are hospitalized as a result of parental abuse. A disproportionate share of the damage is done to black infants.

In America, systematic destruction of the bonds between mothers and infants has created a black community at war with itself. Reports of brain damage, estimated as high as 40 percent, from these hospital practices have been ignored, and in most cases not even published. The clear and detailed medical studies of autopsies of SIDS victims, 80 percent of whom are black, showing damage due to the violence done to the infant at birth, were ignored. So far the growing violence in our black communities has been largely contained within that community. Black teenagers kill each other with abandon, but there is just as much violence exhibited by black men toward black women, and the anger and fear of women toward their men is all too often taken out on the children. This was not the case when I was young. We blame it all on drugs, of course, or poverty, neither of which is the case. Our black communities in the pre–World War II South knew a poverty far more extreme, harsh, and unrelenting than today—yet their solidarity and extended family held them together. The breakdown we witness today is a result of the violence done both mother and infant at birth—a psychic shock acted out from that point on. Rather than a cause, the drug taking we see is in itself but one of the many fall-out effects of this basic genetic damage.

A high percentage of black children are uneducable, a fact strenuously denied and covered with massive deceptive studies supported by huge investments, lest anyone admit to the facts. Both Mary Ainsworth and Marcelle Geber claimed that children of Ugandan mothers were developmentally ahead of and superior in general intelligence to their American counterparts in 1957.[17] The subtle innuendo-lie that the black ghetto child is less educable because of race be easily refuted by a review of these early studies, as well as the recent work of Marcia Mikulak or Miles Storpher.

Newly formed foundations and groups are trying to bring black infants and mothers back together, only to find, as one report stated, that those mothers don't want their infants. This is an absolute anomaly in human history, as freakish as a two-headed calf, yet rapidly becoming the norm. Because of the work of The La Leche League and others in counteracting the medical community and the corporate promotion of bottle feeding, breast-feeding has increased by some 30 percent in the past two decades except in the black community. According to the United States Bureau of Statistics there is no evidence of breast-feeding among blacks at all. (Ironically, in the old South, wet-nurses for white babies were most often black.)

During World War II the percentage of children born in hospitals in America rose from around 30 to 97 percent; home births were stamped out, midwifery was virtually outlawed, and childbirth became the source of very serious money. Breast-feeding was discouraged even before this, but after World War II it was considered a cultural embarrassment; and home birth, the common practice before World War II, even more of an embarrassment. Thus the nation's psyche was split. Television followed within ten years, then day care came, and shortly after, drugs.

Today we witness the macabre drama of a horde of lawyers swarming in to feed on the vulture-like obstetrical body that feeds on the

128

dying social body. Have you sued your OB recently? This malpractice madness has exacerbated every outrage, increased every invasive technology, and obliterated all remaining common sense. Dark clouds gather for us and for all those "backward" nations to whom we send our "life-saving" childbirth interventions. Japan threw out its ancient midwife system some twenty-five years ago in its major industrial cities, imported all our machinery, and then technologically outdid us; within three years the Japanese set up their first day care centers; within ten years the violence in schools and homes was epidemic, while the "stress level" and rate of alcoholism skyrocketed in the Japanese work force. In a two-week lecture tour there, I was asked most often by older people how young mothers could say they didn't know what to do with their children. "How can a mother not know how to mother?" these elders asked in bewilderment. The answer lies in the arrogance of the male intellect in undermining Nature's wisdom, casting on water a bread returned tenfold.

I think of our Senate passing a bill that hospitals must teach new mothers how to mother and breast-feed. Can you imagine teaching a mother cat how to nurse her kittens and care for them? The tide is possibly turning, though, after all these years. Jessica Mitford has targeted birth in America, and midwives are beginning to catch on to the devious machinations of the obstetrical intellect and are finding out how to maneuver on legal grounds. Women who resent the loss of their personal power to the obstetrical world can take a decisive and effective step simply by supporting Midwive's Alliance of North America (M.A.N.A.). Our civilization, as well as our species survival is at stake here.

CHAPTER 14

Name and Thing

Language has been called the greatest invention of the human mind, but it is hardly our invention. It was certainly not developed as an economic or survival expedient by early primitives to facilitate hunting or group action, as wild-eyed materialistic theorists have made into doctrine. Humans no more "invented" language than they invented an opposing thumb. "Realists" propose that early humans' need for tools for hunting, outwitting the saber-toothed tiger, and such, stimulated growth of our huge brain—a hilarious notion in light of the fact that we use so little of our neocortex even to build rockets, lasers, and other offensive defenses. Language is as innate as digestion or sexuality, a genetic given. The muscular response to phonemes is as automatic as the knee-jerk reflex, begins at the seventh month in utero, and is functionally complete by birth. The response is obviously hard-wired into our neural circuits, only needing the appropriate environmental stimulus.

Language is a shaping force in our reality, even as our reality shapes our language. We are constantly creating language by our spontaneous adaptations of it to new situations, many of which arise from our creative use of language. Through naming the things and events of our experience, we help to create them. Speech gives us dominion over a world that speech helps create, and its development of necessity follows the triune structure of our brain. The foundation begins in utero, with those muscular responses to phonemes, and continues after birth through the limbic system. Infants are acutely sensitive to the emotional tone underlying speech, thus one of the first words, universally, seems to be that emotionally charged negation: "No!" The toddler can use a single syllable to express, denote, question, or complain, which is emotional communication. We call the infant-child's random practice of phonemes "lalling," and in that lalling we can detect the growth of syntactical shape, the emotional inflection of later speech. The clear shape of a question, an emphatic declaration, a supplication, a thundering objection, can be detected in our infant-toddler's lalling before actual words appear. Phoneme sound as emotional expression gives rise to syntax, the orderly form in which actual words are placed.

Alexandria Luria proposed that the use of a word can synchronize a child's senses and muscles involved in perceiving and/or acting out an event.[1] A verbal command can enhance a child's physical balance and muscular fine tuning. Recall that sound and physical touch are parallel phenomena from the beginning, as are sound and movement in general, and that virtually all perceptual systems funnel through the labyrinth of the inner ear. The first four years of life center around building "structures of knowledge" of the physical world, our relationship to that world, and names for that world's contents and events. The child is driven to taste, smell, feel, listen to, and look at an event to "fill-in" a visual stimulus. In this way neural fields organize as structures of knowledge.

When the infant-child is given a name for an event, that name enters into the neural patterns giving rise to and shaping that event. When he or she points to an object, parents tend to name it, and that name becomes an integral part of the structure of knowledge the child is building. Physically interacting with an object or responding to an event and getting a name for it completes a structure of knowledge of that object or event. The neural fields that process the event lock in the name as a major ingredient of that experience. Though the child might not use that name for some time, the name enters into the conceptual shaping of the perception. Without this final ingredient of name, events are not lifted out of potential into the orderly structures of our perception.[2]

So words are not addendums to the perceptual text, but the principle motifs that act on and coordinate all the other parts of the play.

Most infant-toddlers start pointing quite early, with a broad arm-fling gesture that becomes more specific until finally a finger points precisely at an object of inquiry. Pointing at an object is both a "reality-check" to see if the parent is sharing that event and a request for a word for the object-event pointed toward. The incessant query "Whazzat Mamma, Whazzat Daddy" begins. Around the home any object can spur a drive to fill in the visual pattern with a full sensory report, including taste, touch, smell, and so on, and build a permanent structure of knowledge of that object. Out in the world, however, our predator-wary mammalian background fires in and caution is the watchword. The unknown can be dangerous. When toddlers encounter an unknown event outside they stop, silently point toward the object, and look intently at the parent. (This same phenomenon is found among all young animals and their mothers.) Parental recognition signals that it is safe to interact with that object, ask what it is, and build a "structure of knowledge" around it. If say, it is a flower and we smile, the toddlers break the pointing stance and go to grasp it, rub it on their faces, smell, listen to, talk to, stuff it in their mouths to taste-identify it, and so fill in that long-range visual stimulus, which initiated the maneuver, with close-range tactile information. This "roughs in" all the materials for that learning. If the parent hasn't given a name for the object, the toddler demands and expects it. Neural fields translate and set up life-long dynamics around the name, which acts as the final coordinator of the event and provides the trigger for recalling it.

A name generally carries with it the emotional state of the parent at the time of that learning. We smile when our children point to flowers, and their structure of knowledge will include the emotional nuances of our sanction. If our children point to a mangy, dirty old mongrel dog, we recoil and shout, "Don't dare go near that dirty beast!" Unless their will has been broken, they dutifully break their stance and rush to taste, touch, smell, feel, listen to, and talk to the dirty beast. We shriek and snatch them away, which is built into the resulting structure of knowledge as the emotional-tone or value of that event. Whether positive or negative, a name has been given and sensory information concerning its nature is locked in. The emotional brain coordinates and shapes the senses into a gestalt completed by the emotional state or "relational attitude" provided by the parent. The parent's positive or negative reaction doesn't alter the effectiveness of the learning, but is registered in the resulting structure of knowledge.

The situation changes markedly when the parent makes no response at all to a "pointing event" in a strange setting. Blurton Jones, researching this, was struck by how often toddlers go through this pointing routine when neither Jones as the observer nor parent could tell what the child was pointing at.[3] When toddlers get no sanctioning response, they will not interact with whatever attracts them. Children may, in frustration, try to drag a parent to the encounter, so critical is the need to get sanction of the event before interaction. Without that sanction, however, there is no exploration. Many times my five children at that stage would demand "Whazzat Daddy," and I couldn't answer because I couldn't see and/or didn't know to what they were referring.

Blurton Jones found this "pointing-at-nothing" so frequent and common an occurrence in toddlers in all societies, that he coined the term "quasi-hallucinatory phenomenon" to describe it. What was puzzling to Jones (and to any observant parent) is the child's lack of discrimination between these quasi or partial events and those we recognize as real. Note, however, that in those episodes we label "quasi-hallucinatory," the children do not build a structure of knowledge of that event. They do not follow through with the tactile interactions needed to fill in the visual stimuli with content, such as tasting, touching, smelling, and, above all, naming. Such phenomena remain "quasi," rather than structures of knowledge reinforced with every repetition of the name. That whole category of event, including similar phenomena, may then remain only potential, selected out by our highly selective brain on behalf of the welter of sanctioned events waiting to be discovered and processed. On becoming parents, our once "quasi-hallucinating" children will also make no response should their children point to and ask for a name for a phenomenon in this unactualized potential-field. Such a deficiency might be passed on to the next generation ad infinitum; lots of other potential abounds, but realizing it depends invariably on nature's model-imperative.

The power of a word to "call up" an event is probably the most valuable aspect of language. Speak the word and the child expects the named thing to appear. If not, the name alone can activate the corresponding neural network and call forth appropriate sensory responses for a quasi-reconstruction of the original event, with the mind filling in as best it can with a memory. This is the foundation of learning, imagination, and creativity, and one of the major reasons for language itself. Remembering is a rough facsimile, a "re-cognition" of the event with a name as its central trigger. This "concreteness" of language will be seen to be the central core of play, on which all higher learning rests. In the young child to think is to remember, most of it in imaging. Later in life the opposite is true, to remember is to think, also involving imaging.

For the first seven or so years (often much longer) children talk to themselves constantly while playing. Word and imagery are part of the child's general worldview. Imagination, the ability to create internal images not present to the sensory system, is intricately tied with language. Ancient theories that the name for a thing-event is inherent in the frequencies giving rise to that object or event is true, if only after the fact. The name is an integral part of thing because name and thing build up as a single neural field or fields early in our life.

In this concrete language, the word not only denotes a sensory object, but participates as a major structural part of that object. Ask two-year-olds to say the word *hand*, and they will move a hand as they say the word. Such language can then be used as a referent, but its referents will always be physical. All early language, though a product of our neocortex, relates to the physical reality afforded by our reptilian brain, and, as we grow, our mammalian, emotional brain. Semantic language is a different matter entirely and appears around age eleven or twelve. This is the language of our highest cortical structures, where a word need only refer to itself, and so can be used by our intellectual, creative thought distinct from the two lower systems. In this semantic language the word can be a thing-in-itself, not referring back to any thing other than the thought. But it is important to remember that in the concrete language of early life, word and thing tend to give rise to each other: Two-year-olds move a hand when speaking the word. The adult can use the word in an abstract form, often forgetting its concrete origins.

A child's structure of knowledge of the physical world and the concrete names given it is about 80 percent completed by around age four and by age seven essentially finished, an autonomous intelligence at our disposal. A child is then "lifted out" of these entrainments and can become objective about them, using the relation between word-and-thing to manipulate or operate on those named object-events themselves. This is "operational thinking," another developmental stage, possible only because name is an integral part of the event's organization. Even this objective use of early language doesn't make it any the less concrete, however. Word and thing are still a unit. A separated word, able to stand alone as its own referent, begins to function with the great shift of intellect at age eleven. A major cause of trouble in our day comes when we demand an abstract understanding of the young concretely oriented child.

Note the critical role of parent-model and child in all this language-world construction. John Kennell and Marshall Klaus found that the child who is bonded to its mother has a more powerful vocabulary than the unbonded child simply because the bonded mother speaks much more with her child. She spontaneously furnishes names for her child at every interaction, through her rapport and instinctive nurturing response. To nurture the human is to nurture intelligence, of which language is foundational. Thus the bonded child is generally more intelligent than the unbonded one. Close parental rapport, monitoring, and sanctioning events in the child's experience, determines to an immeasurable extent the depth of that child's cognitive ability, sensory awareness, general alertness, and educability. Marcia Mikulak found that children in non-technological societies have some 25 percent greater sensory awareness of their environment, its people, and ongoing events than children in the United States. Average "primitive" children can name hundreds of plants in their immediate environment and tell you their uses; they can sense the general atmosphere, emotional and environmental, and are, in general, simply more alive. Sound and touch, word and thing, are two interpretations of the same underlying frequency. The touch-starved child, sensorily and emotionally deprived, brought up in a mechanical environment, will be language deficient as well. No later abstract language *can* form without the solid foundation of a concrete language.

Children who are able to name and recognize the hundreds of plants around them are in a better position to grasp such abstractions as $E=MC^2$ when the time comes, than children forced into such abstractions prematurely, with no concreteness on which to base them.

The right hemisphere of the brain retains this initial concrete language, where words denote affairs of the sensory-motor and emotional systems, even after the left hemisphere and its abstract use of language becomes dominant. Our right hemisphere has a richer neural connection with the two older, object-oriented brains than its neighboring left hemisphere. The right hemisphere has been popularly considered the "holistic" hemisphere, but it is holistic only insofar as it integrates the two lower systems into service of the higher. Its primary direction is downward, in effect, keeping the threefold system intact. Its secondary direction is lateral, toward its left partner, which holds within its potentials a far greater "holism."[4] Thus we note that when the right hemisphere is dominantly active we tend to be anxious and defensive. When the left hemisphere is dominant and active we are more relaxed and euphoric. The left is evolutionarily superior to the right; it is the last to be developed by the child and provides a means for moving into realms beyond the physical entirely.

Somewhere around age six to seven, as we begin our first objective operational thought, nature begins creating that "semantic language" by abstracting words out of their concrete referents. *Hand*, for example, can have a much wider, metaphoric meaning in an essentially left-hemisphere language where a word need not refer to anything other than itself. All development is from the "concrete to the abstract" as Piaget said, which means, in effect, from reptilian stimulus-response to higher, neocortical creative action. In this progression, words planted in material soil can grow and flower into pure thought. Our sense of self moves accordingly, from one embeddedment to another, each progressively less physical.

Nature has programmed these progressions with care, allotting to each stage time for development, assuming, of course, that the proper environment is given. While the stages vary in each child, there is a general statistical movement of them, which is wise to keep in mind, lest we, for example, fail to recognize the concreteness of a child's orientation in the early years and assume he or she can grasp abstract language or thought. In the next chapter we will explore this issue of concreteness as observed in the "cycle of competence" by which learning unfolds. In the cycle of competence we may find more evidence that the neural loss at age eleven is excessive (remember that only a scant 2 percent differential separates us genetically from the higher apes).

CHAPTER 15

Cycle of Competence

Mechanical excellence is the vehicle for genius.

WILLIAM BLAKE

Nature's agenda for us is to learn procedures, so we can participate in the creative process. Products, such as information, answers, thoughts, and things are cheap; process is priceless. People with I.Q.'s of 25 can give infallible answers and voluminous information. In reversibility thinking, considered by Jean Piaget to be the highest level of intellect, we solve a problem only to retrace our steps to see how we arrived at that solution. Then we can "abstract" that ability from its original context and apply it to a wide variety of new situations. The actual solution is incidental to learning the process, as when an infant grasps for an object; gaining the object (the stimulus) is secondary to learning how to grasp.

Most learning, deliberate or not, follows a threefold "cycle of competence." Observed by Greenfield and Tronick at Harvard's Center for Cognitive Studies many years ago, this cycle seems more significant then ever, in light of the triune nature of our brain. The cycle involves: (1) roughing in, (2) relating and filling in, and (3) practice and variation.[1] In our earliest years this cycle is an entrainment that demands every bit of attention. An entrainment is a sequence that unfolds in lock-step fashion, one step leading to the next. We speak of being "embedded" in an entrainment until it completes itself, since it leaves no room for a separate awareness. We can't even process other sensory information when an entrainment is in force (as when, absorbed in writing, I sit oblivious to the smoke from the supper I promised my wife I'd watch). Once the cycle of competence has run its threefold course, our self-awareness becomes general again and can attend to other stimuli.

Indications are that our personal-self represents only 5 to 10 percent of our total consciousness. As a free-floating point of attention, our self can act like a super target-cell to activate any of the intelligences and abilities available. A mature self-system can embed in an activity, allowing 100 percent of one's energy to be applied, or, equally, can dis-embed completely from an engagement and move on. A fragmented self remains partially embedded in various systems, unable to fully detach from any of them, and so, is unable to fully integrate its energies into a single entrainment.

The toddler can embed and entrain as nature intended. For instance, the first time a little girl notices her mother open the kitchen cabinet, she goes over to one of these doors, grasps the handle, and pulls as her mother did. The magnetic latch may give and she might fall back, but she gets up and sees that the door is open. She pushes the door closed, grasps the handle and pulls again, keeping her balance this time; again it opens. The light dawns, understanding appears as the roughed-in form is filled in with actual content. Here is how mother does it. Previous neural fields handling similar complex movements start to interact and link up; new neural fields rush into service, filling in the bits and pieces that complete the pattern.

The next stage follows immediately, practice. She begins to open and close that door over and over again with exuberant abandon. After an interminable period of this noisy business, there is sufficient myelination for the several millions of neural connections involved in this total body-mind action to function with the minimum expenditure of energy. This frees the toddler's consciousness from the entrainment, and she can abandon this arena of conquest and look for new worlds to conquer. The critical variation period begins. She notices other doors and repeats the performance on each, spending hours at this. Aware of and enjoying her new-found ability, she plays with it as one would a piano.

Until that practice stage was completed, the toddler was not aware of herself performing the new action, she *was* that action. She was only aware *as* the action, not of it. Her entrainment was so complete that no conscious energy was left over for self-awareness. Only through completing the initial entrainment can she stand back from it, look at it objectively, see what she has done, and apply her learning somewhere else. This is the foundation of reversibility thinking and all further development and applies to us at age seventy as well as seven.

When this sensory-motor phase of the cycle is completed, a higher entrainment takes over, impelling her to extract the new ability out of the context that gave rise to it and vary that learning. She will correlate that situation with other contexts and expand the stable neural fields she has just formed with each new variation. We could say she "stands in" her neocortex and examines what those lower systems can now do under her direction. She looks around for something "doorish" enough to be compatible to her new field of potential, yet variable enough to furnish novel stimuli that will enlarge that new field.

Continued repetition without variation would lead to habituation and prematurely close the cycle. Habituation happens when there is no novelty and a neural pattern–tape loops, it is turned over to the R-system, which can handle that single pattern but without variation. This is nature's economy, but if the R-system takes over too soon, expansion into new relations stops. Since the episode of that single door, by itself, would make for an incomplete learning, the neocortex keeps the ball rolling with its novelty factor.

It is a neat cycle, and variation is the key, when its time comes. Variation disturbs the patterns established by forcing them to accommodate to new possibilities, and this strengthens those patterns. My muscles are all very comfortable and undisturbed, sitting here in my cushy chair. But they will never match those seen in the health magazines if I leave them so comfortable. The word *comfort* comes from the Latin words for *with* and *strength* and originally meant operating from a position of power—different from what it has deteriorated to mean today: to avoid all action and "flake out." Ilya Prigogine claims perturbation or disequilibrium is necessary for learning and growth. A smug, satisfied system goes static. Marian Diamond points out that the brain stays flexible and powerful all our life if sufficiently challenged. Habituation is the enemy of growth. Perturbation, or disturbance of established patterns, overcomes the tendency toward this inertia. The minute we establish a pattern we would rest in it, were this variation impulse not built into the cycle. The dynamic between our reptilian and mammalian systems tends toward habituation and will avoid novelty since those limbic-R-system dynamics are not built to handle novelty. The dynamic between our emotional and intellectual brains, however, impels us toward novelty. Our constant tension between our lower and higher natures is partly this tension between new and ancient neural structures, between avoiding and seeking novelty, between equilibrium and disequilibrium. Even when we choose novelty, we want to rest at each achieved point and habituate the novel state. The highest point of life may be to live in a state of pure flow, a "now-state" without past or future, in which prediction and control are not factors—a state of continual, instant-by-instant adaptation to the unknown, which is just about as far beyond the reptilian state as one can imagine. This is the state the active, learning child actually lives in (by default; we habituate later), and what we must recapture in spiritual development.

In our toddler's variation stage, any possibility for variation now becomes the stimuli. Once ability is gained it can increase. This keeps the fields of potential seeking out new relations and compatibilities. The increase must follow on the heels of the initial learning, while the entrainment is in effect. Myelination will now take place between categories of experience, between related neural networks. Now the new field of potential assumes some autonomy, as though it were an independent intelligence, and seeks out all areas of compatibility in the environment. Some correlations our toddler makes will be clearly compatible, others less so, as she extends to quite different forms of doors—a variety of hinged objects, the potty seat, the lid to the music box—then to tops or coverings in general, such as box tops and jar tops. The initial category, once formed, continually expands as the dynamic broadens; sub-categories form and relate, and so on.

Consider a common variation on the above scenario, however. In the midst of this all-encompassing practice period, while the entraining toddler is banging away on the door, getting that myelin going, the phone rings. Mother says: "Stop that, dear, I can't hear." The child doesn't even slow down. Mother shouts, "Stop this instant, I am on the *telephone!*" But not a flicker of response. Bang, bang. Mother puts down the phone, rushes over in a rage, picks the toddler up, and smacks her hand. "When will you learn to mind me?" shouts mother, putting the shrieking toddler down and returning to the phone.

The toddler didn't respond to her mother's request because an entrainment leaves no energy for processing other forms of information. She literally didn't hear her mother. Having her hand smacked simply breaks the entrainment as a non-sequitur, an illogical interruption of an instinctual, hard-wired response. The learning is now canceled and she will have to begin all over again, more or less. The problem is that, after a few such interferences, the child learns that following the hard-wired entrainment of learning can lead to disaster, a no-win situation that strains the parent bond (a major fear of childhood). Confidence is the essence of intelligence. *Confidence* means "with faith." Faith in one's self is built in; fearfulness and timidity, being counterproductive, must be learned. After a few episodes of reprimands and conflicting parental demands that break the child's learning entrainment, she must, of necessity, split her attention between the learning at hand and the environment at large, since that environment has become a source of unpredictable fear and pain. From that point on, the toddler will have one eye on the "door" or whatever the learning target is, and the other on her parent, or, later, teacher, lest she suddenly get smacked (for no reason she can comprehend). A learning cycle gets 50 percent of her energy (at best), the defense mechanisms get 50 percent, and learning becomes a halfway, divided effort. Most of us grow up split in this way. "I can't seem to concentrate" we say, and, indeed, we can't. We can't trust our world enough to entrain on anything. We can't put 100 percent of our consciousness into any action, since that would leave nothing left over for our defense system. Thus we are scattered and fragmented between what we are trying to learn and our feelings of anxiety.

So a good learning environment for children must be safe and free of reprimands, fear, and pain, and one in which stimuli to initiate cycles of learning are provided and the children are allowed to complete those cycles.[2]

Estimates are that 95 percent of all learning takes place below our awareness. The pregnant mother just carries on her speech as usual, and this activates the infant's built-in, hard-wired speech pattern. You can't stop children from learning to speak if they hear people talk. The same is true of many intelligences. Surprisingly little learning takes place from willful, forced attempts to make a child learn. Just provide a child with the appropriate environment—one with acceptance, love, protection, and appropriate stimuli—and you can't prevent the brain from learning. Learning is what it's designed to do.

Our toddler, still trying to gain some control over those ungainly muscles and limbs, is not available for a discussion of quantum physics or evolution. Similarly, the adult still locked into a body-world identity and low-level defense postures is not available for a discussion of the evolution of spirit. A scientist, locked into and identified with a reality consistent with his electronic-physical devices in the laboratory, can hardly be blamed for a lack of enthusiasm over my reports of a unity-state of consciousness or meditation experience.

My meditation teacher said "You can never really occupy this body until you can move beyond it." Examined in the light of learning in general, "moving beyond the body" is the logical conclusion to the lengthy process that occupies our childhood: discovering and learning to use our physical bodies in the larger body of the world. William Blake commented that mechanical excellence was the vehicle of genius. You can't get into the music, a great pianist said, until you can get beyond the notes. Through mechanical excellence in a subject we rise beyond it and can play with it creatively. Thus, nature's goal for us seems to be dominion over the creative process itself. This may be an audacious suggestion, since it means moving beyond creation itself, but it follows logically from the cycle of competence nature has arranged for us.

CHAPTER 16

Will and the Terrible Two

Our eighteen-month-old points at things, demands their names, bangs doors, and tastes everything to build a structure of knowledge of her world. Eighty percent of this will be accomplished by age four through the child's natural curiosity, exploration, and play, activating and developing each of the three neural systems in their respective evolutionary order.[1] Early physical and emotional learning, though hard-wired into our two primary systems, is registered by neural fields of our neocortex. This gives us the means to modulate and humanize those lower behaviors later on. As we saw with language, any higher brain activity must be established in the two primary structures first. So sensory-motor and emotional development must be in keeping with the nature of those two animal brains that unfold first, as foundations for the higher, human one. This is why any education for children should be presented in a way compatible with the nature of these early "animal-systems," essentially "sensory-motor" with emotional security.

A brain growth-spurt at birth equips newborns to adapt to their new environment, and they are completely "embedded" in and identified with this R-system task. The infants don't "have" a body, they *are* that body; they don't "have" a sensation, they *are* that sensation. There is no separation of subject and object simply because the entrainments called for are so complete that no energy is left over for a "self-system." That subjective self appears only with the opening for full development of the limbic system around the end of the first year, when visual fields mature and a stable world forms. At this point, which Piaget called "object constancy," another brain growth spurt takes place, and a parallel development of the limbic system unfolds. Infancy ends, and early childhood begins; *will* unfolds and an independent self-system appears. This ego-self will encompass the emotional and cognitive intelligences and behaviors of the limbic system and strive to build a structure of knowledge of the world, self, relationships, and language.

Our structure of knowledge of the world is built through a coupling of mind and environment. The first environment is the mother herself, the second the home. For all mammals the nest is the safe space for exploration and gives the infant a stable frame of reference. Consider, however, that our toddler spots the new antique figurine on the coffee table and makes a beeline for it. Mother calls out "Don't you dare touch that figurine, it's priceless." Toddler, startled, turns and looks at mother, but proceeds to toddle blindly toward the unknown object, his eyes still fixed on her face. Mother, seeing her toddler stare straight at her and yet do exactly as he is told not to do, goes into a minor rage, shouting, "You touch that and I'll spank you." Toddler looks alarmed, but, still locked in on mamma's face, clumsily reaches toward the figurine, probably knocking it over. Mother rushes over, grabs him, shakes him, smacks him about, and shouts "What is the matter with you, didn't you hear what I said? Are you deaf, stupid? When will you learn to do as you're told?" Later she recounts the episode to neighbor, husband, or mother-in-law, saying, "And that little devil looked me square in the eye and did exactly as I told him not to do." (How many times have we heard just this, and how much wilder is father's reaction to such "disobedience.")

The reason for this devilish turn of events lies in a baffling drive called *will*, which is one of the limbic system's behaviors. We are familiar with and somewhat tolerant of the erratic emotions that begin at this time; those mercurial polar shifts from like to dislike, love to hate, joy to sorrow, or exuberance to tears are the primitive aversion-attraction of the R-system incorporated into the far more complex emotions of the limbic system. We are equally familiar with but far less tolerant of this force called will, which also appears at this time, as an intelligence for overcoming obstacles to development. It is a non-volitional power, that is, the toddler has no say in it. Will acts

145

like an instinctive, hard-wired impulse driving the R-system to do the limbic system's bidding. Development in the first four years is equally sensory-motor and emotional, but the emotional system is a higher and more powerful evolutionary structure. It drives the motor system to "do its will," just as the neocortex later drives both the emotional and sensory-motor systems. So when our child sees the figurine, an entrainment is activated to explore that new object and build a structure of knowledge about it. Countered by mother's command, two equally strong, but opposing forces are now in effect, the bond to mother and this powerful drive. If the parent blocks learning, the will fires in to move him through this obstacle to his development. When that obstacle is his own mother, the very source of life, a classical double bind unfolds. Driven by his will, his body stumbles along toward the target while he, as a consciously aware self, looks back at his mother, "square in the eye," trying to maintain that threatened bond while his body does its thing.

With some moral effort we adults can, with our developed ego, modulate those mammalian instincts (curb the tendency to do violence to spouse, child, or boss, for instance). But the toddler, whose ego is still bedded in his limbic and R-systems, has no such moderating influence. Toddlers don't *have* emotions, they *are* that emotion-of-the-moment. So his body moves toward the target, silently looking back at his mother, caught up in two conflicting major instinctual drives, neither of which he has any control over.

The best solution is to "baby-proof" the home in the first place and keep valuables or unsafe items out of the toddler's reach. Failing that, we can gently remove him from the situation, substitute another object to take his attention and, when things have cooled down, replay the situation from a more constructive angle. Punishment and rage break the child's will—the capacity to overcome obstacles and explore the unknown, which is learning itself. They leave him with no self-confidence, no faith in himself, and he will fumble or retreat at every little difficulty or challenge. Repetitions of this kind of double bind, like the previous example of breaking the cycle of competence, split the psyche. That youngster will grow to be one of us, thinking one thing, feeling another, and acting in a way disconnected from both.

Michael Gazzaniga thinks the environment (of parents and society) is generally inhibitive to the child's learning.[2] A lack of stimuli and maximum of frustration and inhibition means that only a minimum of neural fields will be myelinated and available for future development. Nature worked out the intricacies of a physical world long before we arrived on the scene and gave us more neocortex than we needed to manage ourselves in it. Going beyond such elementary stuff as this well-established physical system, the rest of our new brain offers us the possibility to move into pure potential or other realms of being. First, we need the capacity to overcome obstacles, the "will to persevere," the curiosity and courage to enter the unknown. We also need to have established a sufficiently mature neural base by physical interaction with a nurturing and stimulating environment.

The development of our two primary structures must be given top priority in the early years, so we have a foundation for these later, greater ventures. Our lower animal structures are designed to meet not only our physical and emotional needs, but to lay the foundations for the eventual needs of the neocortex. Nature prepares us for this years in advance; intent precedes the ability to do, as illustrated by the muscular response to phonemes in utero, but this same pattern holds for all forms of neocortical action, particularly for the intelligence that appears at age four.

CHAPTER 17

Intuition:
Seeing Within and Beyond

Around age four another growth spurt takes place in the brain, adding even more neural connections and field potentials. By now 80 percent of the child's language, worldview, and ego-structure are complete, and the other 20 percent should be filled in by about age seven, as provided for by this growth spurt. Among the potentials opening for development at age four are music and that twin of imagination, intuition: the ability to "perceive information not present to the physical senses." Music stands some chance of being developed, so I will concentrate on intuition, which is almost never developed and generally misunderstood. It crops up continually. A five-year-old's mother went to town. She stopped by an empty laundromat to telephone home to the baby-sitter and see how things were. Her five-year-old got the phone and asked, "Mamma, why are you in the laundromat when you didn't take any clothes to wash?" Mamma wonders how he knew where she was. A four-year-old comes in from play announcing that daddy was calling her; the phone rings and it's daddy, just thought he'd call and talk to his little girl a minute. Or, recall my son's theological discourse—essentially the same sort of play of energies. The connection is through the implicate order, and the relationship involved is quite clear.[1]

Intelligence is the ability to respond for one's well-being. Intuition is an intelligence from "higher upstream" in the evolutionary scheme and offers information related to one's physical or emotional well-being when that information is not available from the immediate physical environment. Intuition employs the dynamic between the limbic system and neocortex, whereas ordinary environmental information comes from the limbic-R-system dynamic. Each structure of our triune system has its own domain or frequency realm. Information is available from each on its own "lateral" level, if we can "sense" it. As William Blake said, we can sense far more than our physical senses allow. The physical, however, is as far as we generally go in development.

A study was made of original Anglo-Saxon settlers in the southern mountains of the United States, isolated for generations, who used "telepathy," as the research people called it, without self-conscious awareness of the novelty. Virtually all these "telepathic" communications involved the general well-being and emotional bonding within the family unit: the mother calling the family in for dinner, sensing family members in distress, or whatever.[2] Such native intuition could be developed into a powerful, extensive, and workable structure of knowledge, such as the Aborigines' Dream Time, if a society decided this were important. A simple case in point is the classical study of bonded mothers in South America and Africa who don't use diapers for their infants, carry the infants in a sling, yet are never soiled by them. They sense when the infant is ready to urinate or defecate. This, of course, is but a part of the intuitions that open in the mother on bonding with her infant at birth.[3] (How ironic that disposable diapers are now a major landfill pollutant and toxic threat in America.)

As soon as the child develops a majority of its physical body-world knowledge, around age four, nature opens this non-physical domain as an instrument of physical well-being. This high form of mammalian intelligence centers in the limbic system as employed by the neocortex. Most animals use some form of intuition, since it is vital to survival, but they can't develop it as we could.[4] The four-year-old is still very much a "child of the dream," dwelling in both physical and subtle realms. Now that these systems are 80 percent complete, and energy can be spared for the effort, nature prepares the child to move up the triune ladder. The neocortex has been fully active from the beginning, of course, but only peripherally, imprinting the respective developments of its lower neighbors. When the new brain becomes available for development at age four, the mind can employ the dreamlike realm of the implicate order in new ways. The first job of any higher intelligence seems to be to incorporate the lower and put it to new use.

Our right hemisphere, recall, has richer neural connections with its limbic structure than the left and maintains a unified connection of all three levels thereby. Concrete language is retained in this right hemisphere and will be drawn on by and incorporated with the left hemisphere's more abstract forms later on. From the objective stance offered by this right hemisphere locus, we can directly access information out of the limbic system and its implicate order. The mind can extract information about its physical reality, taking shape within that nontemporal implicate order, before that subtle potential becomes explicate through our perceptual system. (This, of course, is how Targ's remote viewing of future targets takes place.) From the right hemisphere we can draw on the formative wave-fields of relationship available through the limbic system and get information about our environment ahead of time, or outside our immediate time-space boundaries. The mind seems to do this through a dynamic between the limbic system and the temporal lobes. Providing information for our well-being when that information is not available to our physical senses is a most logical step for nature to take, directly in line with development, and physiologically self-evident in brain construction.

Intuition seems to fade around age seven if it is not developed, and developing it requires modeling and nurturing. The function fails to unfold either through lack of recognition and guidance, or through direct discouragement, as when parents consider such events to be pathological or psychotic. The word *providence* comes from the Latin *pro-videre*, "to see ahead." Intuition in the four-year-old is the first stage of this "seeing ahead"—a capacity we fail to develop and then "divinize" as we tend to do with any undeveloped potential. Lacking this intuition, we will remain partially embedded in the limbic-R-system, restricted to physical-sensory information as our only way to relate to our earth and each other. If physical perceptions are all we have, we are grounded in matter. By the time we are informed of our physical world, that world already has acted on us. If we have only physical reports to go on, nature must compensate by intensifying our attention to them.

Were this early intuitive system developed, as part of our intelligence for maintaining our physical well-being, it would be turned over to the automatic pilot as part of the R-system's larger maintenance system. Without this intuition, we develop an intellect compulsively trying to compensate by engineering our environment and each other. This contributes to our living like "armed crustaceans eternally on the alert" against a world we can't trust and curtails a full development of our highest structures.

Intellect is a specialized and limited form of intelligence, designed for far higher pursuits than physical safety; however, when it is incorporated into our defense system it makes trouble. We try to predict and control an infinitely open and creative system and dominate our earth and each other, all on behalf of a physical welfare seriously threatened by this very activity. We consider the resulting sciences and technologies our highest achievements, indicative of evolutionary "progress," even as these activities pull our highest structure into a lower brain action, which is devolutionary. This blocks development of the intelligences that can lead us beyond any need to manipulate. Were our intuition developed, our right hemisphere, handling the balanced integration with its two lower support systems, would keep our environmental adjustments in fine tune. This would allow mind to move (through the left hemisphere, and probably a general cerebral-cerebellar dynamic) into those mental realms evolution intended for us.

The Australian Aborigines developed intuition to an exceptional level.[5] They based their mythical cosmology as well as practical worldview on this non-localized form of awareness. Dream Time was far more than a primitive "trance state." It was the next logical stage of development beyond the limbic-R-system and was foundational to later stages of operational thinking. The Aborigine doesn't appear to *us* to have developed such later stages as we in the West have, but we develop this operational thinking without the foundation of this critical intuitive thought and so recognize only operational thinking that "operates" on our material world as valid, which, again, may be devolutionary.

The higher up the evolutionary ladder we go, the less physical and stable and the more subtle and fluid the energies are, and, strangely enough, while more powerful, they are equally more fragile, more difficult to establish, and harder to sustain. Evolution points us toward a state of consciousness in which we are beyond the physical, yet these states seem to be critically subject to physical disruption until stabilized. Millions of years of genetic encoding embed us in those stable matter fields of the R-system; they happen to us automatically by the nature of our conception and birth. Habituation to them is more comfortable and natural to us than adaptation to unknown possibilities beyond time-space. It is our own "nature" we must go beyond, here. Higher evolutionary possibilities are fluid, relational-causal fields that have no fixed reality or structure. They do not "exist" but form as we interact with them and according to the nature of our interaction. They are unpredictable and incompatible with previously established patterns and measurements, and we retreat from such insecurity by embedding more tightly in our ancient physical stability that is ironically only fleeting and transient for us fragile creatures.

Developing the intellect to logically analyze and intervene in the natural order may not have been evolution's intent at all but rather its gamble. Since our highest brain is novelty seeking by nature, the natural tendency is to seek the novelty available through our lowest system, rather than exploring the potential of the highest. In order to merge with creation-as-process, we must be able to operate on higher creative levels, and intellect is nature's tool for this. So it appears that nature must both develop this intellect and at the same time entice us to use it to move beyond the powerful allure of our ancient, stable physical systems.

Nature's goal seems to be to integrate our intellect into an intelligence that will use it in a balanced, logical way. This is the heart's intelligence, which can guide intellect in its movement into the unknown; and we must recognize that the unknown is unknown even to that highest intelligence. The unknown forms as intellect probes for novelty. We have lost contact with this higher intelligence, though, probably through intellectual interference itself; the risk intellect presents is its ability to cut itself off from its polar dynamic. In this alienated state we develop intellect as an ally with the physical-sensory system and its primitive defense postures, producing brilliant thought in reptilian personalities. And the more brilliant the human reptile, the more precarious our situation.

152

The capacity for entering this higher evolutionary realm of potential isn't well enough established to be statistically available. Access to that state is difficult to attain or maintain on any broad level as long as we remain entrenched in our animal natures, served by an intellect developed through a devolutionary setback. The combination is disastrous to evolution and to the societies caught in this reverse dynamic.

Development unfolds on nature's schedule, nevertheless, and process is nature's goal. Access to process is possible through our newest and highest structure, just as access to product is given by our older, lower structures. By age six or seven, nature's intent is that our product orientation, our physical knowledge, be well established, allowing us to look at it objectively, begin to understand it, and eventually come into dominion over it. So nature provides a new brain growth spurt in our sixth year, giving our seven-year-old four to five times the neural connections available at eighteen months. (Gazzaniga claims the neural system is six to seven times more densely packed than before.)[6] Loaded with a massive amount of new neural materials, our seven-year-old enters into the first, concrete phase of operational thought. If our current research is correct about the astonishing extent of neural connections in the brain at this age, the possibility for development is limitless. The only boundary is nature's model-imperative, a boundary that proves as restrictive as our parents and society.

The concrete operations beginning at this age are so important that we will discuss them in their own chapter. But first, because they can't be developed without the foundations that are built through child play, we will review that initial creative action, play, in our next chapter.

CHAPTER 18

Play

If you want your children to be brilliant, tell them fairy
tales. If you want them to be very brilliant, tell them
even more fairy tales.

ATTRIBUTED TO ALBERT EINSTEIN

Play is the foundation of creative intelligence, but, like any intelligence, it must be developed; in keeping with nature's model-imperative, the child who is played with will learn to play. The child who
is not played with will be unable to play and will be at risk on every
level. One of the foundations of play is story telling. Even before
they can speak, infants will listen raptly to adults speaking or telling
stories. Understanding the words is almost incidental in the beginning, it's the sound of those syllables that fascinates. In his memoirs
one gentleman recounted how as a toddler he loved to snuggle into
his grandfather's lap and listen to him read the great philosophers,
lofty words that predisposed that young mind toward higher things.

Time-honored children's tales are equally vital to the child's development. The child listens to the storyteller with total entrainment; he grows still, his jaw drops, his eyes widen, and he stares
fixedly at the speaker. His vision, however, turns within where the
action is, for the words of a story stimulate the creation of corresponding internal images. A little girl told me she liked radio more

than television because the pictures were so much more beautiful. The radio words gave the stimulus; the beautiful pictures were her own creation. This imaging is the foundation of future symbolic and metaphoric thought, both concrete and formal operational thinking, higher mathematics, science, philosophy, everything we consider higher mentation or education.

The word *metaphor* comes from the Greek *metapherien*, "to transfer." The word *meta* means that which "stands between, comes after, or stands for." A metaphor is an image that can create a bridge between different meanings, showing a likeness between them, or representing something else by transferring meaning from one object or event to another. Metaphoric thought can create new meanings by relating images in different ways and suggest new directions for creative action.

In the story *The Three Bears* Father Bear wears a suit of clothes and carries a cane. He is a metaphor in that he is an animal figure representing a human one. He is symbolic of the father archetype. The word *symbol* comes from the Greek word *sumbolon*, meaning "to throw a token." We throw or cast symbols forth as tokens of a greater action, thought, or larger structure. A symbol points beyond itself, toward a state, condition, or concept in which the symbol participates. For instance our flag, the bald eagle, and Uncle Sam symbolize the United States; the cross symbolizes Christianity; the six-pointed star of David, Judaism. Suzanne Langer pointed out that symbols are "vehicles for the conception" of things. When we hear words about something, we have conceptions of those words. "It is the conception, not the things, that symbols directly mean."[1]

The symbols presented in story telling are the foundations for later conceptualization. Metaphoric-symbolic figures can represent, stand for, or point toward states of being. They can participate in meanings or suggest connections that open new areas of thought. Metaphoric-symbolic language can suggest subtle states that can't in themselves be articulated. This is why poetry is a powerful tool for moving the mind beyond its embeddedment in matter. It can evoke or call up feelings, longings, or aspirations unavailable to discursive thought, logic, or description.

Almost surely the limbic structure, in conjunction with the neocortex (that combination involved in dreaming and imagery), is involved in developing metaphoric-symbolic ability. Each of our three brains has its own lateral form of imagery, representative of its function: from the physical images of the R-system's outer environment to the dreamlike inner images of the limbic system to the abstract images of neocortical thought. The gap between the R-system's localized thing-events and the abstract conceptions of our neocortex is bridged by the limbic system. As poet George Franklin points out, the higher realms of imagination, as explored and championed by such poets as Coleridge and Blake, go beyond mere imagery. They can move us into a realm where metaphor is causal, not merely emotional but "cognitive-epistomological," ushering us into creation itself.[2]

Inner imagery acts metaphorically to bridge our sensory-motor and creative-intellectual systems and transfer the production of each to the other. Recent research suggests that all thinking involves imagery. The dream world the early child lives in is a hybrid between the transitional implicate order and the explicate order of her or his environment. The limbic system on which all this centers must adapt and transfer physical signals to the neocortex as well as interpret and transfer its concepts back to the R-system. For example, written symbols, such as those used in alphabets and mathematics, are perceived only as physical images, contrasts of dark and light, chalk on a blackboard, print on paper, by the R-system. To be *conceptualized* and meaningful, these perceptions must be transferred to the neocortex. The translator and transference medium is the limbic system.

A simple error in our interpretation of this brain function underlies a great deal of educational failure. The R-system can send environmental signals directly to the parts of the neocortex that form neural patterns of concrete experience in our early years. Through this we can respond to common sensory signals with our higher intelligence, such as interpreting with lightning speed the logistics of an oncoming vehicle or projectile and timing our getting out of its way. But to assume that the printed symbols of mathematics and alphabets or highly abstract instructions follow the same route is a major error. All metaphoric-symbolic action must be *translated* from R-system to the neocortex by the limbic system.[3] Thus our memories of what we learn in school retain the emotional states in which the learning took place.

The foundation of this metaphoric-symbolic capacity is the principal task of early childhood and is established through play. In this, story telling plays a major role. The spoken word has played a vital role since the child was in the womb. At the appropriate time and place the right words stimulate the brain to create a corresponding flow of images. This creative act is an enormous challenge to the brain and involves virtually every neural field; this is why young children seem "catatonic" while listening. The entrainment needed for this flow of images is so total that no energy is left over for anything else. After age five or so children become more active listeners because their capacity to create images in this fashion has developed well enough to operate on much less energy. Since each new story requires an entirely new sequence of neural field interactions, children want to hear the same story over and over again, not to "learn" it—most children remember a story after one hearing—but because repetition causes the interweaving neural fields involved in the image-flow of each story to myelinate. Each new story requires an entirely new set of connections and new fields of response. Thus, the more stories and their repetitions, the more neural fields and connections between them are brought into play. The stronger and more permanent the capacity for visual-verbal interaction grows, the more powerful conceptualization, imagination, and attentiveness become, while the scope and flexibility of neural capacities in general increases. (Waldorf Schools wisely repeat all stories a half dozen or more times, or even "live with" a story for days before moving to another.)

Once the imagery fields of a new story have stabilized, children, no longer embedded in the action, can stand back from this function and take charge, as in the cycle of competence. They are ready to reverse the process: take the internal image-flow of their own making and overlay it on an appropriate external stimulus. They want to modulate their outer world with an inner image, a first step toward creation itself. (And think how early this begins.) We tell our toddler the story of the three bears over and over as she sits glassy eyed and still. One day, however, we sit down to dinner, and our little bear says, "Oh, its too hot," pushing away her "porridge." "We must go for a walk in the forest." And she insists that we take part in her play, leaving the table and going for a walk, real or pretend. Or, following the story of the three pigs, a knock at the door elicits, "Oh, its the big, bad wolf. Run and hide." Each of us becomes the target of imagery overlay, taking our part in the outer casting of her internal production.

She has created an inner world around the story, extracted its essence, and applied it to a different situation. This completes the dynamic. Her outer play feeds its concretization back into her creative world. Her implicate has been made explicate. "Inner world" means the limbic-neocortical dynamic; "outer world" is the limbic-R-system dynamic. In play the R-system responds to orders coming from higher upstream—patterns that will integrate the triune system and ego-self—and through such actions she learns that her own thought and imagination can make a difference in her world.

Symbolic play follows the same pattern. The five-year-old sees a "road-roller" rumbling down the street mashing everything flat. In his mind's eye our five-year-old sees himself as the road engineer but he doesn't have a road-roller. Here in Mother's sewing kit he finds an empty spool, "a road-roller!," and for hours on end he plays, making all the appropriate diesel sounds, giving orders, exercising dominion over his private world. He extracted from his concrete experience of a road-roller his desired object, and plays it over in his inner-image world until he finds an external object onto which he can project his internal one. His inner image projection fills in the bare outlines of that spool that becomes the mighty road-roller, and he moves in a modulated world of his own creation.

In functional illiteracy a person can "read" a word, speak it, even write and spell it correctly, but, when asked to give the meaning of the word in a context, is vague and unsure. The written word is, again, but a contrast of light and dark to the perceptual system, and speech but a muscular response. To understand what those signs mean the neocortex must be given that signal in a form compatible to it; this requires a metaphoric-symbolic capacity, established through play, that equips the limbic brain to bridge the R-system and neocortex.

Note that a majority of the characters of early-childhood stories are humanized animals. (Authors such as Thornton Burgess, A. A. Milne,

Beatrix Potter, Joel Chandler Harris come to mind.) Children have an uncanny rapport with animals, and stuffed animals are as loved as dolls.[4] An affinity with animals is part and parcel of early childhood because those structures of brain being developed to construct a shared world are shared neural systems. There have been countless accounts of "telepathy" between humans and animals through the ages, and many of us could add our share. Our mammalian brain is *the* mammalian brain.

Down through the ages animals have played a prominent, indeed critical, part in the mythologies of all cultures. Generally these animal images are metaphoric, they represent human beings or are symbolic of human characteristics. In both mythology and fairy tales a fluid exchange takes place between animal and human forms. Ignoring the high levels of symbolism involved, note that the beautiful king becomes a terrible beast, the handsome prince an ugly toad (until delivered from such punishment by various forms of grace). In C. S. Lewis's *Chronicles of Narnia* a lion is a Messiah figure. In many myths the mouse stands for timidity, the lion courage, the owl wisdom. Carl Jung was fascinated with the constant recurrence of such animal archetypes.

Walt Disney intuitively presented his humanized animals with oversized heads and benign smiles. An oversized head is a characteristic of childhood (when our body-head ratio is quite out of balance), giving his archetypal human-animals an early-childhood cast and instinctively playing on both our ancient heritage and nurturing response to the young. This intuition was picked up by Madison Avenue. Most advertising concerning the pre-logical child uses bunnies and kittens just as bikini-clad women adorn adult advertising.

Recent sleep-dream research reveals that most of the characters in pre-logical children's dreams are animals. These dream-animals are symbolic and/or metaphoric of the people in the child's actual daily life. Around age seven, these animal characters disappear from the dreams and are replaced by humans.[5] By then nature has completed her long development of the two animal brains and integrated them into the neocortex, where development will thereafter concentrate.

The reason why upward of 90 percent of all childhood dream images are animals who act in a metaphoric-symbolic capacity, why a majority of the characters in children stories are animals who talk, and why a crossover between humans and animals is a major issue in myth and fairy tale, lies, then, with our threefold structure: Each brain has its own inherited agenda. Although each is reshaped when incorporated into the service of its evolutionary superior, each must be established within its own genetic agenda. Millions of years of genetic encoding can't be dismissed lightly. Transformation of the lower into the higher is not possible until the lower is complete enough to be transformed, as educators of mind and spirit should remember.

Current research indicates that we share 98 percent of all our chromosome encoding with the higher apes. That 2 percent differential we have seems small, but it gives us a light-year leap beyond our cousins. We must, however, have a firm foundation for that leap, which lies in that shared 98 percent.[6]

So Father Bear, wearing a suit, carrying a cane, and speaking authoritatively, is compatible with both our ancient animal systems and our higher human ones. The single image serves to bridge two worlds, as a metaphor should. Add to this the power of language, which transfers humanness to the bear and lays the groundwork for the higher abstract usage of language years later.

In imitative play the child sees her mother making cookies and wants to take part. The bowl and spoon are too big and out of reach, so she finds a jar top and a stick, puts some mud or sand into the jar top, and mixes with the stick, voicing all the appropriate words for making cookies. Two major metaphoric acts are made here: The toddler has represented an external act with an internal image and then transferred it onto objects accessible to her (jar top, stick, mud) that she can manipulate. This cycle of external to internal and out again integrates imagery transference in the triune system.

So metaphoric-symbolic thought develops through story telling, acting out the characters, and representing one thing for another, as when the match-box becomes a bed or truck, or the clothespin a doll or rocket ship. Throughout this period the child talks constantly and aloud (if allowed). Recall that all early language is concrete—words are a structural part of a neural pattern concerning things. When word is spoken the image of the corresponding object is reconstructed in some fashion; if not present to the physical senses, it is created within. In play, the child's own speech enters into the construction of the inner world.

There is no breakdown in logic in child play. The child is well aware that the spool is not an automobile or truck, but is struck with what a beautiful automobile the spool makes. Just as the physicist uses "h" to represent Planck's Constant, so we can "see" how the inner world of the atom functions, or the poet uses a metaphor (the lake is a sapphire) to get us to see something in a new light, the child holds up the battered match box and says: "See my beautiful boat." This is seeing creatively, not passively, the capacity William Blake and others retained all their life and developed to a high art.

Each and every form of play is an exercise in metaphoric-symbolic thinking, the foundation of all literacy and higher learning. An abstract mathematical symbol such as $E=MC^2$ has no meaning at all in itself. We "see" what something stands for only if we can manipulate that imagery on a mental level. As George Franklin pointed out "metaphor and symbol can operate vertically and laterally," linking the three realms of mind or operating within any of them individually. "Metaphor can be in the service of the causal level, building lateral connections between geometrical-archetypal images, as in the imagery in Dante's *Paradiso*. Symbolism in its highest sense usually has a causal aspect, and can become one with a numinous source"— that is, participate in creation.

Around age seven, we leave the world of the dream and move into an objective view of the physical world. Our early foundational forms of transference should be fully stabilized, leaving us free to move beyond them. Although these early functions will be overlaid with far more sophisticated forms later on, leaving Father Bear behind, we must remember how important he is to our foundation. Our muscular response to language forms in utero, becomes micro-kinetic and unseen, yet is the foundation of Shakespeare, *The Bhagavad Gita*, the Song of Solomon. That is what evolution is about. Foundations are structures in their own right, yet are built only to be covered up and overlaid with higher structures, and no superstructure is possible without its foundation.

After age seven, stories shift as does play. Animals are just animals to the middle child, and they want stories of animal and human

161

relations. Stories of magic, mystery, and extraordinary people are equally powerful, and the child plays at being the fantasy figures or acting out the hero model. To a child, reality is whatever one makes of it. At age nine, with a battered old cowboy hat, a homemade six-shooter sawed out of a wood shingle with a split spool for a cylinder, and a gun holster made from a scrap of old car seat leather tied about my waist, I was transformed into the likes of Buck Jones or Tom Mix, the cowboy giants of the screen before whom I sat in awe and wonder on those Saturday afternoons when I had been lucky enough during the week to earn the huge ten cent admission.

Those heroes, and the characters of the stories I read and had read to me set the parameters of my own possibility. And my possibility seemed infinite and open; no matter how lean things got in our Depression world of the 1930s, our inner world was wondrous, our future bright. We had hope. Our nine-year-old logic was fluid, ambiguous, indeterminate: "Bang! Bang! you're dead!"; the dramatic bullet-riddled collapse on the ground; the instant resurrection for another round. (Thus we also wrestled as best we could with the concept of death, which articulates at this period.) As we identified with our model we acted the representation out, preparing to move into that adult world as an integrated and whole self.

Competitive team games have nothing to do with middle child play. Everyone wins in child play, and, as Bruno Bettleheim has made clear, no child *should* ever have to lose.[7] All the middle child learns from losing is to be a loser. Winning and losing appear spontaneously later and serve different functions. Play to the middle child is fluid, loose, unstructured, and open. Hide and seek, chase games, cops and robbers may be transitional as we shift toward formal operations at age eleven, when the focus toward organization, the formal structure of play with rules and regulations, is a major concern. In my day, at age eleven or twelve sand lot baseball or football was our passion. Simply dividing up sides fairly took a disproportionate part of our play time, for being fair was a critical issue. The games themselves were divided between action and passionate, intense arguing about that action: "You're out!" "I'm not!" "You're not being fair!"

This play of the eleven- and twelve-year-old is based on one overriding principle: self-restraint, the reasons for which will become apparent shortly. The wide-open possibilities of the middle child give way to the constricted, rule-ridden organizations of the late child because puberty looms ahead: adolescence, leading to becoming a functional member of society; sexuality, with its possibility of becoming the parent—responsibilities requiring maximum self-restraint. We gathered on the sand lot to hammer out the rules and regulations of getting along as a team, a group, a society, all of which is critically dependent on our voluntarily accepting parameters imposed by group-need, willfully accepting self-constraint on behalf of a larger body. Giving over our individual, innocent, dreamlike, and magical freedoms to the needs of the social group, we also require that the group be fair and equitable in turn. Thus we spend half our time in passionate argument about fairness, the other half in play—but it is *all* equally play; we turn a primitive "herd-instinct" shared with all mammals into the social instincts and awesome dimensions of human civilization. For this late childhood period, the great myths, heroic legends, and biographies of great people, with their noble tales of sacrifice, virtue and restraint, forbearance, and overcoming great odds, are crucial.

At age eleven we can no longer afford the luxury of anything and everything being possible. The open parameters of childhood close to the disciplines of formal operations: learning the "body of knowledge" of one's culture, the selective, disciplined learnings we call higher education. Nature prepares us for this through childhood play, which enables us to enter the next phase with excitement and joy.

CHAPTER 19

Play's End

Play develops intelligence; integrates our triune nature; prepares us for higher education, creative thought, and taking part in and upholding a social structure; and helps us prepare for becoming an effective parent when that time comes. Play is the very force of society and civilization, and a breakdown in ability to play will reflect in a breakdown of society. We are a tough, resilient species; our capacity to compensate for damage is enormous. Our children could compensate for hospital childbirth and the ensuing separation anxiety of day care and its abandonment, but children can't compensate beyond a point, and we went beyond that point years ago. Some ten years after we began to systematically separate infants from mothers in hospitals, eliminating bonding and breaking down development of the limbic-heart dynamic, we introduced television. The major damage of television has little to do with content: Its damage is neurological, and it has, indeed, damaged us, perhaps beyond repair.[1]

First, television replaced story telling in most homes, and it changed the radio from a storyteller to a music box.[2] When television is criticized, its apologists point to similar warnings made when radio burst on the scene early in this century, but radio as an endless storyteller sparked the imagination of and helped give rise to a generation whose creativity changed the face of the earth (for better or worse). Television, on the other hand, has now been with us far longer than radio was before television's introduction, and its programming has deteriorated at an astonishing rate for the same reasons that it damages us.

Television also replaced family conversation in general. The television tray replaced the dinner table and its captivating table talk. Carol Gilligan points out that grandmothers used to sit and relate their childhood stories to a rapt audience of grandchildren.[3] That remarkable series of books by Laura Ingals Wilder grew out of her parents and grandparents "telling their stories." Gilligan saw this as a primary need that grandmothers had (a recapitulation that rounded out their lives), but grandmother tales filled many needs: They provided a continuity between generations, gave children a sense of history, and established a continuum of meaning to life. I heard both my grandmother's and grandfather's stories either directly or indirectly through my parents. And I knew my mother's childhood as I did my father's by their reminiscing, which would hold us spellbound on a winter's evening or at the table. I clearly saw my father's boyhood on the river at Milan, Tennessee, so clearly that to this day those images, formed as he told his tales, shine so vividly in my mind I mistake them for my own childhood. I see him as a little boy skipping school to play with his handmade boats, harbor, and wharf; when he forgot them one evening and the river's rise carried them all away, the loss felt like my own. My mother's childhood played out in such clear images that the last two decades of the nineteenth century were as real to me as my own day. Both my paternal and maternal grandmothers' far less gentle stories of escaping the Yankee armies in the Civil War made that conflict intensely real, my very own struggle. In passing their stories on they gave us tradition, continuity, place, and meaning. We knew who we were and where we came from, our lives had significance, drama, meaning. "Tell me about when you were a little boy" my daughter begs, and never tires of listening (even to my repetitions and elaborations).

Second, with television on the scene, parents rarely played with children. All sat around the box, and even playing among siblings disappeared. Thus no capacity for play and its internal imaging developed. Nintendo does not and cannot replace imaginative play.

Third, and perhaps most critical, television floods the infant-child brain with images at the very time his or her brain is supposed to learn to make images from within. Story telling feeds into the infant-child a stimulus that brings about a response of image making that involves every aspect of our triune system. Television feeds both stimulus *and* response into that infant-child brain, as a single paired-effect, and therein lies the danger. Television floods the brain with a counterfeit of the response the brain is supposed to learn to make to the stimuli of words or music. As a result, much structural coupling between mind and environment is eliminated; few metaphoric images develop; few higher cortical areas of the brain are called into play; few, if any, symbolic structures develop. $E=MC^2$ will be just marks on paper, for there will be no metaphoric ability to transfer those symbols to the neocortex for conceptualization, and subsequently, no development of its main purpose: symbolic conceptual systems.

An equally insidious effect is habituation—the natural condition of our two animal brains with their hard-wired response to "concrete information."[4] Unable to adapt to novelty, these primitive systems avoid it. They seek out compatible stimuli and feel "comfortable" with familiar input unless moved by the novelty seeking of the neocortex. Recall how a new story told to a child ties up a majority of the neural fields and locks in all three systems to create a flow of new imagery matching the new stimuli. Repetition brings myelination and stabilizes the creative action. That imagery pattern becomes an integral part of the neural system and is then played out on the external world, part of the general reference maps called on in an expanding world. Note that each new story requires a whole new set of patterns to accommodate the new stimuli, requiring entrainment of all three brains over and over. The brain is challenged anew and continually enlarges the number of neural fields involved in new image-pattern flows.

Television, on the other hand, as a source of paired image and sound, can be assimilated by a single set of neural fields. The same neural fields initially worked out to handle such a paired stimuli can assimilate all further stimuli of a like order. Each time that stimuli-source fires in, that singular field responds. Note that we *habituate to television within a few minutes of viewing,* from the very first exposure on—since no creative response to such stimuli need or can be made. That response is already part of the stimuli coming in. This means, in effect, that those six thousand hours of television the average child in the United States sees by age five might as well have been all one program.

Recently groups of five- and six-year-olds were shown a number of regular television shows designed for their age group. For this experiment, the sound tracks were switched so that the sound did not match the imagery on any of the programs. The children did not recognize the discrepancy.[5] The reason is that the brain habituates to the single source of stimuli; primary autonomous processes take over at any repetition of that stimuli, regardless of its apparent variety. So the nature of the stimuli, the program, is beside the point, and so much for the wonderful information and learning programs often proposed for those six thousand hours.

Habituation also pacifies the brain, puts it to sleep, since the stimulus includes the brain's own response and so demands almost no output of energy from the brain, while it occupies the mind so that no other stimuli are sought.[6] This again indicates that habituation is a primary reptilian response. Paul MacLean shows that the R-system takes over all learned physical patterns of the neocortex. Once the R-system can handle a source economically, it doesn't need to carry the signals higher. With the rapid turnover of imagery, the apparent novelty of the programming fools the novelty seeking aspect of the neocortex. Combined with the habituation, we have difficulty turning away even when we hate the program playing.[7]

Failing to develop imagery means having no imagination. This is far more serious than not being able to daydream. It means children who can't "see" what the mathematical symbol or the semantic words mean; nor the chemical formulae; nor the concept of civilization as we know it. They can't comprehend the subtleties of our Constitution or Bill of Rights and are seriously (and rightly) bored by abstractions of this sort. They can sense only what is immediately bombarding their physical system and are restless and ill-at-ease without such bombardment. Being sensory deprived they initiate stimulus through constant movement or intensely verbal interaction with each other, which is often mistaken for precocity but is actually a verbal hyperactivity filling the gaps of the habituated bombardments.

The average child in the United States sees six thousand hours of television by their fifth year, at which point, in the midst of what

167

should be the high point of their dreamlike world of play, we put them in school, prevent bodily movement (most purposive learning is sensory-motor at this age), and demand they handle highly abstract-symbolic systems (alphabets and numbers) for which most of them have no neural structures at all. Driven by nature to follow their models, they try and can't. Their self-esteem collapses and failure and guilt give rise to anger. Even after beginning school, they continue their time-percentage of television viewing unabated. They spend more hours looking at television than attending school, and our national daily viewing time grows year by year.

Having no inner imaging capacity leaves most of the brain unemployed, and a child who can't imagine not only can't learn but has no hope in general: He or she can't "imagine" an inner scenario to replace the outer one, so feels victimized by the environment. A recent study showed that unimaginative children are far more prone to violence than imaginative children, because they can't imagine an alternative when direct sensory information is threatening, insulting, unpleasant, or unrewarding. They lash out against unpleasantness in typical R-system defensiveness, while the imaginative child can imagine an alternative, that is, create images not present to the sensory-system that offer a way out. True playing is the ability to play with one's reality. Thus imagination gives resiliency, flexibility, endurance, and the capacity to forego immediate reward on behalf of long-term strategies.

Forty years ago, along with the epidemic of day care and television, a new phenomenon burst on the American scene: the toy store. Until that time, the average American child had a maximum of some five toys. I can recall each of mine; they were precious. Christmas, the only time we ever got a toy, was a time of near unbearable excitement. My Flexible Flyer Sled was secondhand, but lasted my whole childhood. My Radio Flyer wagon was new when I got it and lasted from my fifth year until my twelfth year as a major item. My Rollfast skates were new and lasted until my fourteenth year. I used them hard. (A new pair cost 79 cents, no small sum.) I bought, for $2.87, my bicycle at age eleven, an ancient relic for which I saved for two years, and it lasted till I left home at fourteen. I never heard the word bored until I was in the armed service in World War II. I never knew a bored child in my own childhood. There was far too much to do, yet we had only a few toys.

When today's toddler sees her mother making cookies and wants to take part, she need not resort to jar top, stick, and mud, like some primitive. She probably has a complete miniature kitchen, scale-model perfect with battery operated appliances. When a five-year-old sees the road-roller he doesn't need to find an old spool: The massive toy industry provides a complete road-roller, exact in detail, battery powered so that the child can watch passively as he does when the same item is advertised on television. Children are inundated with objects that don't stand for something but already are. A clothes-pin need not be draped with an old rag to make a doll; our daughters have shelves bulging with dolls of every description—life-like, sexy, indeed complete with all the organs for real precocious sophistication if you like. Where is the metaphoric-symbolic learning or the dream-world of play-acting the adult?

The electronic toy that does everything at the push of the button itself habituates. Boredom sets in immediately; what's next? Even playing with such objects children often merely act out the images advertised on television. When they identify with the television children playing with the same toy they feel some group authenticity, a belonging not found elsewhere. Television, of course, is the way to sell those toys that then represent the television images flooding the young brain, reinforcing the television stimulus when that stimulus is absent.

The 30 percent or so of our children still capable of learning in school have been read to and played with by their parents, generally in addition to television and mountains of plastic junk. This shows how little attention is needed to nourish the brain and get its creativity going. While the screen itself prevents neural development its content affects behavior. By 1963 studies had shown a direct one-for-one correspondence between the content of television and behavior. Violence on television produces violent behavior in young people. Everyone knows that. Once one has habituated to violence as a way of life, however, anything less is boring. There are sixteen acts of violence per hour of children's programming, only eight per hour on adult's.[8] By the time our children become teenagers, they have seen an estimated 18,000 violent murders on television, their primary criteria for what is "real." Life is shown to be expendable and cheap, yet we condemn them for acting violently.

One final point that needs mention in this parade of intellectual interference with the intelligence of childhood is minor but has its effect too. In the last chapter I showed how play in the pre-puberty and early adolescent period centered around the concept of *us*, group action, and the need for self-constraint on behalf of us, the team, club, or organization. My concern here is over our sand lot football, baseball, and street games. Sometime after World War II, society suddenly had no room for children, our quiet childhood streets filled with speeding autos, many new communities had no sidewalks; yards were status symbols, and children's play was relegated to playgrounds with professional playground supervisors. Child safety became a paramount concern. Supervised play replaced child play. Adult rules, regulations, and decisions began to replace our passionately defended personal criteria and judgments.

The high point of this adult intrusion on childhood centered in Little League. Gone were the choosing up of sides, the striving for fairness, arguing the rules and infringements, the heated hammering out of decisions. Everything was managed by adults: They created the teams and provided the uniforms, which of course soon carried advertisements of "sponsors"; adults made the rules and regulations and enforced them; adults called the shots, children stood, grim-faced and serious while parents on the sidelines shouted invectives for victory at all costs. This new child carried the team, sponsor, parents, and social image on his or her shoulders into victory or defeat. Insidiously, Little League targeted younger and younger children, until even the little tots were dutifully marching out in full advertising array to do battle with the enemy. Whatever might have been left of play after television was killed by Little League and other organized sports leagues, substituting a deadly serious adult form of win-or-lose competition for what had been true play. Gone are the invaluable social learnings, self-restraint, and ability to decide.

There are many other facets to the current collapse of childhood. I have touched on the issue only briefly, but one thing is clear, our schools have deteriorated because they must deal with damaged goods. Most responsible for this damage is hospital childbirth; second comes television. Next comes day care, which fosters television and is a result of hospital childbirth. Premature schooling runs fourth. (A fifth must wait a bit for discussion.) And as our damaged children grow up and become the parents and teachers, damage will be the norm, the way of life. We will habituate to damage. Nothing else will be known. How can you miss something you can't even recognize, something you never had?

CHAPTER 20

Concrete Operations

Development moves, Jean Piaget observed, from the "concrete to the abstract," which means from our knowledge of matter to our knowledge of mind's process. Long before that concrete world is fully formed, our early child overlays external objects with inner images, seeing the match box as a boat, and so on. Now at age seven, with a complete world structure, the child can take a further step and actually change a concrete object to conform with an inner idea. Piaget called this concrete operational thinking.

We operate on objects in this fashion through using one physical process against or in conjunction with another, or, under exceptional circumstances, directly, without using mediation. Unmediated operations are always exceptions to the norm, rather random, and essentially savant-like. In 1983, for instance, John Hasted, physicist-mathematician at the University of London, published a study concerning dozens of children, averaging age nine, who could, given the right conditions, bend simple metal objects without touching them.[1] In 1982, at Robert Monroe's Institute in Virginia, twenty-five of us, ranging in age from five to seventy years, sat in a circle and, under the guidance of a United States Army Colonel, bent stainless steel into various shapes by stroking it. Children led the way that evening, tying knots in knives, rolling spoon handles up into the bowls, bending the bowls of spoons into neatly creased halves. A five-year-old youngster tightly corkscrewed his heavy fork from tine to shank end as we watched. We grownups followed suit after a time.

A physicist at Melbourne University bent metal bars sealed inside glass cases. Spectrographs were made that demonstrate how the steel, once bent in this fashion, had a chemical-molecular structure different from the same metal unbent or bent by mechanical pressure. In investigating the interaction of mind and matter, Robert Jahn found that ordinary people could influence electronic devices in classically "impossible" ways, and stated that we must "rewrite the laws of physics." In the 1970s Bryan Josephson, a Nobel Prize–winning physicist, witnessed bars of steel bending, or disappearing completely and reappearing in another room of the laboratory, when placed some twelve feet away from an English boy. Wired up to an electroencephalograph (brain-wave recording device), and surrounded by a dozen physicists and psychologists, this youngster, Matthew Manning, underwent several weeks of testing, prompting Josephson to announce that we would have to "rewrite" the laws of physics.[2] Manning was brought to the University of Toronto where Dr. Joel Whitten worked with him for some six weeks, always with the electroencephalograph attached. At the moment of each non-ordinary event the brain-wave recorder showed a burst of activity from Manning's R-system and cerebellum.[3] This is intriguing in light of what we know of the R-system and Sir John Eccles's claim that the cerebellum is the "seat of the mind."

Recently Michael Sky wrote a remarkable account of his many years experience leading groups in "fire-walks," walking over forty-foot-long beds of white-hot coals. Some people walk leisurely up and down, sit, or even lie down on the beds. Occasionally a walker gets burned, but none seriously, and a fundamental shift in personal attitude seems to occur.[4] In Shri Lanka the situation is a bit more robust. In two previous books I have quoted from scientific studies of fire-walking there, a practice followed for millennia in honor of a local god, Kataragama. Walkers are carefully selected by the temple priests and prepared for three weeks. The walk takes place in the central courtyard of Kataragama's temple. The recessed fire pit, six feet wide and twenty feet long, creates enough heat to melt aluminum on contact. Onlookers can't stand closer than twenty feet for any period. Yet, hundreds walk the fire each year; some rush across, others stroll or sit, some women pour handfuls of coals over their hair and face with no sign of discomfort or damage. Each year an average of 3 percent of the walkers fail, however, most of whom die in spite of the attendants with long wooden hooks who try to get them out of the pit. The cotton clothing worn doesn't scorch or singe, except in that 3 percent, whose clothing and hair burn at the moment of their failure. *The National Geographic Magazine* did a photographic essay of a similar ceremony to Kataragama at a private home. It was an amateur ceremony, so the heat was less severe, yet optical pyrometers registered 2300 degrees Fahrenheit interior and 1380 Fahrenheit exterior, which should be warm enough for any deity.[5] (The end of a cigarette burns at 1380 degrees Fahrenheit.)[6]

These brief examples of unmediated concrete operations are not the kind found in textbooks, but they show our potential for intervening in our world. We can do without such esoterica quite well, but we can't do without developing the textbook variety. Around age six or seven, when development of our limbic and R-systems is complete, our neocortex becomes the focus of development. Nature provides another massive brain growth spurt to accommodate the new intelligences unfolding. Remember that the six-year-old's brain is two-thirds of its adult size with five to seven times more neural connections and available fields than it had in early childhood or will have as an adult. Nature provides an abundance of material for the vast potentials available in the new operations.

One of Piaget's classic (and safely academic) examples of operational thought is the Law of Conservation, which pre-logical children can't grasp but logical seven-year-olds can. Take a tall, thin pint flask and a short, fat pint flask, and demonstrate that they hold the same amount. The practical perception of pre-logical children tells them "tall is most," and no amount of pouring back and forth convinces them otherwise. Their "magical" explanation is that "some just disappears" as you empty the tall into the short or "more just appears" when you empty the short into the tall, sufficient to their pre-logical common sense. With the shift into concrete operations around age seven, the newly opened conceptual system automatically corrects the perceptual system. Children recognize that the liquid is "conserved," that it remains the same in spite of appearances. The same logic automatically applies to similar situations.

So operating on our concrete reality need hardly be esoteric: tossing some flour, salt, shortening, sugar, and eggs together and having the results come out of the oven as cookies is a very practical and devel-opmental concrete operation. In this the middle child discovers how to change the nature of concrete information according to an abstract plan, and is hungry to do this. Even an Erector Set offers opportunity for concrete operations. We use such operational thought when we "see" how a particular device works or how some mechanical job should be done. Our graphic arts, sciences, and technologies are es-sentially concrete operations, some serving more advanced formal thinking, which we will discuss in the next chapter.

The period from age seven to eleven is the optimum time for "mak-ing things and singing" as my seven-year-old proclaimed her goal of life to be. Making music, as in the body-movement-singing games presented by the Richards Institute's *Education Through Music* (*ETM*), is a form of early child play and concrete operations combined. *ETM* is of enormous benefit in that it creates a state of mind open to learning. Spontaneous play, making things and singing, involvement in daily life with the imagination operating freely, keeps the options open, utilizes the new neural fields, and is the perfect education for this middle stage. Margaret Mead once said no education would work unless based on art. That is, art is not a subject to be taught, but the way in which all subjects should be approached. Waldorf Schools base education on art, just as Grace Pilon's Workshop Way is art itself. The children of Nyack, New York's Blue Rock School and the Sudbury Valley School in Massachusetts learn through art, play, and explo-ration.[7]

Crafting a concrete representation of a pure mental idea or feeling is the heart of operational thought. With an infinitely open neural ca-pacity, seven- to eleven-year-old children have no limitations and consider all possibilities equally valid. The only qualification is na-ture's imperative that they be given appropriate cultural models and environment. Ernest Hilgard points out that this middle child be-comes acutely sensitive to suggestions concerning personal possibil-ities. This susceptibility to suggestion peaks around age eleven and closes by about age fourteen in most of us. The subtle suggestions, implications, even hazy ideas held by parents, peers, or superiors con-cerning who we are and what our possibilities are or aren't pro-foundly impact children. They pick up our inherent beliefs and social notions whether expressed or not, and automatically reflect them.

175

Their limitless possibilities for new patterns of conception and perception will be limited by the nature of their models, with no one the wiser.

Bending objects without touching them, walking through fire, or other "mind over matter" displays, are not developmental—you can't *do* anything with them or improve on their random factor. They are still concrete operations, however, and strictly biological. Recall that the right hemisphere has a much stronger neural connection with the limbic system than the left, and that concrete language is made of word and its object as a combined structure of knowledge. The right hemisphere retains this concrete language, giving that hemisphere its "holistic" unifying connection with the two lower world-self systems. The left hemisphere, largely isolated from the limbic system, uses its connection with the right hemisphere to draw information from, and communicate its abstract ideas to, the rest of the system. The route is: left to right to limbic to R-system. Remember that direct muscular movements, as handled by those new brain neural patterns imprinted to such action, is a different modality than employing the intellect of the new brain to change structural processes in the lower two systems.

The two hemispheres are connected by a huge bundle of nerve fibers called the *corpus callosum*. This corpus callosum, which begins its development after object constancy, around age one, and becomes complete between ages four and five, may be a functional decision-making organ in its own right. It not only bridges the hemispheres, it may control the traffic on that bridge, sending information either way, making decisions, closing traffic when the left hemisphere needs privacy to do its abstract work, and so on. Through its possibility for isolation, the left hemisphere's lateral actions can be independent and not subject to the general rules governing the integrated brain. This means the left hemisphere doesn't have to answer to the organic intelligence governing life as a whole, as the lower structures do.

So the left hemisphere can draw material from its lower world-system and operate on it within its own lateral functions, answering to no other part of the otherwise integrated system. Using abstract ideas coming not from matter as it is, but from the mind's ideas of what might be *done* with matter, we modulate, mutate, or change the concrete information. Children must be given models for such action if they are to develop the capacity, and the capacity unfolds according to the nature of the models. Children soon come up with endless and ingenious notions of their own, devices seen within their mind's eye. Generally a child's imaginative ability runs far ahead of any capacity to put those ideas into action, which can be frustrating. As Jerome Bruner said, intent precedes the ability to do.

Through this operational mode of mind we can come into dominion over the world given us through those lower systems. Coming in "higher up" on the evolutionary stream we can even reverse or cancel the natural order on which reality is based. In earlier childhood an inner image is superimposed on an outer image, as when the spool of thread becomes the road-roller. Then one plays in a "modulated reality" in which nothing physical actually changes, all is in the mind's eye. After age six or seven this higher, causal level of the neocortex is activated and becomes an integral part of the ego structure. Then the inner image (the idea) can be superimposed on the external object (the concrete information) and, in certain circumstances, can actually modulate and change that information. The supra-implicate, when the structures for translating it are developed, can change the implicate, which in turn changes its explicate display. With development, Alexandria Luria pointed out, different nervous centers gain in dominance, and the hierarchy among behavioral functions alters.[8]

Michael Gazzaniga observed that "nothing happens psychologically until the appropriate brain region has become physiologically functional." Recall, from our brief sketch of quantum physics, that non-localized wave-fields give rise to localized particles whose history changes the non-localized wave-fields giving rise to them, back and forth in dynamic. Meshes of resonant wave-fields give rise to bonded particles that can be shifted in their locus or changed in shape. Metal, as a lattice-work of bonded particles, can be shifted as a unit, or its form altered, through the non-localized implicate fields giving rise to it. Those implicate fields involve our limbic system and can be shifted in such a manner only through supra-implicate orders of energy, which become operational in the neocortex around age seven. This is but an extension of physicist Paul Davies' observation that "self-organizing systems that are open rather than closed . . . can exchange energy, entropy and material with their environment

... where general organizational principles apply to a wide range of complex systems . . . [that] transcend subject boundaries."[9]

Intervening in the natural dynamic between wave and particle is one of the things our brain can do since it *mediates between* wave and particle. Once the physical and emotional systems are fairly stable and we move into the causal new brain, the mind can employ that median between wave and particle and change the relations between particles, or, later, between wave-fields themselves. The relation between limbic and R-system changes in concrete operations. One walks through fire with impunity when an abstract idea from the causal neocortex impacts the wave-fields of relationship accessible through the limbic brain, changing the nature of the relationships on a particle level, the level that is interpreted or perceived through the R-system.

For immunity to fire, one need only shift the relations within the fields of experience—a personal, inner play. One bends metal or interferes with the workings of a machine without touching it by the same process, but this esoterica involves the matter-fields universally shared with others, which is a different issue. Ego-intellect is a personal, matter-oriented self-system, a product of or at least subject to the emotions of its limbic and R-systems, a recipient rather than instigator on deep formative levels. We would have to be free of identifications with and stand outside of our two lower structures to willfully operate on matter in a way involving general potential fields. (For instance, saying to the mountain, "Remove to the sea" and having it comply.) When interventions in that common world do occur, as they do randomly, a higher intelligence is picking up at that point for reasons of its own. "It" may or may not respond when the nine-year-old tries to bend metal, the remote viewer tries to see, or the devotee enters the fire pit. Thus much of the paranormal seems to occur randomly.

Esoterica such as firewalking or bending metal may have little utilitarian value, but phenomena of this sort can break through the stranglehold classical scientific and religious thought have placed on our self-images and personal possibilities. Intervening in our physical world without intermediaries is only a play of one part of our triune brain with another, but through such a play we can discover that our reality is an inner construction of our self-organizing system and subject to our participation to an unknown degree. The only way we could intervene in reality in such unmediated ways is if our brains acted, as I have proposed, as an intermediary between wave-field and particle display, and if those three neural structures, physical, relational, and causal-potential, were each operating on its own respective frequency level of successively greater power.

We seem to stand in relation to such non-ordinary acts about as the savant does to his strange accomplishments. A random factor keeps us on the edge of uncertainty. This is why Targ, Jahn, and others face such frustration when trying to get these very real but quasi-random phenomena accepted by their fellow scientists. Matthew Manning never knew when something was going to happen to the object of his attention, nor did he have any idea what would happen when it did or how, only that things tended to happen if he intended it. "It" bends the metal or allows us to walk through fire. "It" raises a blister an hour after the hypnotic experience. "It" can breathe the body in meditation. Consider the statements of creative persons that at the final moment of insight "it" breaks through with "its" revelations as a grace. We have only to allow and not get in the way. "It," in these cases, is the possibility of concrete operational thinking. Any label will do since "it" isn't a semantic proposition.

Evolution's intent for us lies far beyond exercises of "mind over matter" though we need to know of such capacities. Our job on earth is not to mutilate our earth matrix, but to nurture and maintain her as she nurtures and maintains us. We need to develop the intelligences needed to go beyond this matrix before we are buried under it. The sage changes nothing but hearts and minds. A truly mature society would leave few traces of itself. On reaching such a maturity that we could willfully change our "ontological constructs" (miracles in the classical sense), we would have no inclination to perform them, as there are far greater themes in evolution's score.

CHAPTER 21

Formal Operations

Around age eleven some momentous events take place: The brain releases a chemical that dissolves all unmyelinated neural fields, removing 80 percent of the brain mass available at age six. Formal operations begin that, in turn, depend on a semantic language that unfolds parallel to it. Semantic language can denote qualities, attitudes, values, or states of mind, words such as *truth, beauty,* and *virtue,* for example. Children may use semantic words before this time, but now they gain a functional grasp of abstract concepts; they can understand mathematical systems based on qualitative value, not just quantitative number, or they can metaphorically transfer meaning from one abstraction to another. Just as concrete language participated in physical object-events, semantic language participates in thought. A word can now be an intermediary between ourselves and our own thought and can allow us to look at it objectively. From this we develop a self-awareness through which we can see others' points of view, stand in their shoes as it were. Even greater, through this way of thinking we can discover levels of awareness beyond physical reality.

The mind of the young child is quiet. Inner chatter arises in adolescence and is non-volitional. We might occasionally choose what to think about, but stopping thought is virtually impossible. This nonstop inner dialogue is a myelinated abstract language system with its "engines idling" as neural structures must. All stages are temporary and meant to be gone beyond, however, including this state that we seldom question, in which our compulsive thoughts constantly spring forth. Our capacity to grasp and describe abstract concepts or states of mind, can, if we receive the right stimulus and guidance, be the very instrument to lead us beyond our natural "embeddedment" in word thoughts. The quiet mind, free of "roof-brain chatter" is rare since it comes with a high level of maturity.

Jean Piaget considered reversibility thinking the highest intellectual achievement. This is the ability to "consider all possibilities in a continuum of possibility as equally valid, and return to the point from which we begin." Middle children (ages seven to eleven) can consider all possibilities equally valid, but have no need of a stable point of reference nor are their thoughts restricted to a disciplined continuum. In reversibility thinking the continuum considered is itself a category of possibility based on logical relationships. Within those accepted parameters we can explore all possibilities while keeping our formal structure of thought intact. This crucial "point of return" requires a stable frame of reference. So the open stage wherein anything is possible is phased out, nature removes all uncommitted neural fields and brings the house to order.

We are then ready to learn our society's "body of knowledge," that threefold system of ideas on which all societies are based: a cosmology (philosophy or religion), an art (music, poetry, literature, painting, sculpture, and so forth), and a science (technology, agriculture, crafts, the mechanics of dealing with physical matter). These are our abstract ideas concerning the actions possible within our triune system. Today this formal structure of thoughts about thought, feeling, and action, is passed on through a schooling that relates only to the physical environment, which seems only common sense. However, in developing abstract thinking only as needed to analyze, predict, and/or control physical matter or each other's behavior, we lock our highest neocortical structures into alignment with and in service of our R-system by default.

Formal operation is the first stage of causal thinking. Intellect, a variable of intelligence, undergoes its greatest development now, and can detach from and then dominate the physical intelligences leading to it. If developed, we can intellectually modulate our earlier animal emotions and be a bit more reasonable, humane, and civi-lized. Fully developed, intellect can move us beyond our embedded-ment in all the structures of knowledge built up to this point.

Each part of our triune system has its own independent block of abilities and behaviors, and these open for development sequentially. Our self-sense is embedded in each until it is developed, at which point, theoretically, we are lifted into the next evolutionary stage. Each developmental period functions on two complementary levels: Its inherent behaviors must be developed according to genetic en-codings, yet must resonate with the higher structure they will even-tually serve. Our R-system, with all its physical encodings, dominates and orders lower ganglia into its service, and it does so according to the needs of the higher systems it serves. The limbic sys-tem orders those physical instincts into a correspondingly higher order of operations as will be needed by the neocortex. The unifying right hemisphere (operating in conjunction with the left) utilizes the limbic structure for intuition and imagination. At age seven the left hemisphere becomes dominant over and employs the right for con-crete operations. At age eleven the new locus is probably the cere-bellum, the seat of the physical mind and final point of perception. Development of formal operations will both fulfill our human po-tentials and ready us to move into a correspondingly larger frame of reference.

The "wisdom of the body," that intuitive intelligence found in all life forms, involves the heart and its limbic connections. Intellect, as it opens at age eleven, is a first-stage causal or supra-implicate en-ergy, able to modulate all lower systems, including that biological intelligence of the heart. Intellect and its operational logic can draw on and modulate all lower structures, and here nature takes so big a gamble we need to understand what is at stake. Here thought begins to break with our overall, species-wide organic intelligence, that limbic-heart dynamic that keeps the body and its internal and exter-nal environment in balance. Ideas bred in our intellect can function outside that intelligence, and so we can either benefit or harm our-selves or our whole planet. It was this capacity that led Arthur Koestler to conclude that in leaving our left hemisphere largely dis-connected from the limbic system evolution had made a dramatic error. While virtually all our disasters do, indeed, result from this apparent omission, Koestler failed to grasp the far greater stakes nature has in mind.[1]

With an abstract, semantic language we can create thoughts "out of the blue," thoughts that arise from the act of thinking, rather than from response to objects themselves. Walking on beds of fire is a concrete operation, but the idea originated in our ancient past from a formal operation of mind. Fire in itself could never suggest its not burning. We can extract information out of context and operate on it with self-created ideas that are discrete and self-referring, rather than balanced within a larger frame of reference. The last chapter outlined how we can feed these left hemisphere activities to the right hemisphere, through the corpus callosum, and, through the right hemisphere's connection with the limbic structure, change the relational fields that give rise to our sensory world. At age eleven, an intelligence opens that can, if developed, stand outside this capacity and operate on and so change the structures of thought.

Formal operations, incorporating concrete operations into its service, could bring us dominion over the physical world so that we could use that world as our launching platform to go beyond it. We get caught up, however, in using the capacity only to dominate our world and so lose sight of anything more. Formal operations can lead us to causality and give us our foothold in creation, a way of becoming one with creative intelligence. This process alone can integrate us and our intellect into a higher form of well-being and counter the destructive tendencies of an immature intellect.

The nine- or ten-year-old floats in a continuum of possibility, with relative and fluid rules and regulations, while the eleven-year-old is subject to a reasonable logic that is consistent within itself. Formal thought encloses an infinitely open and random field with a specific set of controllable factors; it selectively lifts order out of chaos. To do violence to one's formal logic or idea system is to violate one's intellect and self-integrity, a threat worse than death. Intellectual worldviews center around the semantic language system with which we identify, and in which we embed in order to develop. Many a war has been fought defending such worldviews, which are equally self-identities.[2]

Play in the eight- or nine-year-old is spontaneous and open-ended, its logic flexible. The nine-year-old plaintively asks: "Is it a fun game or a winning game?" Around age eleven or twelve, however, competitive group games of a tightly defined order come into the picture. Play becomes a serious issue based on a growing sense of logical cohesion, balance, equality, and justice—part of the sense of moral and ethical rightness and clarity of thought that seems part of the pre-adolescent agenda. Critically important in social organization and cohesiveness, this same sense of balanced, self-imposed restraint, reason, and order gives the frame of mind needed for disciplines such as chemistry, mathematics, physics, grammar, art, and so on. A discipline (which comes from the Latin word for "follower") requires us to learn what is and is not admissible and what does and does not work. Further, this stage prepares us for full sexuality and parenthood, surely requiring the greatest self-restraint. There is no way such discipline could be developed if "any and all actions were equally valid," and no way we would be willing to give up our autonomy on behalf of a group unless we understood its dynamics and believed the sacrifice and effort worth it.

To *belong* is a serious biological need of late childhood and adolescence. Our social ego first emerges at age seven, blossoms at eleven, and bears fruit from fifteen or so. To be a member is an inherent mammalian "herd instinct." By eleven we prepare to leave the nest and enter the mainstream of society. The foundational bonds for this should have been built through the years. This is the thrust of civilization and should incorporate all our preliminary intelligences into higher cortical structures and potentials. Not being a member is dreadful to the pre-teen and teen age child, and rightly so. Sexual needs and the "gene pool" aside, without membership in the culture and access to its cumulative knowledge, passed on verbally, we would have to re-invent the wheel, generation by generation; and no generation would last long enough to get much of a vehicle rolling. Further, the power of a group is greater than that of the individual, on all levels of energy. So we are (or should be) eager to submit to society's disciplines, take up where our predecessors left off, and move on. It is like inheriting a fortune with which, since money makes money, we can amass ever greater fortunes. (A generation "rebelling" against its own social body is a major anomaly.) An efficient, powerful society, in line with the flow of evolution and intelligence, where nature is getting what she is after, would be extremely stable and long-lived.

At age eleven, when nature cleans house by dissolving all unmyelinated neural connections, she clears the decks for a much more refined and apparently restricted but more powerful level of operation. Yet, loss of 80 percent of our neural mass is disturbing because we end up, neurologically, with what we had at age one. Overproduction is nature's way, but such a massive neural loss is not; the only other comparable losses are immediately replaced by brain growth-spurts.[3] This loss is a culturally induced phenomenon, both the direct result of and the direct cause of our dysfunction and cultural disease. Perhaps such a loss has long taken place, indicating an ongoing failure to become what evolution intends, which is all the more reason to look for a way beyond. The causes of our breakdown, technological childbirth and day care, for example, become self-replicating fields of potential, rapidly taken for granted, with the resulting fear, anger, and general helplessness accepted as our natural condition. The causes of our grief become our frames of reference.

In middle childhood we build a structure of knowledge of creative possibility according to our models. Any and all things are possible, but that which becomes actual is determined by the usual structural coupling. Studies show that a teacher's underlying belief about seven-year-old students has a profound impact on them. Children do well under a teacher who believes in them and "knows" they will do well, and poorly under a negative teacher whose opinion of the children (and probably self) is low.[4] Just as our own attitudes, of which we need not be aware, can impact our health and relationships, they can impact our children.

For whatever reasons, we enter into our formal operational stage with 20 percent of the neural structures available four years before. And, that 20 percent was almost surely established before age seven, with only minor elaborations added thereafter. Instead of building new structures of knowledge during the intuitive and concrete operational stage, the child seems to only expand on earlier learning, filling in the gaps. No learning that demanded new neural structures *could have been* introduced during this middle period or we would not end up with the "neural weight" we started with in infancy. Surely there is a general "tightening up" of neural fields, eliminating redundant connections, making greater use of remaining ones, as happens in maturation.[5] In no way, however, can this account for an 80 percent reduction, but rather the opposite. Nature wouldn't add huge volumes of neural mass only to help tighten up and make more efficient the fields already in operation. Neither of the growth-spurts at ages four and six produced very much. Surely our worldview is far more sophisticated by age eleven, but with no more neural circuits than we had when we entered early sensory-motor development. The implication is that we added nothing significant beyond physical-sensory emotional experience and left the higher system largely dormant.

In chapter 5 I presented recent research suggesting we develop only a fraction of our neocortical potential. The prefrontal lobes are a very recent evolutionary addition and are the last to be developed in childhood.[6] Researchers suggest that our intellect is developed for and devoted to manipulating our physical environment. Even science, no matter how rarefied its mathematics and hypotheses, is oriented to strictly physical processes. The character and nature of everything taught to us between seven and eleven (and indeed beyond) directly relates to our consensual world of outer objects, events, and processes, for which we already had made our constructions of knowledge *by* age seven. Since the unquestioned assumption of our culture has been that no dynamic exists between mind and environment, every aspect of that learning from age seven to eleven could, as a result, be assimilated to previously developed neural patterns, those of our concrete thinking. Most of our neocortex is not resonant with and can't be utilized on behalf of our physical-sensory system. So we can't unlock our potential on behalf of more scientific or technological expertise, and evolution's thrust just might not be for better lasers or greater GNP's anyway.

Jean Piaget was intrigued with the discontinuities between each of the child's stages of growth in the first fifteen years. Each new stage opens capacities beyond those of the previous stage. Although in retrospect we can see clearly how everything in a previous stage prepares for the next, no period in itself suggests the powers to come. Nothing in the first four years would in any way explain intuition; nothing in the first seven years suggests the stunning capacity of operational thinking; concrete operations in no way suggests the richness of formal operations. These discontinuous leaps, each one opening new vistas of possibility beyond the reach of its predecessors, follow a kind of Richter scale exponential increase. If we started with the infant mind, compared it with each successive stage computing corresponding increases in ability all the way to adulthood, and then computed on a like increase beyond, we might gain some indication of the power inherent in us.[7] The nature of such a new form of intelligence couldn't be known other than by being it, and nothing we are doing now indicates the nature of such a quantum leap of creative being. Even if we had models to demonstrate it, who could grasp what was offered? A four-year-old can't understand the law of conservation, nor an eight-year-old formal operations, nor the average adult anything of post-operations. As William Blake observed, cups can't "conceive beyond their capaciousness."

Our current use of intellect is proving destructive to our life and planet and creating problems which that intellect is hopelessly incapable of solving. Since the higher transforms the nature of the lower into that of the higher, it should be obvious that the intelligence inherent in our undeveloped neocortex is one that would incorporate and use this astonishing intellect of ours, transforming it automatically in the process, leading us to a lifestyle in which our current problems would not exist. Intellect, driven by novelty, asks only, "Is it possible?" Intelligence, driving for our well-being and fulfillment, asks, "Is it appropriate?" A fully developed and integrated intellect could not, by its nature, make any move that was not for the well-being of self, society, and world. We would, by the very nature of our minds, be incapable of even considering dumping 100 million tons of violently toxic chemical waste on our own nest, or spend enough on armaments in one day to adequately feed the seven million or so children who starve to death each year.

In the next chapter we will briefly examine adolescence, where nature plays her last ace. Statistically, that ace never seems to pay off, but an individual is always the non-statistic. A fourth or post-operational intelligence is intuitively expected from adolescence on, and we spend our lives waiting for it without knowing what we are waiting for, harboring a hidden, inner conviction that there is something more to do with a life than eat, drink, sleep, beget, and be buried.

CHAPTER 22

Great Expectations

Adolescence is an arbitrary, contrived category. In past eras children were children until the early teens wherein, through some rite of passage, they were ushered into and took their place in adult society. Today there is no economic place for young adults and no rites of passage. We have, instead, created a holding stage that keeps young people in a limbo, into which children enter earlier and adults stay longer year by year.

Social needs are intense during this period, so this excluded group forms its own subculture based on models who ostensibly stand against the main culture and "for" the alienated young. These models are carefully engineered for commercial exploitation of this age group, however, and make astonishing fortunes by feeding on the adolescent's lack of other models and his or her need to belong. Like the underground in the novel *1984*, our counter culture is produced by the culture. The resulting "generation gap" is equally a new phenomenon in history. In previous times young people wanted to take part in adult life and looked forward to plunging in to "prove themselves." Throughout history the young have followed the footsteps of their elders, and created history. The word *discipline,* from the word *disciple,* a follower, means "to follow the exemplar." A breakdown in discipline in young people is a breakdown in our genetically encoded agenda for following the model. A rebellious adolescent refusing or reluctant to take his or her part in society is a biological anomaly.

Consider, though, that the encoding to follow the model is the constant, the model is the variable. Just as the failure of bonding at birth is the adult's responsibility, not the infant's, the failure of adolescents to follow our discipline is the fault of the adult models.

There are three characteristics of adolescence that are not part of the accepted scene, but may ring a responsive chord. They are felt-states, emotional pressures with no specific content, neither easily spoken about nor understood. Because they are qualitative, we can resonate with them, but not being quantitative, they defy precise description. Writers and poets have tried to give them voice, as J. D. Salinger in *Catcher in the Rye* or Thomas Wolfe in *Look Homeward Angel*.

First, starting at around age eleven, an idealistic image of life grows in intensity throughout the middle teens. Second, somewhere around age fourteen or fifteen a great expectation arises that "something tremendous is supposed to happen." Third, adolescents sense a secret, unique greatness in themselves that seeks expression. They gesture toward the heart when trying to express any of this, a significant clue to the whole affair.

What "it" is that is supposed to happen at this age remains a mystery, for though it may linger like Thomas Wolfe's "grape bursting in the throat," it never happens. George Leonard spoke of an anguished longing so acute he knew it could never be assuaged. A university student said that since fourteen she had waited for a momentous happening that didn't happen. (Were the issue sexual it would not be an unknown.) A student wrote his parents that he loved his third year of college but had awakened one night with "the cold hand of terror clutching his heart." Since about fourteen, he reported, he had felt that something tremendous was supposed to happen. Now approaching twenty-one, he had been waiting for seven years and it hadn't happened. Suppose, he had asked himself at that late-night awakening, it never happens, "and I never even know what it was supposed to have been?" a possibility that struck him with despair.

It may be difficult to accept that adolescents are idealistic: often they seem crass and cynical, following obvious anti-heroes. Betty Staley, from the Rudolph Steiner College, explains in her book how a noble idealism automatically unfolds in young people, impelling them to search for some model or expression of it.[1] They uncon-

190

sciously look at society, parents, and teachers through the prism of that new criteria, seeing, as for the first time, our feet of clay. This is not willful disrespect but a need within them for a model of new horizons, a need pushing them like the will that appears in the toddler.

The third characteristic, that secret, hidden greatness, complements the first two. Feeling uniquely selected for some great task, some ultimate challenge, the young person looks for a vehicle that will express that specialness or a person who represents such a potential. In times past, most societies inherited and passed on myths and folk tales of heroes of great stature, which young people heard as part of growing up. In Europe, centuries of people were brought up on the heroic figures of the Old Testament; the ethereal near-mythical figure of Jesus; the Knights of the Round Table and the search for the Holy Grail; the Norse Gods. The stained-glass windows of the great cathedrals burned into the minds of the illiterate a larger-than-life image of great beings that lifted one beyond the perishable world. The Gothic Cathedral in itself was a didactic device, designed to lift the individual spirit up, beyond our lower, animal natures, into higher realms.

In Greece, the pre-Socratic myths and Homeric legends were of people only a bit less than the gods, sharing both our attributes and those toward which we could aspire. India lived in the light of three great epics, *The Mahabarata*, *Bhagavatum*, and *Ramayana*, accounts of superhuman feats by godlike men and women, weaving into miraculous exploits the highest spiritual teaching. The power of these great epics lay in the paradox that the highest reaches of humanity arose from people depicting every human failing, failings so magnified as to be unmistakable, yet finally overcome. Incorporating god-like greatness, which we long to possess, and human weakness, which is already ours, these models of transcendence meet us where we are in order to show where we can go. Our evolution toward greatness begins, after all, in a most animal-like body. The bridge in childhood is between a specifically mammalian brain and a human brain, while in adolescence the bridge is between the human brain and the human spirit that can transcend it. The great and lasting cultures of history held before their young people symbolic figures who rose above their lower natures, making transcendence the highest and most noble of all quests, the ultimate achievement and model for becoming.

Brought up on models of such stature, we identify with a general, if inarticulate notion of a "higher aim of life." These images act as an attractor; even when no one achieves such goals all are lifted up just by the acknowledged presence of them. And for some, at least, such images act as the first stage in the cycle of competence: a rough model about whom we feel impelled to "fill in the details" and to become like through practice.

In our early years we developed each block of unfolding intelligence by our entrainment-embeddedment in it. As each stage matured, nature extracted our self-sense out of this stage and moved us on into a more expanded potential. At age one we *were* our reptilian system, at four our mammalian, and so on. By fifteen or sixteen, with sexuality in full swing we are "all hormonal," yet engrossed in our logical intellect and involvement in society. We literally feel immortal, too, which is why the eighteen-year-old makes the best soldier and this age group has the highest rate of automobile accidents. This pervasive "intimation of immortality" persists even though by around age twenty-five our body peaks and starts its slow decline.

At around age fifteen or so, the hemispheres have myelinated, and research indicates no further brain growth spurts or detectable change after that. If we have at that point developed no more than 10 percent of our neocortex, as many have proposed, our adolescent feeling of something more is intuitively correct. Bear in mind that the house cleaning of neural patterns at age eleven removed axon-dendrite connections, but apparently not neurons. Those neurons can, as our six-year-old shows, support six to seven times the axon-dendrites we adults possess. Were the young person given the appropriate stimuli, a brain growth spurt would take place around age fifteen, ushering in the new block of intelligences obviously waiting. No matter how ethereal our longing might be, however, nature's model-imperative holds.

As it is, all further development we undergo after fifteen or so, our "higher education" and lifelong learning, is but an extension of or adaptations of the foundation of intelligences developed in those first fifteen years. And all these are centered on our physical, social, and world bodies, which is the nature of the models and pursuits our society offers thereafter. Every "career" or life-path is, at its core, commercially motivated; someone stands to make money on the young person's response. If a proffered pursuit doesn't have a dollar-commodity basis, it is considered unrealistic and impractical.

Evolution's pattern is that every development be incorporated into the service of a higher function: An animal intelligence is designed for service to a greater human intelligence, which must, logically, find its own higher fulfillment. Perhaps we can't utilize more than ten or so percent of our highest cortical structures for physical pursuits simply because *only a small percentage of the neocortex is designed to operate on those lower frequencies.* The neocortex is so powerful that only a little of it is needed to modulate or change the lower, and the issue is what is the other hypothetical 90 percent for?

Our first fifteen years were devoted of necessity to products of the creative system. Nature's agenda for us after adolescence is to discover and become one with process, which pursuit will activate and incorporate the rest of our neural structures, bring us in balance, and lead us where evolution intends. Dr. B. Ramamurthi, president of the International Congress of Neurosurgery, proposes that our unutilized portion of brain is designed for exploration of an "interior universe."[2] Ten percent of our neocortex can take care of the exterior world, since that is a previously established, stable creation, while the interior is vast, open-ended, and infinite. This is similar to the contrast between the enormous challenge the image-flow from story telling presents to the brain, and the habituated, narrow spectrum of neural stimulus television presents. The unknown is a potential we define and create as we enter into and participate with, the ultimate challenge and the opposite of habituation.

The more advanced an intelligence, the more intense the need for guidance and a protective ambient, and the longer development takes. The higher up the evolutionary ladder we go, the more difficult and arduous is the journey. If the relative length of stages found in the first fifteen years were applicable after adolescence, development of a post-operational intelligence would entail a major portion of our adult life, and its employment all of our later years. This would mean a life continually opening into greater realms of experience, knowledge, and understanding—not a bad prospect.

A fourth level of intelligence is at stake in this post-operational potential, and it needs to be activated and established by our early twenties. Otherwise, that intelligence goes dormant again, just as language or intuition will if not developed within the first seven years. If it goes dormant, the search for an ultimate model gives way to cynicism; the great expectation fades, our hidden greatness isn't revealed, and we resign ourselves to a life of quiet despair. Overwhelmed by the "real world" we look back on the fantasies of adolescence as we do the fantasies of childhood. We give in to the social common denominator and knuckle down to purchasing the endless stream of substitutes that keep us locked into that R-system. These temporary possessions and pleasures ease our longing only briefly, which impels us to seek new ones and keep the wheels turning.

For decades the highest percentage of suicides took place in the early twenties age group, particularly among men. Though dormant, that fourth-level intelligence never rests; it is always waiting, and, occasionally, when we get quiet for a moment we become aware that it is still there: a vague uneasiness, a restlessness of heart.

CHAPTER 23

Compensation and Dying

Something tremendous that was supposed to happen didn't, and, though we wait not knowing for what, we knuckle under to the only models and criteria offered. These prove paltry indeed. Considered but dollar commodities in the gross national product, our self-worth is measured monetarily; we are schooled accordingly while we view six thousand hours of television by age five (and maintain the same percentage after starting school). With sixteen acts of violence per hour on children's programs and eight on adult, we witness 18,000 murders by adolescence and learn, in effect, that life is violent, and people, including one's self, are expendable. Any noble stirrings are subtly scorned. Money can't be made off virtue and restraint.

A major magazine had an article on Madison Avenue's discovery of four- to seven-year-old children as a lucrative new market. With the right stimuli, "these tots prove to be just as materialistic as adults." National chain stores with miniature check-out stands and merchandise racks for this post-toddler set were predicted as the new vogue. Further, the article went on, psychologists have determined that, given the right inputs and programming, by six years of age a child's buying habits can be determined for life. Millions of dollars for research into the kind of advertisements and programs needed to set those young minds properly will be followed by millions more for the actual programs later, a small price for establishing one's market well ahead of time.

An article on the editorial page of *The Wall Street Journal* urged industry to start investing in education, since an illiterate working population is undermining our industrial fiber. The president of a major corporation sponsored a series of advertisements in the same journal, concerning the crisis in education, explaining that it was equally a crisis for American Industry, and urging reform. As of 1990, every day in the United States 135,000 school children bring guns to school. Every day ten children die at the end of a gun barrel, while thirty are wounded. Every 78 seconds a teenager or child attempts suicide; every day six succeed. Every day 1,512 teenagers drop out of school and 3,288 children run away from home. On any day 1,629 children are in adult jails, while 2,556 children are born out of wedlock (with virtually no support for the mother from any direction).

In 1987 newspapers ran full-page accounts of the rise of our prison population in the United States. Using 1976 as a typical date to project from, at the present rate 30 percent of all white males born in that year will be in or have spent time in prison by age 29; while 80 percent of all black males born in 1976 will be in or have spent time in prison by age 29. As of 1990, 23 percent of all adult black males in the United States are either in prison, awaiting sentence, or on parole from prison, with a 96 percent recidivism rate; and the figure increases each year.[1]

Recently a rap group published a recording that sold over a million copies before some adults paid attention to its contents. The average age of the buyers of these rap records is twelve, and they listen in groups. One of the enlightening songs on this "smash-hit album" described in explicit, though hardly intelligible language, the male singer's various forms of anal-oral sex with a twelve-year-old girl. Attempts by some local authorities to take the record off the market brought not only a cry of infringement of rights and economic freedoms, but a huge increase in the sale of the record. (Plato said that if he could determine the music young people listened to, he could determine the shape of society.) Harvard's Carol Gilligan spoke of our young girls as "confident at eleven, confused at sixteen." She observed a clarity, purity of mind, and strong self-image in the eleven-year-old that was smashed in those intervening years. Millions of dollars are made from this destruction, and the destroyed child becomes the destroying but consuming adult.

History doesn't necessarily repeat itself. Phenomena have appeared over the past fifty years that have no historical precedence, for which our genetic system can't compensate, and that have so altered our mental makeup that we are blinded to the obvious relation between cause and effect. I have detailed here some of the damage of hospital childbirth, day care, television, and the erosion of child play. Schooling contributes its share and will continue to do so since vested interests view the shambles only as economic or political opportunity. No national "solution" yet forthcoming has moved beyond a politically motivated or "financially viable" position. The massive thrust for computerized education, capturing the public fancy by design, is a case in point. A computer on every desk, software for the millions and billions for the investors, will be the final straw in damaging children beyond all educability.

Since a majority of older children are uneducable, our focus has shifted to very early academic schooling based on mastery of abstract metaphoric-symbol systems. Our earliest "reading-readiness workbooks" for kindergarten children involve formal operations designed by nature to open once all the support systems are complete, somewhere around puberty. These capacities are genetically inherent within their respective evolutionary structures of brain (just as females are born with all their several million eggs complete in the ovary). We can force a child to prematurely employ these abstract intelligences to some extent, but at a price. Demanding that the young child prematurely develop symbolic capacity means the programs which nature intends for that period, as detailed here in the earlier chapters, are severely neglected. Ironically, these early programs are the foundations we need for true abstract, symbolic capacity later. Since nature's imperative is to follow the model, however, children have no choice but to try. With no neural structures developed for this capacity, a majority of children are defeated before they begin. Guilt and a loss of self-image results from their inability, while we continually test them to show how they fail to measure up.

In forcing academic intelligences ahead of time, even though we fail to develop what we are after and prevent what nature is after during that period, we get parallel behaviors we could well do without. Formal operations, timed for pre-puberty and adolescence, is part of a general program that includes the encoded sexual behaviors designed to open then. Forcing one, we get the other. Our push for premature abstract ability generally fails, while premature sexual activity too often succeeds. About seventy years ago Rudolph Steiner warned against starting children in formal academics too early (Europe and America were moving first grade from age eight to seven) and warned that the first result (though it takes a while to show) would be premature sexuality. Fifty years ago pregnancies in eleven-year-olds would have been a gross anomaly. Twenty years ago pregnancies in eleven-year-olds were epidemic (there were zero cases fifty years ago, then a few, then hundreds, now thousands); today the epidemic is down to age nine. Menarche, the beginning of menstruation is now commonly seen in eight-year-olds; hostile rape of females by males under age ten has grown from zero cases fifty years ago to epidemic levels today.[2]

Television also contributes to premature sexuality through its content. Most adult television has a sexual basis, the eternal male-female tensions found in drama and literature, and advertising is heavily dependent on it. Most children's viewing is of adult programs, placing sexuality as a major focus of attention and the casual, accepted norm, rather than the world of play and fantasy filling childhood in our past. The Barbie Doll, a blatantly sexual television concoction foisted on the viewing public years ago, largely replaced the baby doll for whatever play a child might undertake. The significance of this is clear. Little girls do not act out mother roles (many have had little enough mothering to begin with) but the role of sex object, as befitting the roles seen on television.

The major contributor to premature sexuality, however, was a World War II achievement in chemistry. Chemists synthesized the hormones accompanying or causing the extraordinary growth spurt at adolescence. Industry quickly introduced these to animal feed to speed up the growth process. By 1946 frying chickens could be marketed in six instead of thirteen weeks, at half the cost of feed. Egg production likewise increased and the price of eggs and chicken fell dramatically. Before World War II the average cow gave 800 pounds of milk annually. With the addition of this hormone to dairy feed, the amount jumped to 1500 to 2200 pounds per year—a 200 to 300 percent increase. Introducing the same hormone to the feed of animals being fattened for slaughter (beef, pork, and lamb) greatly increased the productivity and lowered the costs of such production.[3] This forced growth also seriously destabilizes the metabolic, homeostatic, and immune systems in mammals, so antibiotics to counter this have long been a staple in all animal feed, ushering in a raft of problems beyond our discussion here.

The addition of hormones took place at the very time we eliminated 97 percent of breast-feeding in the United States, substituted cow's milk or "infant formula" for mother's milk, and began early feeding of high-protein prepared infant foods, including concentrations of eggs and various meats. We had an immediate unprecedented explosion in the growth patterns of an entire generation. Postwar children suddenly towered over their pre–World War II parents and beds were suddenly too short, which we attributed to our improved diets; and, with our cultural assumption that more is always better, were proud and unquestioning of this sudden generation of giants. Indisputable evidence has been established for years now that these artificial hormones accumulate in the body, inducing premature sexuality; they are, after all, sex hormones.[4]

All bonding springs from the same mammalian source; the hospital-induced breakup of bonding has brought about day care, the breakup of families, and a sharp increase in child abuse. Close to a million children a year receive medical attention (and possibly more should) from beatings and maltreatment; some five thousand or so a year die. The average age of the victims is between two weeks and two years. Sexual abuse of children has likewise proliferated, not so strangely coincident with the widespread ingestion of sex hormones from birth, television imagery, premature schooling, and so on. A "sexual revolution" was inevitable from such a combination of factors, while the collapse of family life ushered in the casual "new family." A turnover of random male partners for divorced mothers became common, temporary fathers "moved in" with their own weight of sexual troubles, rubbing elbows with sexually precocious, disturbed, confused, and emotionally starved children—an explosive mixture. Often an abusing adult's inherent anger, serious fear of discovery, and dire threats against the child's telling creates an emotional atmosphere far more damaging to the child than would be just the physical act itself.

These destructive forces constitute the very woof and warp of our current social fabric. They are interdependent and self-reinforcing, ingrained into our very worldview and opening whole new avenues of exploitation. By commercializing and capitalizing on the R-system's basic survival drives for food, territory, and sexuality, we keep our young people locked into and identified with these lowest order behaviors. Creating a nation of radically immature adolescents as a way to keep the wheels of industry turning unleashes on society behaviors in adults typical of the two-year-old. Irritating enough in the toddler, these are terrifying in a grown population. Like the Sorcerer's Apprentice Goethe foresaw, we have unleashed far too great a power for our meager intellectual-political capacities to control, damaged a majority of our children past the point of educability, and left too few to mind the store. Industry is, indeed, in trouble.

The Scottish physicians and cellular biologists Scott Williamson and Inez Pearse observed three major states of our lived experience: function, compensation, and dying.[5] In function we operate optimally in mind, body, and spirit. Compensation begins at any point of functional failure, anything less than optimal. Dying begins when compensation breaks down. Compensation breaks down through overload, and overload happens gradually. We habituate to each gradation of compensation, until we are compensating for compensations, so caught up in each exigency that we seldom notice the steady deterioration of the quality of our life. Dying, the third state, can take place over years, even occupy a lifetime, its gradations even more elaborate than our labyrinthine compensations. Williamson and Pearse spoke of cultural-social bodies as identical to individual ones. They rise and fall, too, nearly always by their own hand.

In 1974, Herman Epstein, of Brandeis University, showed a clear decline in the number of children achieving formal operational thinking, with a similar but lesser rift with concrete operations. In American universities at large, the general faculty complaint has been that the caliber of the student body has been deteriorating year by year. In 1988, 80 percent of all academic honors and scientific awards in the United States went to foreign born students, a mere fraction of the student population. Fifty percent of all Ph.D. researchers in the United States are foreign born.

In a major western university, the psychology school devised and administered a test to determine the incoming freshmen's capacity for formal operational thought and found well over 50 percent not capable of such operations at all. The percentage declined steadily so a similar test was designed for the junior class, to observe the effect of three years of university study; no change was detectable.

In 1983 a Midwestern state department of education hired me to give a one-day workshop to some 400 teachers taking part in a week-long training for teaching exceptionally bright and gifted students. I quickly lost three-fourths of my audience though I slowed up, adopted new tactics of explanation, gave concrete examples of every issue as best I could, and used visual aids copiously. Nothing helped. The rest of the teachers, about 100 strong, easily followed. These were mostly middle aged and had taught for upward of twenty years. The 75 percent I lost averaged about age twenty-five. They couldn't sit still, listen, attend, and gave no sign of comprehending what I was talking about. Had they behaved as students in a class as they did in that course, they would have been considered hyperactive, with "attentional deficiency." Once gone, the absence of formal operational thought would be no more detectable than could the lack of music be to a deaf species. Those young teachers were victims and products of our dying system. "And if the blind lead the blind shall they not both fall in the ditch?"

PART *three*

GOING BEYOND THE WORLD WE KNOW

CHAPTER 24

Post-Operations

> . . . toward which the conscience of the world is tend-
> ing, a wind is rising, and the rivers flow.
>
> THOMAS WOLFE

There are two stages to the development "that should have happened but didn't."[1] The first stage parallels the Piagetian periods of the first fifteen years much as a wave-state parallels its particle complement. Under ideal conditions this first phase of post-operations would follow the same seven year cycles and be completed somewhere around age thirty, as a natural course of events. However, though stage-specific to late adolescence on, the potential for this post-operation stays open and we can complete it at any point.

Our first fifteen years centered on "products" of the creative system, while post operations center on process, creative action. The first stage is rather open-ended, offering a continuum of "non-ordinary" phenomena by default, just as concrete operations did earlier. Movements or groups arise that point us beyond our ordinary time-space framework, such as Charles Tart's mutual hypnotic experiments, the shared lucid dreaming of the Poseidon group, Robert Monroe's Hemi-sync program, and aspects of "parapsychology." The Christian contemplative and higher meditative paths are direct thrusts in line with evolution's end. The first group can give us experiences of the wave-side of our reality dynamic, move us temporarily from locality to non-locality. The second can lead to and include the second stage of post operations, which goes beyond all dynamics.

Given the appropriate stimulus, a brain growth spurt would take place around age fifteen; given the appropriate nurturing environment, post-operational development would unfold from it with no more fanfare than is found in the shifts at ages four, six, or eleven. Just as formal operations may not be possible for all children, however, post operations may be even less available. Post-operations are rare because of incomplete earlier development and/or lack of a model-stimulus and nurturing environment as needed at adolescence. The procedure may be rare and difficult because it is still "in-progress" on the evolutionary scene, and its procedures not yet worked out. Recall Luther Burbank's observation that new cellular groupings open new evolutionary directions. Perhaps nature has opened a new direction by adding frontal lobes offering an unknown possibility. The well-established neural systems of the two primary brains, giving us our physical world and contributing to ego-self, are formidable competition to a formless unknown awaiting discovery.

This is probably why nature added those problematic "novelty chemicals" Cloninger reports. She is pushing us into new territory. Those undeveloped frontal lobes, locus of the first stage of post-operations, are not only evolution's latest addition, but the last developed in late childhood; not only are they more complex, but more fragile and susceptible to damage than other parts of the brain. "Many cells of the frontal lobes are still forming connections and laying down circuits during childhood. . . . The dorso-lateral pre-frontal cortex is notably unfinished and unfunctional. . . . Certain brain cells don't finish developing until early adult life."[2] A full post-operations must await the maturation of this higher cortical area, and the completion of the necessary supportive structures childhood should provide.

Recall that Paul MacLean associated these frontal lobes with a larger, more empathic, humane intelligence and thought development of them was appropriate to later adolescence, when the needed support systems were mature enough. The brain's cleanup at age eleven is primarily of axon-dendrite connections. Those neurons had six to seven times as many connections at age six and could immediately produce a like quantity and offer as many new fields at age fifteen, or fifty, if conditions were met. All evidence points toward a potential brain growth-spurt somewhere around our mid-teens to inaugurate a new developmental period. This would be what the young person is waiting for, but nature's model-imperative holds, "interaction with appropriate environmental support systems."[3]

The progression from "concreteness to abstraction" noted by Piaget is clearly seen in the behaviors and capacities inherent in each of our evolutionary brains. We are born embedded in matter and move toward that matter's wave-form as seen in the progression through our triune system: from the limited physical experience of the hard-wired R-system, on to the more fluid and powerful subtle-emotional limbic system, to the limitless causal realm of the neo-cortex. Each of the Piagetian stages requires more nurturing, is more difficult to complete, and is paradoxically more fragile in its potential state though more powerful once functional. Each stage is discontinuous; nothing in one developmental set in any way suggests the quantum leap of capacity found in the next, yet each clearly prepares for its successor since it is the foundation. The inner-world and modulated play-world of childhood; our intuitions, ordinary dreaming, our Eureka! experiences giving outreach beyond the mind, all point us beyond our physical matrix.

Carlos Castaneda's many books concerning the "non-ordinary" world of his sorcerer's apprenticeship, whether factual or not, are an accurate description of the open-ended nature of our mature creative system. He shows the intense disciplines needed to allow creative potential. Both Castaneda and Robert Monroe perceived non-ordinary domains in an ordinary way. Monroe considered those realms established worlds in their own right (which may or may not be the case), while Castaneda was aware that a creative power shaped each event as he entered into it, making his response critical.

In my mid-thirties I underwent an experience that brought me two years or so of tranquility and freedom from fear, but this eventually dissipated, and my fragmentation surfaced again. Around forty I had an experience of overwhelming magnitude, however, that took place in a normal wake-state: An exterior presence-force formed directly against me. It was, I feel sure, the anima figure Carl Jung

207

discusses (though he radically underestimated its scope). This force, which was the most ancient part of me, more familiar than my name, yet more feminine in form, texture, and psyche than any living creature, fused into me cell by cell, became me and wrapped me in a prolonged and indescribable state of completeness beyond anything I had experienced before or since. Eventually the state faded and my greater half left as it had entered, leaving me devastated. That such a state of completeness could exist, yet happen only once and be unattainable again was something I never quite got over. I worked intensely to regain the state and had an ongoing series of rhapsodic episodes, generally through early morning sessions of silent longing (I had never heard of meditation) during which the world would fall away and I would be briefly lifted into a spiral of love and power, but these were only faint echos of the original unity experience.

Years later I met a teacher and undertook a disciplinary path that brought a slow and systematic change, which all those sporadic experiences, dramatic as they were, did not. Recall how my teacher made me aware of my "subtle body" by lifting me out of my physical body thereby shifting my attitudes and orientation. I have recounted several non-ordinary experiences in this book, and while mine were occasionally ecstatic, most were didactic—teaching me something new, shifting my point of view. This book itself originated from such a teaching. In 1979 my teacher explained to me at length how the world I perceived was generated within my brain-mind-body, projected onto the "screen of my mind," and dutifully sensed as out-there by my perceptual system, which is the reverse of common sense and classical physiology. He claimed that vibratory frequencies within us create our perception of volumes of space, which then fill with the light and objects perceived as our outer world; he stated that the vibration giving rise to sound gives rise to vision and gives those visual patterns their dimensions, placement in space, and movement. He spoke of language as a shaping force of mind and reality, and urged me to discover the source of *word* within me. There I would find the very source of creation and core of my self.

This psychology-cosmology struck me as a quaint creation myth of a bygone age, and I neither believed nor understood him. He gave me ancient texts to read and though I wrestled with them for weeks I believed no more what I had read than what I had heard. My teacher resolved the matter through a teaching method common to Sufi and Yoga masters. He simply *gave* me a direct experience of the creative process. Abruptly and without warning a weight seemed to descend on me, "pressing me" into the deepest state of meditation. My perceptual world and personal history vanished, yet my awareness was intact. Then the entire creative process unfolded from my point of awareness, exactly as he had described. Sound vibrations arose, created volumes of expanding and contracting space, determined by the strength and duration of the sound. As the volumes expanded, so did my awareness; space and my awareness of that space were one. These conscious spaces then flooded with light articulating as objects that took on three-dimensional form located within the moving spaces. Recognition flooded in, each of these sound-vibrations both originated from and gave rise to an actual "outer" sound from my environment. As I recognized each object of my world by name, it "detached" and became objective to me, the world forming, re-forming around me.

A protracted and delightful period of absolute amnesia followed. I knew I had a name and a personal history, but I had no access to it. As I realized how superfluous that name and history were, however (and I had thought that they were the *all* of me), they rushed in as though anxious to fill their niche. My wonderful detachment faded; I identified with and became that name, limited story, and worldview—my usual self.

I knew many things from this episode. I knew there were people who could inject an experience into the neural stream of another; that I had experienced how creation does form within us; that the core of authentic self-awareness was not dependent on memory, personal history, or a physical setting; that I was indeed more than my physical body and everything connected with my named history; that a higher state of awareness lay beyond these personal characteristics. (I found, however, that getting rid of this baggage permanently was a major task.)

My teacher later told me that within ten years the scientific community would provide all the research needed to explain this creative process in scientific terms, which has proved true. He urged me to resume writing, now from my meditative position, which I dutifully did. His ongoing work on me centered on breaking my identity with

209

this body and its related emotions, a break essential to the first phase of post-operations, and allowing me to *be* in this world fully. He operated out of love, which is not a sentiment but a power, that intelligence of the heart that moves for our overall well-being. Love extends far beyond our notions of bliss and good-feelings, which stem, after all, from our limbic reward system.[4] Our first-stage post-operations are often ecstatic and blissful, as we discover the rewards of non-physical relationships. Nature uses our limbic reward system to shift our notion of reward from physical to non-physical. Higher states themselves leave all emotional rewards behind, since these are effects of our animal brain, and, following a rather blissful early period on the spiritual path, as nature entices us away from our ordinary notions of reward, we go into a very dry "desert" where nothing seems to be rewarding at all. We have to discover the rewards based on non-physical perception.

Our natural embeddedment is in the limbic-R-system alliance which gives rise to our personality with its prejudices, fears, desires, ambition, every facet of self as recognized by both ourself and others. This identity is a critical part of our childhood and young adulthood. When such a temporary identity becomes permanent, however, it is our enemy, and drags us down to death and despair, causes social grief and disaster, and blocks our movement into evolution's higher agenda. This is difficult to grasp since we *are* our identity of the moment. As Bernadette Roberts points out the eye can't look at the eye. This ego-self is all we know; it constitutes every fiber of our being, and we can't recognize it for we have no other position from which to view it. A threat to this aesthetic-emotional bundle of desire is more direct than a knife at the throat. Our greatest fear, as Susanne Langer said, is that our ideation, our notions of who and what we are, might fall into chaos. So we can as ego-selves neither self-analyze nor self-correct. Only an "outside" force, something other than our ego-self, can bail us out of our impasse, but this "outside" force is actually "inside" us, the authentic force of our life. It is "outside" only in the sense of being absolutely other than our passionate and desperate ego-self clinging to what it knows.

Recall that neural structures form in utero for precise needs, but are eliminated before birth so they don't impede the next stage. An ego-self forms throughout the first fifteen years to serve critically important ends but should be superseded by a higher intelligence in later adulthood, just as the terrible two's *will* is a critically needed developmental device, to be eventually replaced. Daily we read of atrocities committed by adults still caught in the two-year-old's emotional web.

The same applies to our passionate, fearful ego-self. Post-operations must incorporate this mammalian-based awareness, with its thorough grounding in the physical body, into service of the late forming structures of the neocortex, an incorporation that will result in an integrated self system bearing almost no relation to the earlier one. The first form of this is when thought, feeling, and action fuse into a single intelligence. Until then, we have no power or effectiveness in life, being a house divided. Eastern psychology refers to three behavioral sets, *Tamas, Rajas,* and *Satva,* which are identical with those of MacLean's triune system. *Tamas* is our R-system self, habituated, inflexible, sluggish, resistant to change; *Rajas* our limbic system self with its passionate resolve, wild energy, and insatiable appetite; *Satva* is our highest cortical self with equanimity, poise, control, and "dominion over the earth," which means freedom from all aspects of the "lower selves." From this high perspective we can literally manipulate our physical world, which is our limbic-R-system dynamic. This last state, merger of the lower self with the higher self may be our classical notions of union with God, the rarely achieved aim of most spiritual systems.

My teacher said "you must develop your intellect to its highest possible extent, in order that it be a proper instrument of the intelligence of the heart. But only the heart can develop intellect to its highest extent." Post-operations involve an intelligence that lies outside and beyond brain systems, even though the first stage of its development utilizes the rest of our neocortex as the vehicle of that higher intelligence. Once operative, this higher intelligence will fully develop intellect as its own instrument.

Our overall agenda can be seen as three stages of this heart-centered power and its constant presence within: The first, cellular and hormonal, maintains us physically from birth on. Developed, this first-stage heart keeps our three-fold system in balance and works for integrity of ego, bonding, and physical well-being. The second stage of this heart-intelligence should unfold in mid-adolescence,

211

ushering in post-operations. This would lift us out of the dictates of our ancient "animal heart" with its primitive emotions and compulsions, and transform those systems into servants of the higher systems as needed.

Paul Muller-Ortega, professor of religion at the University of Michigan, studied Kashmir Shaivism for many years and wrote a major work, *The Triadic Heart of Shiva,* on this psychology-cosmology. Through his publisher, he met my teacher whose meditation system is directly descended from this ancient science. In an intense three-day meditation course, sitting in a dark hall some fourteen hours daily, Muller began to experience in clear moving diagrams the "wave-forms of Shiva." (*Shiva* is the name for the primordial source in this system.) Muller saw, in the finest detail, the wave-fields cross-index and create interference patterns out of which arise the frequency realms that in turn give rise to our universe, our speech, and all experience. At each break in the course, he would rush to write down and describe the experience as best he could. This three-day "Eureka!" experience concretized and clarified twenty years of study.

Under his mentor, don Juan, Carlos Castaneda's experiences, while equally post-operational, arose from a radically different tradition, giving them a completely different flavor or texture than discipleship and sainthood. Sorcery depicts the creator as a grim Eagle devouring billions of souls in an insatiable appetite for "awareness." The job of the sorcerer is to slip past the Eagle and enter the unknown beyond. Plotinus experienced a state of union several times and spoke of God creating universe after universe in an attempt to express a "superplenitude of love," a love always exceeding its expression. This is about as far-removed from a devouring Eagle as imaginable, yet the function underlying both viewpoints might be identical, the radically different metaphors arising from different perceptions and, indeed, experiences, of that function. Carlos Castaneda experienced this very "archetype of love" at one point of his journey, and wept from the enormity of it. His mentor, don Juan Matus, was contemptuous of such sentiment. Any path beyond the world of folly is inordinately difficult, particularly don Juan's, where the need is for "unbending intent and impeccability" (to be free of sin—that which stands between self and God, or in this case, goal). One's intent would be fragmented by such sentiment or emotional indulgence from another system as Carlos reported. Don Juan knew the ego unconsciously attempts to "play the field" and keep its integrity intact, resisting change while playing at change.

The sages spoke of our "fleshly heart" as "looking down," since it encompasses within itself the primary intelligences of our animal heritage and keeps our physical being intact. The job of the intelligence of the higher, "subtle" heart, is to "devour the fleshly heart," a striking metaphor for breaking our identity with emotion and sentiment. The higher, subtle heart, looks "up," bonding us on a universal level and eventually drawing us beyond our biological selves. Here is the "crosswise line" the sages saw, with impulse below and forward movement from above. Incorporated into this higher heart our intellect could not work against our well-being as it now does. Impulse from below with no forward direction from above breeds disaster. Were our intellect serving an intelligence which moves only for well-being, not one facet of our current personal-social-ecological crisis could exist. "The intelligence of the heart never solves problems" according to my teacher, "it just dissolves the situation in which problem exists and gives a new situation."

This second-stage "subtle" heart will activate and utilize the rest of the neocortex and the unknown block of intelligences and potentials inherent in it. The nameless lump in the throat expressed in adolescence is our primary physical heart longing for its "union" with this higher heart. Once achieving this, another stage awaits: A final, highest "heart" resides within us at the fontanels at the top of the brain. The reason for calling it a "heart" is that this is the primary pulse of life, the Spanda, the base frequency that gives rise to all the frequencies to which our triune structure and physical-subtle hearts respond, the "frequency-realm" out of which our world-self experience is spun and the reason "the whole of creation lies within us."[5]

Our first heart stage is intimately connected with the limbic and R-systems. Our second heart stage is connected with the potentials of our neocortex, the causal realm of pure potential, creativity as itself. The third heart is the point from which all springs and for which we have neither neural structures, nor anything else with which to approach, imagine, or achieve it. "It," that ultimate point, must arc the gap and incorporate *us* into *its* being. We can, by enormous effort,

Joseph C. Pearce

take the rest of the kingdom by storm, as ordinary yogis and sorcerers do, but not this final citadel. Union with it is the gift or grace of that citadel itself. This realm of insight-intelligence becomes as each person who becomes it, yet "it" is always the same. Meister Eckhart claimed that when God took birth in his soul, he became none other than God, but God, at that moment, also became Eckhart. The magnificence of unity in diversity as a complementary system is that you and I and each diverse variable are both uniquely "that" and the unity from which "that" springs.

CHAPTER 25

Access to the Field

... the gods are later than this world's creation ...

THE *RIG VEDA*

Developing a language requires accessing the language field through stimuli given by a developed language in the environment. The open field closes according to the nature of that model (French Mamma, French-speaking infant). The neural fields developed for this translation are at some point indistinguishable from the field of potential translated. The discipline of science determines, to an indeterminable extent, what people in that discipline can and will discover, and carefully excludes "non-scientific" material, that which can't be controlled within the system and so is an embarrassment or threat to the system's integrity.

Even the ultimate source is a field of compatible-variables. Each of us is a variable of that field, and the field *is* in each instance according to the nature of its variable. To access that ultimate ground and become it, rather than just expressing a variable of it, is a different matter. Each of us is a part of God, an expression of God, in God, but to *become* God is something else. Though the goal of our evolution, this entails process. We can access that field only through some path, frame of reference, or means of access, and the means we use determines to an indeterminable extent the nature of the field we

215

then find. Even as the person accessing the field becomes that field, the field equally becomes that person according to the nature of both the person and the access by which the person achieves the field.

The gods are later than this creation since they arise *from* it as definitions of that creation. The assumption that we "create" our gods is as wrong as that we create our world; however, both result from the same "structural-coupling" with which we are part and product. In Kashmir Shaivism, Shiva is the still-point of witness; Shakti, his consort, births the universe for her lord to witness. They are an indivisible conscious power but through an instant-by-instant separation and union, Shakti's creation appears a play or illusion. According to Shaivism, each of us, as expressions of that union, are both Shiva and Shakti by simple default. Our goal is to become aware of who we are, at which point we become the play and the play takes on a new cast and plot.

In Vedic theory the creative force is called Prakriti. Like Castaneda's Eagle she functions without reason, judgment or compassion. An ancient writer observed that "Prakriti needs humus," humus being organic material for her soil of endless creation, and we humans are that humus—unless we get beyond Prakriti. The *Vedas*, however, point beyond Prakriti to a witness who observes her creation, since without the seminal act of witnessing, creation is barren. Whether the witness gives rise to the goddess as something to witness, or she gives rise to the witness, is similar to the wave-particle issue, a paradox our *Hymn of Origin* leaves hanging.

Through an inordinately difficult and complex apprenticeship the sorcerer, like the yogi, slips past Prakriti, or the Eagle, into creation ✶ God itself, through developing the "Eagle's gift"—that very "Prakriti" power within all of us of since we are her product. The sorcerer steals her fire, in effect, but she responds to him equally as with any witness and, as is her nature, spins before him a path of "breathless wonder." What she spins, however, reflects the sets of expectancy built into the path of access the apprentice followed. Don Juan Matus, Castaneda's mentor in sorcery, came from an ancient lineage of sorcerers, which determined the nature of what Castaneda in turn experienced.

Process has no criteria, judgment, or logic, just procedure. So sorcery, like some of the "lower" yogas, can take the kingdom by storm,

216

to a point (for I believe that what is found this way is only the first stage of post-operations). The saint, on the other hand, through an equally difficult but utterly simple discipleship, allows Prakriti to devour him, "gives up his life for a greater life," a sacrifice that can move him beyond Prakriti to the witness, who can be no other than the saint himself. "What you must realize," my teacher said, "is that God cannot turn out to be anything other than you."

There are two main paths to the witness state, that of Eastern meditation or Christian contemplation. They are structurally parallel but texturally quite different. Bernadette Roberts achieved the highest state through the contemplative path and experienced nothing similar to accounts of eastern saints. She points out that we can only enter this journey from a "frame of reference," a path, or means for accessing the goal.[1] Yet, Roberts also points out that the goal toward which we move must always, of necessity fall outside any frame itself. Our goal lies beyond our "cosmic egg," yet only from a cosmic egg can we find the crack that leads to the goal. Frames of reference "come later than this creation," and arise out of our experience, feed back in and become parts of that creation, while evolution's end lies beyond all creation and so all frames of reference. A frame of reference is necessary to get there, but will only carry one so far.

At one point I was convinced that the path of meditation was its own goal because the rewards from it were so rich. And I was right in one way while wrong from a broader perspective. The word *yoga* means union or yoke. The word *religion* is popularly held to mean relationship, but its literal meaning is "to bind fast," which is a bit more stringent form of tie than yoga or yoke. Religion can only exist so long as separated parts long for union. Should the parts achieve union the religion would disappear; however, religions, being our intellectual creations sustained by people investing their life in them, tend to bind the separated parts tightly to the religion itself. The frame of reference becomes its own field perpetuating itself, and, while the rewards of the relationships unfolding can be immense, the goal of evolution can be lost. "I must create a system of my own," cried poet Blake, "or be enslaved by another man's."

Those who break through the "fast-binding" of a system are generally suspect within their own tradition. Nothing so upsets the Bishop as the rumor of a saint in his parish. William Blake, having no sectarian ties, was considered mad by his social peers. Jesus broke with his frame of reference and so literally outlawed himself in the eyes of his society and was hung as a common criminal. Bernadette Roberts, as her predecessors Eckhart and John of the Cross, inadvertently broke with her Catholic frame of reference in order to fulfill her longing, but she fulfilled that Catholic frame in so doing. We would have no Eckhart, John, or Bernadette Roberts were it not for their Catholic frame though each of them had to struggle with and go beyond that frame to fully express it.

In the *Bhagavad Gita*, Krishna tells Arjuna that trying to achieve the highest state without a teacher is virtually impossible. The path of the "formless guru," a teacher long gone or simply an ideal held in the mind as a model, allows our ego-intellect leeway to entertain ideas of change rather than submit to change itself. The living teacher, having gone before, models the goal, and guides us around the devious ways of our ego-intellect in its unconscious moves for survival. Bernadette Roberts, however, broke through into the highest of all states without a visible guide, model, or, worse, any clear idea of what was happening most of the time. As a nun in a convent from the age of seventeen, she had achieved "unity with God" in the classical sense as a "subject adoring an object." That, however, was only half the journey. God is not object, even of adoration, and adoration is emotion, a limbic function. No sooner was this bond with God sealed than she was impelled to leave that safe haven and re-enter the world (just as a well-bonded child grows up to leave the nest and become independent). A second journey began, which took some twenty years to bear fruit, which was the loss of her warm, inner unity, along with both sense of God and self, leaving only a singular point of witnessing, without emotion, judgment, reflection, or anticipation. Relationship was no longer an issue, not even with God since that was all there was. She couldn't turn within to that still center for the witness can't witness itself any more than the eye can view the eye. All she could do was look without while a powerful, incredible intelligence within her did everything, as it had all along.

She never overtly "broke with her church" as an adolescent rebel might. She was simply moved beyond its ordinary parameters by the power of this inner guide, which she would probably never have discovered except through the church. She continued to observe the sacrament of bread and wine, the heart of Catholic practice, and during her "passage," when her sense of self was being annihilated, she carried the host (the bread representing the sacrificial body of Jesus) with her at all times, and from this her strength and guidance apparently came.

George and Charles, the calendrical savants, played with that little brass perpetual calendar in their otherwise impoverished childhood, knowing nothing of its purpose. The device triggered into play neural fields that were then open to that category of phenomena. (All experience, remember, is a "peak of activity in a population of neurons," and that population must be brought into play through structural coupling, the stimulus-response dynamic.) If a mechanical gadget can function in such a way as to predispose a neural system toward a field effect larger than imaginable within the "symbolic-gadget" triggering that field, consider the effect the Christian sacrament of communion offers. This sacrament was established through one of history's most dramatic events, has been observed by untold millions for two thousand years, "canalizing the access" and expanding the power base itself. Consistently taken as the most significant act of life, by a person of extraordinary intelligence, with a sustained, concentrated dedication and passionate desire to know the meaning or power behind that ritual, as was Bernadette Roberts's case, why should the maneuver not function as designed? In fact, how could it fail? Any other field would function by responding, and all *do*, as evidenced by physicist Gordon Gould's laser "breakthrough" or mathematician William Hamilton's "quaternions."

Roberts felt no relationship with the historical person of Jesus, nor the larger symbol of Christ, however. Her love affair was strictly with God. This seemed to keep the goal constantly singular and all else supportive. The host, that sacramental bread, provided access to the "field of all fields," that is, it ushered her into the field rather than becoming itself a field to her. On taking the veil the nun "marries" Christ, the body of the church. Many a nun, in her lonely cell, contemplating her Lord, dwelling on his wounds, suffering with her savior (the word suffering means letting, allowing), "buys into the field" through such concentrated devotion. But the field she buys into is a devotional field. She may well experience the stigmata and bleed precisely at those wound marks depicted in all those countless crucifixions adorning churches over the centuries. The field responds according to the nature of the access to it, but this bears no resemblance to the unknown Bernadette Roberts fell into, which lies beyond all fields.

I found reports that Eastern devotees drink the water in which their guru's feet are washed rather revolting, but then considered Jesus' statement that his followers must "eat his body and drink his blood." The account is that "many fell away from him" saying "who can stomach this?" and surely I would have fallen away first. Christians counter that Jesus' statement was symbolic only, and in that they are both right and seriously mistaken. Recall that symbols participate in that toward which they point; they enter into our conceptualization, cognition, understanding, and reception of what is involved. To say "just a symbol," as Christians have tended to do, is to miss the power. Carl Jung proposed that symbols "lose their power," but we rationalize away the power of the symbol in order to play at it emotionally rather than submit to it. Real symbols access their field of potential. A symbol offers a dynamic that must be both invited in and entered into, at which point our conceptual capacity is operated on and changed by the power of the symbol. When a symbol is presented in a "concrete" form, with which we can interact in as tangible a way as eating it, for instance, we open to the power within the symbol, its "abstract" form. This is the way of all learning, and the reason why there is such power in tangible "hosts" as the Eucharistic sacrament or drinking the "waters of the Guru's feet." The cross as a functional symbol works only in conjunction with its necessary complement, the Eucharist, the communion through bread and wine.[2] It might be that you can't have one without the other.

Carlos Castaneda's mentor, don Juan, considered peyote and other hallucinogenic plants to *be* the gods, not to "stand for" them. These were "power plants" and power is action, movement, energy. One devours the god not to have an experience but to take on his power, become him. This is a serious ritual, carried out under the strict "rule" of that system and guidance of one who has travelled that path. One then uses the power only to develop the power of that path.

The thrill-seeker looking for a chemically induced experience or the half-baked spiritual seeker looking for easy access to power may instead have their brains burned out for their sloppiness. If Christian communicants simply observe taking bread and wine as a sentimental rite, as I did as an Anglican, or, as Catholics do following "Pascal's wager" (that the church just *might* be right and transubstantiation true), trying to cover their bases and protect their self-sense, the power of the Eucharist, though still there, won't be revealed.

The two millennia gap between Jesus' time and today has no affect on the power of the sacrament since all fields are non temporal-spatial. Consider that for months methadone blocked the bruises and pain of an accident, prompting Lippin to ask "where was the bruise and pain all that time?" Consider how a post-hypnotic suggestion plays itself out after the specified time, and we ask "Where was the blister and sensation of burning during that time?" These are small effects within constricted subtle fields, but it is sobering to realize that all power can function in this way.

The word *sacrifice* (meaning, like the word *sacrament*, "to make whole") has taken on strangely negative yet understandable connotations. To become whole all parts must be left behind, for a whole is not the sum of its parts but a different state entirely. Eckhart spoke of "all named objects" being left behind when one enters that unknown. We must go beyond the fragmentation of parts and leave the world of diversity to discover the single unity from which all springs. Bernadette Roberts recognized that Jesus became whole only at that moment of abandonment on the cross, when he cried "My God, why have you forsaken me?" That "Father within," his source and guide, having, in effect, lured him into this awful deal, ostensibly to *maintain that very inner relationship*, disappeared, leaving him with nothing. Note, however, that he had followed this inner guide with total obedience and from that discipline had gained the strength and conviction to follow it anywhere and do anything necessary to maintain that contact. (Evolution knows how to use that reward-syndrome built into the limbic system long ago.) He gambled everything on this inner relationship and set up the whole operation as directed from within. This included his last meal with his followers and the commandment to "eat his body and drink his blood" to maintain *their* relationship with him. All this he did to maintain *his* relationship only to have it blown away and his own self with it. For relationship is between separated parts. The first awareness of *becoming* "it" was to feel utterly abandoned. All that was left was a witness, where anything witnessed is God.

Just as planned, however, in becoming that ultimate goal, Jesus' rather awful symbol for getting there offered access, the "passage" as Bernadette Roberts calls it, to that goal. The intelligent force propelling him into this episode concretized at that point, burning its way into our historical psyche with unforgettable force. Regardless of our aesthetic, intellectual, or religious response to the cross and communion, from that point on there resided in us, along with a mathematical, musical, or any other field, this power that could, if followed, lead us beyond all fields.

The force that seized, tricked, and became Jesus and he it, is the issue. St. Augustine said there was never a time in history when that called the Christ was not present among us. Jesus said "Before Abraham was I am." In Eastern psychology this Christ-Principle, which Augustine saw as the underlying structure of history, is called the Guru Principle, *guru* meaning "teacher," the one who leads us from the darkness of ignorance to the light of knowledge. (The word *rabbi,* the title given to Jesus, likewise means "teacher.") Since all learning is from the concrete to the abstract, this principle has been concretizing, taking flesh and blood form down through the ages, as Augustine recognized, "before Abraham" and today.[3]

In the Synoptic Gospels, Jesus remarked that he and his Father were "always working," and in a post-crucifixion appearance account in a Gnostic Gospel, Jesus said, in regard to his coming back, "I am always becoming what you have need of me to be." In the *Bhagavad Gita,* Krishna tells Arjuna that he is always working and says, "age by age I come back to you to bring you back to the supreme self." This is evolution in its constant attempt to break through with a new mode of being and why we know that behind the apparent randomness of creation lies a perfectly clear intent. The following account indicates that this appearing, or "theophany," goes on all the time and always has.

The anthropologist Adolf Jensen gave us this account given him by an Apinaye hunter from the Ge tribe of eastern Brazil. The hunter recounts:

I was hunting near the sources of the Botica Creek. All along the journey there I had been agitated and was constantly startled without knowing why. Suddenly I saw him standing under the drooping branches of a big steppe tree. He was standing there erect. His club was braced against the ground beside him, his hand he held on the hilt. He was tall and light-skinned, and his hair nearly descended to the ground behind him. His whole body was painted and on the outer side of his legs were broad red stripes. His eyes were exactly like two stars. He was very handsome.

I recognized at once that it was he. Then I lost all my courage. My hair stood on end, and my knees were trembling. I put my gun aside, for I thought to myself that I should have to address him. But I could not utter a sound because he was looking at me unwaveringly. Then I lowered my head in order to get hold of myself and stood thus for a long time. When I had grown somewhat calmer, I raised my head. He was still standing and looking at me. Then I pulled myself together and walked several steps toward him, then I could not go any farther for my knees gave way. I again remained standing for a long time. Then I lowered my head and tried again to regain composure. When I raised my eyes again, he had already turned away and was slowly walking through the steppes. Then I grew very sad.[4]

This is a perfect example of the teacher-principle always becoming. "He" appears to the hunter as the perfect hunter, because he *is* the hunter himself, in his perfected form. The hunter instantly recognizes him, as he could not have recognized Jesus and his cross, Krishna and his flute, or the Madonna of Medjagorge. "He" has been appearing like this down through the ages, offering the yoke, the union that will carry us beyond our state. Had the hunter been able to accept that yoke, make that address as he intuitively knew he must, and accept the invitation to enter the projection of his greater self (which terrified him as it would you or me) he would have returned to his village transformed. He would have *been* the perfect hunter and the model for a new phase of consciousness in his people. "If I be lifted up I draw all to me." (Throughout the ages countless societies have been lifted in just such a manner.)

For centuries people have foolishly speculated on "where" Jesus went to "learn" all his tricks. Everything is within each of us, and, if conditions are right, our perfection "throws out an image" and invites us to enter, each according to some destiny over which we have no control nor the slightest notion of where it leads. "He" or "it," evolution herself, is continually trying to break through into our human psyche. Evolution's end was clearly articulated at the first instant of creation. The end was in the beginning and has already taken place in that non-temporal realm. But the workings-out in time of evolution's intent is another matter, subject to any number of random factors including the whims of our individual egos and wills.

Early in 1979, my inner journey had bogged down, my meditation had gone bone-dry, and I was wondering how to find help when I had an unexpected visual experience of my long-held secret ideal, Jesus. My "mythical model" appeared and clearly and powerfully directed me to go meet my teacher, of whose person and whereabouts at that time I knew nothing. This directive came to me so concretely and symbolically, and in a way so compatible with my background, that I couldn't miss the message, though I was appalled over the notion of a foreign guru. My old hero "became what I had need of him to be," by leading me to a living teacher who propelled me into a whole new phase of the inner journey.

Had I been a Catholic communicant as Roberts, with a strong foundation and as steadfast a will as she displayed, my need may never have manifested as it did, or, if it had, it may well have been met by other methods. As it is, after many fruitful years on the path of my guru, my old model resurged and pressured me into yet another shift, a far more radical turning within and cutting off of my new frame of reference, the very lifeline and support system that had bailed me out and brought me to a far stronger position. Evolution's intent gives no guarantees, no resting place to "lay one's head" since the goal is an unknowing.

The statement: "God cannot turn out to be anything other than your own self" represents different aspects of our journey. First is that we are each a definition of God, a definition that could come only "after this creation." God in this sense has no other definition than us—for or to us—so we find him only within. The field of compatible-variables is both never changed by its variables, yet, having no being except through such variables, the field infinitely reflects each variable equally. The question of God and our relation to him has arisen in our minds throughout the ages, but in fact we are God asking that question; the creation has given rise to this capacity to question itself; we are the only way by which such a question could arise; and we are the only answer to that question only we can ask, the real pay-off of the novelty-factor built into us. And God will "exist" for us to the extent of our definition, and we define God according to the nature and character of our models.

Bernadette Roberts did not experience the stigmata, for she felt no "marriage to Christ," nor did she experience anything similar to Eastern mediation symbols. Roberts had nothing to go on other than "it," which moved and breathed her, but the end result is the same—and absolutely different. She clearly progressed through the physical, subtle, and causal hearts, to have the resulting synthesis blown away in order to lift her to the highest heart, the absolutely unknown.

The God who comes after creation, our necessary first journey, evolves as shaped by our definitions. Paul Muller-Ortega traces the growth of the God Shiva from the very earliest and primitive conceptions of a local fertility god on down to the profound insights of Abhinavagupta and non-dual Kashmir Shaivism. Observe the primitive, punitive, judgmental, and murderous God of the Old Testament becoming the God of love through Jesus.

"Who really knows? Who here can say? . . . from where it came—this creation?" the *Rig Veda* hymn asks. Knowledge and the object of knowledge are one. This creation, the *Rig Veda* said, "came before the gods," but out of this creation has come an endless attempt by that creation to define itself, giving rise to an endless procession of gods, each definition giving another facet of it. And each such definition expands the possibilities for those that follow, yet tends to become archetypal, a field within the field, leading only to itself, and so must eventually be broken with and gone beyond.

Ancient dogma decreed that no man can see God, which is true. God is not an object. We can only see *as God*, but then, when we do, God is all we can see. Walt Whitman asked, "How can I see God better than this day?" and claimed to see God on a thousand faces and names in the street. The ancient Rudram, a hymn from the *Krishna Yajur Veda*, sings of the endless names and faces of God, who finds himself as each of us: He is the robber, the desperado, the saint, the slave, the king. Each defines him, and each must then experience his or her definition of him.

As Blake said, anything possible to be believed is an image of truth. Truth is function, not a thing, idea, event, or semantic slogan. Truth is how the creation works. Understand function and you are home-free. The opposite of truth is delusion, the non-functional. My fearful self-sense, a "raging bundle of desire in a dying animal" as William Butler Yeats calls it, is the only delusion there is. All else is God. So the creation gives rise to God as defined, the infinite defined in order to know itself as a self, as you and me. But God as our realized definition is still less-than, still defined. Even so great a relation as me and my greater Self, is a relation and relationship requires separation. So even this rug, the union of individual and God, will be pulled out from under sooner or later. A further stage will open. We will have to leave the safe-harbor of even this highest knowing, since, as Eckhart put it, all known things must be left behind. Only then will we express evolution's end that was in its beginning, which is the opening of a new evolution.

The drop becomes the ocean and the ocean realizes itself as that drop, poet Kabir observed. All is a dynamic, and that dynamic is God. Every person breaking through to the ultimate ground is the whole of that ground, and that ground is all there is. And yet, what then? Then the creative force spins her worlds out before such people, as is her nature. Each person achieving the highest is equally what is seen, the act of seeing, and the seer, yet they simply witness *her* dancing. Each witness enters in, participates, directs, and plays God—but creation does the dancing. Wherever they look worlds form—but creation forms those worlds. Eckhart's soul just "throws the image out to enter into it" but where does the image come from and who is throwing it out? The eternal question and wonder is still there: "from whence it comes, this creation? Just who *is She,* who comes before all things?"

Notes

Note: Full citations can be found in the Bibliography.

ORIGINS

1. Oriental Philosophies, John M. Kolber. (New York: Scribner's Sons, 1985).

INTRODUCTION

1. Going strong in his mid-seventies, Pribram's most recent book, *Brain and Perception,* Holonomy and Structure in Figural Processing (1991, Hillsdale, New Jersey, Lawrence Erlbaum Associates) further explores these parallel processes, though in the most difficult material and mind-numbing concepts I have yet encountered.
2. Gould, Stephen Jay, 1987.
3. Stochasm is a Greek term used by Gregory Bateson in his extraordinary work, *Mind and Nature* (1979, New York, E.P. Dutton). The word means randomy with purpose, and was used to describe nature's way of profusion. "If a sequence of events combines a random component with a selective process so that only certain outcomes of the random are allowed to endure, that sequence is said to be stochastic." Unity and diversity, I hold, operate stochastically.
4. Larry Dossey's *Recovering the Soul: A Scientific and Spiritual Search* (1989, Bantam Book, N.Y.) is remarkably parallel in content and general format to this book of mine, but it was sent me too late to use as a general reference in my work, or I would probably have been quoting him on every page. I can only urge readers to find out what this extraordinary medical man has to say.

1. IDIOT-ENIGMA

1. The twins, George and Charles, lived at Letchworth Village Mental hospital outside New York City for many years, and I came across accounts of them in the early 1970s. I found reports on no more than half dozen such people until Treffert published his accounts.

2. Treffert 1989.
3. William Blake, *Selected Poetry and Prose of William Blake*, ed. Northrop Frye (New York: The Modern Library, 1953), discourse VI, marginalia, p. 453.
4. Gardner 1984.
5. Walt Whitman, "There Was a Child Went Forth," in *Leaves of Grass*, selected by Lawrence Clark Powell (New York: Crowell, 1964).
6. Chamberlain 1989; Cheek 1988.
7. Tart, Puthoff, and Targ 1980.
8. Jahn and Dunne 1987.
9. Pribram 1977 and 1982.
10. General sources: Bohm 1957; Bohm and Peat 1987; Bohm and Weber 1978; Jahn and Dunne 1987; Kafatos and Nadeau 1990.
11. Bruner 1962; Laski 1962; McKellar 1957.
12. Gould, Gordon, 1988.
13. See Pearce (1971) for a full account of the Eureka! phenomenon. See Briggs (1988) for creative process in general.

2. FIELDS OF NEURONS

Epigraph: Eric I. Knudsen, Sascha du Lac, and Steven D. Esterly, *Annual Review of Neuroscience*, vol. 10, p. 59. (Palo Alto, CA: Annual Reviews Inc., 1987).

1. Sternberg 1975. Saul Sternberg's work followed on a theory of Henri Poincare, the great mathematician, who, based on introspection into his own creative work, made such a proposal in 1909.
2. Gardner 1984.
3. Rosenfield 1988.
4. Some theorists believe the neurons "transduce" potential energy. *Transduction* is transference of energy from one state to another without loss or cost of energy. The brain, however, uses far more energy than any other body part, so *translation* may be both more accurate and accessible.
5. Edelman 1987. Gerald Edelman has a brilliant theory of how fields are established. Taubes, 1989 describes this vibratory structure graphically.
6. Gazzaniga 1985.
7. Humberto Maturana and Francisco Varela show why the term *process information* is wrong, since the environment, which is that "information," is part and parcel of the structural coupling taking place. The term is so conventional and convenient, and their more accurate terms so complex, I sadly lapse into "process information" as the best I can do here.
8. Condon 1974. William Condon found no muscular response to phonemes

in newborns of deaf-mute mothers. However, given a sufficient language environment, the response does develop eventually in such children. Combined with the earlier work of Sontag and Bernard, I deduce that the phoneme response must have been developed in the last trimester, since movement response to language starts at the seventh month, and is found fully developed immediately at birth in infants of speaking mothers, but not in infants of deaf mute mothers.

In later work Condon speaks of mother-infant language bonds based on shared univeral structures. In "More evidence for innate language concept," from *BMB Themepack* #11, vol. I and II, 1977, Condon proposes that "basic psychological mechanisms impose perceptual structure from the beginning."

9. See MacLean (1985, p. 414): "Anterior cingulate cortex in human beings is important for the initiation of emotional forms of vocalization." Emotional use of phonemes forms during and following visual stabilization in early months.

10. See Maturana and Varela (1987) and *BMB* (April 4 and 18, 1977) for discussions on blind spots.

11. Berndt, *Nature*, p. 316.

12. Maturana and Varela 1987, pp. 75–79.

13. Fields are compatible in giving rise to their own category of experience; they are variable in that no two expressions are ever identical.

14. Condon and Sander 1974. Hearing infants of deaf parents develop muscular response and regular speech if given a speech environment within the first seven years. See also Woods and Carey, *BMB*, 1980.

15. Beaulieu and Colonnier, *Journal of Comparative Neurology*, pp. 478–94.

16. Bernard and Sontag 1947.

17. Restak 1984, p. 265.

18. While overseas in 1989, I was sent this paper following a university lecture. The paper concerned the relation of neural population and development. It outlined periodic growth spurts wherein new glial support cells and axon-dendrite connections were made, and presented new information that explained a great deal about development heretofore not well understood. I use this information extensively in Part II, and the introduction to Part II, in spite of the fact that the paper sent me was a poor Xerox and the source was not legible. Since its references were excellent, and drew on sources worldwide, and since I have continually found supporting research, I decided to use the information even though I can't cite its exact source. A full defense of its many propositions would be a separate study.

19. Giorgi, *New Science*; Bunge and Eldridge 1986.

20. Changeux and Danchin, *Journal of Comparative Neurology*; Haier 1988.

21. Sheldrake 1982.

3. MIND AND MATTER

Epigraph: Bohm and Peat 1987, p. 186.
1. Muller-Ortega 1989.
2. Shimony 1988.
3. Bell's Theorem arose from a long dispute between Albert Einstein and Neils Bohr concerning non-local influences in atomic structure. John Bell proposed a laboratory test by which the matter might be resolved. Einstein was proven wrong in this case in his denial of non-locality. See Kafatos and Nadeau (1990 and 1991) for a full account.
4. Einstein spotted what looked like a contradiction in quantum physics; his famous comment about "spooky" actions at a distance actually led to the whole issue of "non-locality." For more, see Shimony (1988) and Kafatos (1990).
5. See Feynman (1985) for fascinating research into the electron-photon effect giving rise to physical matter.
6. Prigogine 1984, p. 293.
7. Ibid., p. 41.
8. Bohm and Peat 1987, p. 183.
9. The suggestion of such an organizing or governing force is an embarrassment to classical thought. Bohm's proposal lost support at this point simply because of its political risk, though this is the point on which our current paradigm shift unfolds. Bohm's eventual vindication is assured.
10. An interesting parallel between non-dualistic Shaivism and quantum physics has been drawn by physicists Menas Kafatos and his wife, Thalia Kafatou. Their work has just been released as I make my final edits here, so I can no more than acknowledge it.

4. FIELDS OF INTELLIGENCE

Epigraph: Shri Guru Gita or Vishnu Saharanama, *The Nectar of Chanting* (SYDA Foundation, South Fallsburg, NY 12779), verse 100.
1. Maturana and Varela 1987, pp. 152–53.
2. MacLean was for many years head of the Laboratory of Brain Evolution and Behavior, National Institute of Health.

5. TRIUNE BRAIN: THE MIND OF THREE MINDS

Epigraphs: Harwood 1904–1905, p. 838; Sheldrake 1982, p. 283.
1. Reprints of many of MacLean's works are available from the Laboratory of Brain Evolution and Behavior, National Institute of Health, Bethesda, MD 20014.

2. For simplicity I have, without doing violence to his presentation, extended Paul MacLean's R-system to include the sensory-motor and basal systems as well as the spinal cord and its "proto-intelligences,"in line with Karl Pribram's *core* brain. All these combined give us our awareness of a physical experience, and all feed to higher cortical structures as needed through the R-system.
3. Just as a hypnotized person might raise a blister if touched with a stick and told it is a hot poker, signals from the higher imaginative mind can seriously affect the limbic-R-system. Use of imagery to combat disease is rapidly growing.
4. Lorber, *Science,* 1232–34.
5. Cloninger 1986. Dopamine for novelty seeking; serotonin for harm avoidance; norepinephrine for reward maintenance.
6. *Witnessing* as used in this context means detaching the mind from the emotions and just observing—a state of freedom that opens a different aspect of reality altogether. Baba Muktananda (1978) and the former Catholic nun, Bernadette Roberts, give the most articulate description of this state.

6. IMAGES OF WAKE AND DREAM

Epigraph: William Blake, *Selected Poetry and Prose of William Blake,* ed. Northrop Frye (New York: The Modern Library, 1953), 100.
1. Siegle, *Trends in Neuroscience.*
2. Hubel 1988, 1983.
3. Sacks 1984, p. 162.
4. Jenny 1984.
5. Prigogine 1984, p. 142. Molecules of water at the boiling point forming hexagons is called *Bernard's Instability.*
6. Fisher, *Journal of Nervous and Mental Disease;* Foulkes 1971.
7. Monroe 1971. This gets into some complicated issues brilliantly analyzed by Robert Monroe, who has made one of the most articulate studies of subtle states ever recorded.
8. Herman 1984. Subjects wearing reverse telescopic lenses during the day dream in tiny figures at night.
9. See Smith and Kelley, *Physiology and Behavior.*
10. I have a friend in Australia who spent eight years with an Aborigine group still living in their traditional Dream Time. She claims that virtually all anthropological studies of the Aborigine are seriously flawed and that the reality shift is far more severe than a Western observer can detect. Another friend, a medical doctor practicing Jungian psychology, has also spent a great deal of time with an Aboriginal group. His experiences, while quite physically real, were of a dimension screened out entirely by other mentalities.

11. Katz 1982
12. Tart 1969.
13. William Blake wrote: "Man, by his reasoning power can only compare and judge of what he has already perceived. . . . From a perception of only three senses or three elements none could deduce a fourth or fifth. . . . None could have other than natural or organic thoughts if he had none but organic perceptions. . . . Man's perceptions are not bounded by organs of perception; he perceives more than sense (tho' ever so acute) can discover." (Blake, *Selected Poetry and Prose*, 100.)

7. SIGHT

Epigraph: Jahn and Dunne 1987, p. 283.
1. Lusseyran 1988.
2. Pettit 1981. Note: Anna Mae claims to have dreamed in color.
3. Von Senden (1960) first reported on this operation's failure to give sight.
4. Kafatos and Nadeau 1990, p. 64.
5. Hubel 1988.
6. Maturana and Varela 1987, p. 162.
7. This is called the *Mondrian effect*.
8. Maunsell and Newsome 1987, p. 371; compare with Hubel 1988.
9. Vasiliev 1977. A blood clot on the optical prominence caused the peculiarity.
10. George Wald (1988) spoke of how the eye was perfected early in evolutionary history and that the eye of the frog, rabbit, and human were quite alike. "But does the *frog* see?" he asks.
11. Johnson 1980; Zimmler and Keenan 1983.
12. Restak 1984, p. 65.
13. Ibid., p. 67.
14. One of Carlos Castaneda's psychedelic experiences was of a gnat hundreds of feet tall. Oliver Sacks related how his injured leg appeared to him as two inches long one instant and twelve feet long the next, as his perception of it began to reconnect following scotoma.

8. SOUND

1. Restak 1984, p. 67; Jay and Sparks 1984.
2. Tomatis 1991, p. 41.
3. Tomatis 1983.
4. Chamberlain 1988, pp. 22, 23. Truby claims that the late-uterine infant practices all the fine motor controls of the voice, including the separation cry, in preparation for birth.

5. Bernard and Sontag 1947; Chamberlain 1988, p. 25; Tomatis 1991, p. 35ff. The cells of the body that *sense* are derived from the tissue that produces the cells of Corti.
6. Chamberlain 1988, p. 22.
7. Tomatis 1991, p. 35ff, 1983.
8. Restak 1984, p. 67.
9. Power 1981.
10. Restak 1984, p. 67.
11. Tomatis 1991, p. 40.
12. Rosenberg 1983; Zurek, *Scientific American*.
13. Brown, et al. 1983. The theory that the brain's steady-state sound is produced by the hair-like structure of the cochlea has been thoroughly discredited, not only by Tomatis. Even common sense says those tiny hairs can't both produce the astonishing range of overtones and volume that are produced *and* do all the other jobs assigned them. In severe tinnitus you can hear the victim's broadcast if you stand within about a foot of them.
14. This primary frequency, from which our sound-broadcast itself arises, is located at the top of the skull at the fontanels and is the Aum sound—the source of all creation—referred to in Eastern psychology. The ringing in our ears is one of the myriad frequencies inherent within this primary one.
15. Tomatis 1991, p. 40.
16. Zucharelli 1981.
17. You can order Holophonic tapes from *New Sense Bulletin*, P.O. Box 42211, Los Angeles, CA 90042 (telephone: 800 553-MIND).
18. Keeton 1977.
19. Landau 1981.
20. Maturana and Varela 1987, p. 244.

9. STATE OF MIND: BODY TO MATCH

1. Muktananda 1978; Muller-Ortega 1989; Pearce 1985.
2. McDermott 1984.
3. "Endorphin system may sidetrack pain below Level of Awareness," from *BMB Themepack* #15 vol. III, an account of Lippin and Methadone, 1977–78.
4. Phantom limb pain has been studied since the American Civil War. It is now generally attributed to maps in the brain, which is probably only half the story; the other half of the story may be that these maps translate through the neural structure but are not contained within them.
5. Sacks 1984, p. 129ff.
6. Ibid., p., 138ff.

7. Gackenbach and Bosveld 1989. In reading Gackenbach and Bosveld, I sense that ordinary dreaming is an undeveloped intelligence.
8. Sheldrake 1982.
9. A direct relationship between the ancient theory of samskara and Sheldrake's morphic fields has been made by *BMB Themepack* #15 vol. VI, 1981 and others.
10. Farber 1980.
11. Becker and Selden 1985.

10. WHO REMEMBERS?

1. Penfield 1977.
2. See Levi-Montalchini 1988; Wong and Miles 1984. A "target-cell" effect is apparently a common brain procedure.
3. Chamberlain 1988, pp. 43, 44.
4. Chamberlain 1989.
5. Poet George Franklin helped me enormously through his edits on an early version of *Evolution's End*. His insights opened new avenues for me time and again, and I can easily say his brilliance has been a major influence on my thinking for the past decade or more.
6. Hilgard 1976.
7. See Holden and Guest, *BMB* 1991.
8. Blake, *The Marriage of Heaven and Hell*, p. 126.
9. Maturana and Varela, 1987, p. 245–46.

PART II   DEVELOPING OUR KNOWLEDGE OF THE WORLD

1. Epstein, Herman 1974. Gazzaniga 1985.
2. Levi-Montalchini 1988; Rakic 1987: Rakic refers to overproduction of neural systems in the developing years and periodic elimination of a large population of cells. Chugain, 1987, reports on brain metabolism at age two as equal to that in adults, by age four twice that of adults and by age six double that. This "supercharged" state falls off around age ten and reaches normal adult levels by age fourteen. The growth spurts may be in glial support cells but largely center in increases of axon-dendrite connections.

11. HEART-MIND BONDING

1. Bernard and Sontag 1947; Whittleston 1978.
2. Attributed to Christian Barnard.
3. Lacey and Lacey 1977.
4. Cantin and Genest 1986.
5. Cannon (1939) coined the term *homeostasis,* meaning "stable-sameness,"

referring to the body's ability to keep its myriad organs all in synchrony and stability.

12. MOTHER-CHILD BONDING

Epigraph: MacLean, "The Triune Brain in Conflict" in *Family, Play, and the Separation Call,* vol. 12, p. 215, 1985.
1. Ainsworth 1967, 1964; Geber 1958; Montagu 1962, 1964.
2. Kennell, Trause, and Klaus 1975; Klaus 1970.
3. Chamberlain 1988, p. 25.
4. Kennell and Klaus 1979; Klaus 1970; Klaus 1972.
5. Hales, et al. 1977; Harlow 1959; Harlow and Harlow 1962. Stress has been emphasized by most research. Connection of this with adrenals is made by simple deduction and research into emotional-cognitive systems.
6. Fantz 1958, 1961.
7. Maunsell and Newsome 1987, p. 389. Many researchers have noted the importance of infant recognition of a face presented within six to twelve inches; this distance is generally attributed to lack of long-range sight in newborn. As important is that the newborn's physical domain has not yet been established; the infant exists essentially in the subtle or implicate "body," which has about a six to twelve inch resonance around the physical body. This is the infant's world and must be entered for contact.
8. MacLean 1985. Paul MacLean shows why larger and more complex brain systems require fewer offspring and longer and more intense care of the young.
9. Montagu 1971; Prescott 1974, 1975.
10. Maturana and Varela 1987, p. 127.
11. Levine 1960, pp. 80–86.
12. Klaus 1972; see also Hull, Klaus, and Kennell 1976.
13. MacLean 1985. MacLean speaks of a behavioral triad: nursing and maternal care; audiovocal communication maintaining maternal-offspring contact; and play. Development of this triad is tied in with the thalamocingulate division of the limbic system, and the prefrontal neocortex. "The cyngulate gyrus of the limbic system (provides) vision for proceeding in a firm way to play out our hopes for our children and our children's children."
14. Justin Call, M.D., from the University of California at Irvine, made longitudinal studies showing breast-fed infants more intelligent. See: Call, Kennell, and Klaus, *Frontiers of Psychiatry* (New York: Basic Books). During my last trip to New Zealand, I read reports from doctors claiming breast-fed infants no more intelligent than bottle-fed. New Zealand has a far more benign birthing system than we have, so there may be other factors involved—or this report could simply have been biased. Again see the work of Geber (1958) and Ainsworth (1967).

15. See Ringler, et al. 1978.
16. Ainsworth 1967; Geber 1958. Of my own children, the one home-birthed and breast-fed achieved object constancy around the seventh month after birth, at least six months ahead of the others.
17. Odent, 1986. The relation between immunities and bonding was a major topic at the Oxford Conference on birth and nutrition in 1982.
18. Sources: International Childbirth Education Association, P.O. Box 20048, Minneapolis, MN 55420; American Foundation for Maternal and Child Health, 439 E. 51 Street, New York, NY 10022; NAPSAC International, Box 646, Marble Hill, MO 63764.

13. BOND BREAKING

1. Sources: International Childbirth Education Association, P.O. Box 20048, Minneapolis, MN 55420; American Foundation for Maternal and Child Health, 439 E. 51 Street, New York, NY 10022; NAPSAC International, Box 646, Marbel Hill, MA 63764.
2. "Operation Task Force Caesarean," 1977. This bulletin is available from Printing and Publications Management Branch, HEW, 5600 Fishers Lane (Rm 6C02), Rockville, MD 20857.
3. Windle, 1969. In underwater birthing, infants have remained under water for up to twenty minutes after birth. I am not recommending this without proper assistance and care, but the fact remains that the umbilical cord continues to furnish oxygen after birth as needed.
4. See Towbin 1968.
5. Windle 1969; also see Brackbill 1979.
6. Windle 1969.
7. Chamberlain 1988, p. 205.
8. Chatwin (1987) pointed out this connection between the separation cry, predators in our ancient background, and the strange quiet of the hospital nursery.
9. Spitz 1965: "I follow Freud's opinion that at birth there is no consciousness, accordingly, there can be no awareness or conscious experience. Thus it is rare to find the smiling response before the third month of life." Nothing persists so long as a bad and wrong idea.
10. Quoted by Beadle (1970). This comment was actually made by Katherine Bridges years ago.
11. Jacobson, et al. 1988; Brackbill 1979.
12. Spitz 1965: "Freud's concept of the neonate as a psychologically undifferentiated organism . . . [lacking] consciousness, perception, sensation, and all other psychological functions."
13. See *The Truth Seeker,* edited by James Prescott, whose July/August 1989 edition (vol. 1, no.3) was devoted entirely to genital mutilation. The issue

was a shock, even though I was familiar with some of the practice. (*The Truth Seeker*, P.O. Box 2832, San Diego, CA 92112-2832.)

14. Full reports are available from NAPSAC International, Box 646, Marble Hill, MO 63764.

15. *An Ounce of Prevention* 1981.

16. Ainsworth 1967; Geber 1958.

17. Full reports are available from NAPSAC International, Box 646, Marble Hill, MO 63764; International Childbirth Education Association, P.O. Box 20048, Minneapolis, MN 55420; American Foundation for Maternal and Child Health, 439 E. 51 Street, New York, NY 10022; NAPSAC International, Box 646, Marble Hill, MO 63764.

14. NAME AND THING

1. Luria 1961.

2. Furth 1973, 1966. Hans G. Furth's studies show that congenitally deaf children progress along the same orderly path of logical development as hearing children, though more slowly. If no such system is given, deaf-mute children will spontaneously establish "signing-systems" among themselves for communicating and agreeing on events of their experience. We do well to remember that sound and touch are but two interpretations of the same sensory experience.

3. Jones 1972. Blurton Jones was associated with Nobel laureate Nikos Tinbergen's group of ethologists (studying animal behavior).

4. Gardner 1985, p. 327; McFarland and Kennison, *Journal of General Psychology*; Otto, *Biological Psychiatry*, 22:1201–15.

   Otto claims that ". . . depression is a right hemisphere dysfunction. . . ." Negative views activate the right hemisphere called the "evolutionary watchdog." Right hemisphere is more intimately involved with arousal in general. Right hemisphere may activate both itself and the left, whereas the left hemisphere arouses only itself.

   According to a report on the work of Richard Davidson (State University of New York at Purchase) in *BMB Themepack* #16, vol. III, 1977–78, "Hemispheres react differently to affect. Positive emotional content activates the left hemisphere, negative the right," and so on. Such research shows the physically "holistic" effects of the right hemisphere, with its closer ties to limbic and r-structures, and thus greater response to and concern over environmental reports, particularly negative. Left hemisphere, more independent, is not subject to such feedback and thus can operate outside and beyond actions of the lower evolutionary structures. It also is not subject to feedback from lower systems and represents a higher evolutionary action. The more abstract intellectual and "formal operations" of the left hemisphere thus open for development later. Further, such research as this shows the lateral, independent actions of different brain structures that are possible, as well as the more integrated functions.

15. CYCLE OF COMPETENCE

Epigraph: William Blake, *Selected Poetry and Prose of William Blake,* ed. Northrop Frye (New York: The Modern Library, 1953).

1. Bruner 1971.
2. Grace Pilon's magnificent "Workshop Way"; Rudolph Steiner's Waldorf Schools; genuine Montessori schools; that extraordinary Blue Rock School in Nyack, NY; and the Sudbury Valley School in Massachusetts are examples of ideal learning environments. Their examples could so easily be employed throughout our nation—at a vast saving of money and minds.

   Education Through Music (ETM), Richards Institute, 149 Corte Madera Road, Portola Valley, CA 94025, or P.O. Box 6249, Bozeman, MT 59771-6249. In Canada: G. McGeorge, Box 1240, Chatham, Ontario, Canada.

   Waldorf School, Waldorf Institute of Spring Valley, Hungry Hollow Road, Spring Valley, NY 10977.

   Rudolph Steiner College, 9200 Fair Oaks Blvd., Fair Oaks, CA 95628.

   Workshop Way, Xavier University of Louisiana, 7325 Palmetto Street, Box 144C, New Orleans, LA 70125.

   Oakmeadow School (Homeschooling), P.O. Box 712, Blackburg, VA 24063 (telephone: 703 552-3263).

   Blue Rock School, P.O Box 722, West Nyack, NY 10994.

16. WILL AND THE TERRIBLE TWO

1. White 1975; also see Pearce 1977.
2. Gazzaniga 1985.

17. INTUITION: SEEING WITHIN AND BEYOND

1. Peterson 1987; Shields 1976.James Petersen has written extensively on *The Secret Life of Kids,* as the title of one of his works reads, listing hundreds of examples of intuitive phenomena in early and middle children.

   Gerald Jampolsky, M.D., wrote of many dozens of four- and five-year-old children who were brought to him by parents who thought the children were having psychotic episodes, when in fact these children reported ordinary intuitive phenomena.
2. Wallach 1990.
3. Ainsworth 1964; Geber 1958. I am told that in Guatemala a mother soiled by her infant after the first day is considered a stupid woman.
4. I invite you to read Ernest Thompson Seton's *Wild Animals I Have Known.* (Berkeley, CA: VBT Creative Arts Book Company, 1987).

5. In my first book, *The Crack in the Cosmic Egg,* I gave a number of accounts of paranormal activity considered normal events by the Aborigine.
6. Gazzaniga (1985) and Chugain (1987) reported 50 percent more synaptic connections in children than in adults. The four-year-old brain uses twice the energy of an adult brain, peaks at age six or seven, falls off around ten, and reaches adult levels around age fourteen. Chugain's ages coincide with other studies, but his estimates of connections are far lower than others.

18. PLAY

1. Langer 1942, p. 60.
2. Barfield 1971; also Northrop Frye, *Fearful Symmetry, A Study of William Blake* (Princeton, NJ: Princeton University Press, 1947). Along with Goethe's reasoning, this line of thought, counter to Cartesian notions, ran throughout the nineteenth century.
3. This might be done through the looped feedback from the neocortex into the limbic system, as well as from R-system to the limbic system to the neocortex—or possibly a mixture of both of these. At any rate, since we know the limbic system is involved in learning and memory, it is definitely the median.
4. I would refer you to Farley Mowatt's account of an Eskimo shaman's five-year-old son who was put with a family of wolves for a day and night. There the child established a life-long intuitive rapport with wolves and was thereafter able to interpret their calls concerning the movement of caribou.
5. Fisher, et al. *Journal of Nervous and Mental Disease;* Foulkes 1971.
6. That we share genetic materials with the higher apes doesn't mean that we "came" from them. We share most of those with wolves and bears as well as monkeys, and some wolves are smarter than monkeys (and some people). Are we to say dolphins "descended" from apes because they too share many biological processes? Worms copulate—after a fashion—but are we to assume Romeo and Juliet "descended" from such a lineage? We should at least recognize *ascent* when we see it.
7. Bettleheim 1987.

19. PLAY'S END

1. Buzzell; Healy 1990; Mander 1977.
2. Michael Toms, of New Dimension Radio and an Acquisition Editor for Harper San Francisco, pointed this out to me.
3. Prose 1990.
4. Buzzell.
5. Hayes and Birnbaum, *Developmental Psychology.*
6. Buzzell; also Mander 1977.

7. Buzzell.

8. A major television filmmaker asked me to consult on a series for children, supposedly designed to stimulate development of imagination. The film company had already signed with sponsoring toy companies who stipulated the "usual sixteen acts of violence per hour" (otherwise, the rationale goes, children lose interest). The filmmaker's concern was how to incorporate that much violence into the programming without having it affect the child. I quietly bowed out.

20. CONCRETE OPERATIONS

1. Hasted 1981.

2. Josephson 1975.

3. Manning 1975. The cerebellum is a complex, largely unknown part of the brain made of each of the three levels but containing perhaps a trillion granular cells rather than ordinary neurons. It receives three times as many signals as it sends out and may well play a major role in perception.

4. Sky 1989.

5. Grosvernor 1966.

6. I have had direct, unbroken skin contact with coals burning at 1380 degrees Fahrenheit for over an hour without blister or harm, feeling only exhileration, but this was child's play compared to Shri Lanka.

7. *Education Through Music (ETM)*, Richards Institute, 149 Corte Madera Road, Portola Valley, CA 94025, or P.O. Box 6249, Bozeman, MT 59771-6249. In Canada: G. McGeorge, Box 1240, Chatham, Ontario, Canada (telephone: 519 674-2555).

   Waldorf School, Waldorf Institute of Spring Valley, Hungry Hollow Road, Spring Valley, NY 10977.

   Rudolph Steiner College, 9200 Fair Oaks Blvd., Fair Oaks, CA 95628.

   Workshop Way, Xavier University of Louisiana, 7325 Palmetto Street, Box 144C, New Orleans, LA 70125.

   Oakmeadow School (Homeschooling), P.O. Box 712, Blackburg, VA 24063 (telephone: 703 552-3263).

   Blue Rock School, P.O. Box 722, West Nyack, NY 10994.

8. See Gardner 1985, p. 276. Luria (1977) points out that different centers in the brain become dominant with development.

9. Davies 1987, p. 41.

21. FORMAL OPERATIONS

1. Arthur Koestler, a friend of Paul MacLean's, considered the fact that the left hemisphere has almost no connection with the balancing limbic system an error of evolution. I would point out it is a gamble of evolution's

but hardly an error. This hemisphere, with its capacity for abstract thought, is a bridge for us to move on into the higher stages of consciousness. The hemisphere's detachment from the earlier systems is precisely its value—and what nature had in mind. That it gives rise to an intellect acting out of balance with the rest of our life-system is our error, not nature's.

2. MacLean 1977. Currently, we are absorbed in the conflict between fundamentalism, rigorous semantic propositions of belief, and paradigm shifts that threaten such "fundamental" propositions. The particular religion involved is beside the point; every ego-system within a frame of reference is concretely threatened if the belief-system giving shape to that worldview is threatened. A major part of a child's education in Islamic countries is memorizing the entire Koran, a difficult feat that requires years of study and shapes the unfolding conceptual system; that knowledge will then be defended to the death. The position of fundamentalist Christians or scientists is essentially that of the Islamic true believer—examples of what Paul MacLean calls the triune brain in conflict.

3. Williams and Herrup 1988; Chun 1987.

4. See Jamieson, *Journal of Educational Psychology.* When teachers were told certain students, chosen at random, were very bright and just "blooming," these students responded with significant improvements in I.Q. in course of the year. In another study, when the teacher of seven-year-olds was told the group was slow, the group did poorly. When another teacher was told the same group was bright, the group did exceptionally well. This has been called the *Pygmalion effect.*

5. Changeux and Danchin, *Journal of Comparative Neurology.* "Learning produces redistribution toward synapses that are more frequently used."

6. From Brown 1988.

7. Alexander (1988) discusses the discontinuity between previous operations and higher stages after adolescence.

22. GREAT EXPECTATIONS

1. See Staley 1988.
2. Rahmamurthi 1988.

23. COMPENSATION AND DYING

1. Mark Mauer, *Young Black Men and the Criminal Justice System.* Washington D.C.: The Sentencing Project. Also, Dr. Jerome Miller, National Center of Institutions and Alternatives.

2. When I was nine years old it would have been impossible for me or any of my buddies to forcibly rape a female. We had no equipment for the operation—such unfolded among us all pretty much at the same time in our

fourteenth year, the statistical time in all past history. Nor could we have conceived of such an operation, as we were far too busy playing.

3. See Schell 1984.

4. In the 1960s Puerto Rico suffered a severe drought: The United States sent, along with emergency food supplies, prepared animal feed to keep their chickens and hogs—the staples of their diet—alive. Within a year, Puerto Rican five-year-olds, both male and female, developed large breasts, and the females began menstruating. Having had no exposure to these growth hormones before, and with no tolerances built up against them, the children exhibited these and many signs of puberty after their sudden large-scale ingestion of the hormones.

5. Williamson and Pearse's major work, *Science, Synthesis and Sanity*, first published in 1954 and years ahead of its time, reads like Zen and the Art of Body Maintenance.

24. POST-OPERATIONS

Epigraph: Thomas Wolfe, *A Stone, A Leaf, A Door: Poetic Excerpts From the Writings of Thomas Wolfe,* (New York: New American Libraries, 1947).

1. I didn't know of such a division until I read Bernadette Roberts, who clarified a whole block of enigmas for me and provided a much needed shift in my "learning curve."

2. Brown 1988.

3. Alexander and Langer 1988.

4. Olds 1958. There is a very precise area of the mammalian limbic brain that is our "reward" center. James Olds discovered this over thirty years ago. Rats with an electrode implanted in this center, able to activate that electrode by pressing a lever, will forego sexual stimulus and need of food or water, and in fact will die of thirst and starvation, in order to keep the electrode activated and maintain this experience. We have exactly the same area in our limbic brain.

5. Time and again in meditation the ringing in my ears shifts to the fontanels where I perceive it simply as a vibration. Occasionally the vibration continues this way for days; I hear no ringing in my ears, yet my hearing is intact.

25. ACCESS TO THE FIELD

Epigraph: Oriental Philosophies, John M. Keller. (New York: Scribner's Sons, 1985.)

1. Readers of earlier versions of *Evolution's End* have asked why I inserted Bernadette Roberts rather abruptly in these last pages of the final revision.

The reason is that I read her book, *The Experience of No-Self*, was convinced of its authenticity since that reading brought a major shift of my life-path, much to my surprise, and I knew that a major evolutionary breakthrough (tired as this cliche sounds) had taken place within her. Since then I have read all three of her books, many times, attended a retreat with her, and am all the more stunned at the magnitude of what has taken place. Interested readers, ready for a challenge, intellectually and spiritually, can obtain her first two works, *The Experience of No-Self*, and *The Path to No-Self*, from State University of New York Press, State University Plaza, Albany, N.Y. 12246. Her third, most important perhaps, and surely most difficult book, *What is Self?* A study of the spiritual journey in terms of consciousness, printed by Mary Botsford Goens, Austin, Texas, 1989, can be obtained from Joseph Conti, P.O. Box 18803 Los Angeles, Ca. 90018.

2. Ordinarily the cross is a symbol of sentiment, which is, again, a limbic system response (connected with self-pity) and not a power. Perhaps this is why Protestantism yielded theologians, religious intellects, but not saints.

3. West (1979) gives a striking argument and strong evidence for the Sphinx of Ghiza, the largest monolith (single stone monument) on earth, being much older than the Egyptian civilization. Before a group of Malumeks used it as a target for their little canon in the early Napoleanic Wars, the Sphinx incorporated three major symbolic figures: a lion's body, a human head, and a huge serpent coming out of that head at the fontanels and curving over between the eyebrows. The Malumeks blew away the great serpent, which represents the creative energy in her ancient evolutionary form. The Sphinx incorporated the three major forms of our triune brain and showed how our evolution's end lay in the bringing of the lowest into the highest—the reptilian breaking through the skull. A sunburst displayed about the head represented enlightenment. A very ancient race understood not only our triune nature but also how our own highest stage depended on bringing into alignment the lower "animal" orders foundational to us. In our maturation lies the completion of evolution's journey from the earliest neural system to a state beyond all neural systems.

4. Jensen 1963.

Bibliography

Note: One of my major sources of information has been *The Brain/ Mind Bulletin*, Box 42211, Los Angeles, CA 90042. I refer to this throughout as *BMB*, or, in some cases, as Themepacks from *BMB*. Themepacks are collections on particular topics available also, and should be of particular interest to new readers of *BMB* who would like summaries covering the past twenty or so years of research. In addition, I have added the primary sources from which *BMB* drew their articles, although *BMB* does not give the dates for the publications cited.

Aggression in non-imaginative children. 1989. *BMB*. Feb.

Ainsworth, Mary, M.D. undated. Deprivation of maternal care: A reassessment of its effect. *Public Health Papers*. Geneva: World Health Organization. 14:97–165.

———. 1967. *Infancy in Uganda*. Baltimore, MD: Johns Hopkins University Press.

———. 1964. Patterns of attachment behavior shown by the infant in interaction with his mother. *Merrill-Palmer Quarterly*. 10:51–58.

Alexander, C. N., and E. J. Langer, eds. 1988. *Higher Stages of Human Development: Adult Growth Beyond Formal Operations*. New York: Oxford University Press.

Arms, Suzanne. 1975. *Immaculate Deception: A New Look at Women and Childbirth in America*. Boston: Houghton Mifflin.

Barfield, Owen. 1971. *What Coleridge Thought*. Middletown, CT: Wesleyan University Press.

Bateson, Gregory. 1979. *Mind and Nature: A Necessary Unity*. New York: E. P. Dutton.

Beadle, Muriel. 1970. *A Child's Mind: How Children Learn During the Critical Years from Birth to Age Five*. New York: Doubleday.

Beaulieu, Clement, and Marc Colonnier. *Journal of Comparative Neurology*. 266:478–94.

Becker, Robert, and Gary Selden. 1985. *The Body Electric*. New York: Morrow.

Berard, Guy. 1983. Hearing and dyslexia. *BMB*. Vol 8.

Berendt, Joachim-Ernst. 1987. *Nada Brahma, The World Is Sound (Music and the Landscape of Consciousness)*. Rochester, VT: Destiny Books.

Bergland, Richard. 1986. *Fabric of Mind*. New York: Viking; *BMB*. Dec. 1986.

Berndt, Rita Sloan. Thesaurus-like indexing of words in brain organized by specific categories. *Nature*. 316:439–40.

Bernard, J., and Sontag, L. 1947. Fetal reactions to sound. *Journal of Genetic Psychology*. 70:209–10.

Bettelheim, Bruno. 1987. The importance of play. *The Atlantic Monthly*. Mar.

Blackmore, Susan. 1990. Dreams do what they're told. *New Scientist*. Jan. 6.

Blair, Edmund. 1988. *Remembering and Forgetting*. New York: Walker.

Blindsight: An alternative mode of vision. 1977. *BMB*. Apr. 4 and 18.

Blum, Jeffrey. 1978. Pseudoscience and mental ability: The origins and fallacies of the I.Q. controversy. *Monthly Review Press*. New York.

Bohm, David. 1980. *Wholeness and the Implicate Order*. London: Routledge & Kegan Paul.

———. 1957. *Causality and Chance in Modern Physics*. New York: Van Nostrand.

Bohm, David, and David F. Peat. 1987. *Science Order and Creativity*. New York: Bantam.

Bohm, David, with Renee Weber. 1978. The enfolding-unfolding universe. *Re-Vision*. Summer/Fall: 35.

Bower, Gordon. State specific learning. *American Psychologist*. 36 (2):129–48; and *Journal of Experimental Psychology: General* 110 (4):451–73; *BMB*. Vol 7. 1982.

Bower, T. G. R. 1966. The visual world of the infant. *Scientific American*. Dec., 1966.

Bowlby, J. 1969. "The Child's Tie to His Mother: Attachment Behavior." In *Attachment*. New York: Basic Books.

Brackbill, Yvonne. 1979. "Effects of Obstetric Drugs on Human Development." Presented at the conference, Obstetrical Management and Infant Outcome, Sponsored by American Foundation for *Maternal and Child Health*. Nov.

Brenner, D., S. J. Williamson, and L. Kaufman. 1977. Magnetic fields in the brain. *Science*. Oct. 31 (19):480–81; *BMB*. Vol. 1 & 2, 1977.

Briggs, John. 1988. *Fire in the Crucible: The Alchemy of Creative Genius*. New York: St. Martin's Press.

Brown, David. 1988. Inside the schizophrenic brain. *The Washington Post*. Dec. 13.

Brown, et al. 1983. Intra-cellular recordings from cochlea inner hair cells. *Science*. 222. Oct. 7.

Bruner, Jerome S. 1971. *The Relevance of Education*. New York: Norton.

———. 1962. *On Knowing, Essays for the Left Hand*. Cambridge, MA: Belknap Press.

Bunge, Mary Bartlett, and Charles F. Eldridge. 1986. Linkage between ax-
onal ensheathment and basal lamina production by Schwann cells.
Annual Review of Neuroscience. 9:305–28.

Buzzell, Keith A. *The Neurophysiology of Television Viewing: A Preliminary
Report.* Available from Dr. Keith A. Buzzell, 14 Portland Street,
Fryeburg, ME 04037.

Campbell, Don, ed. 1991. *Music, Physician for Times to Come.* Wheaton,
IL: Quest Books, The Theosophical Publishing House.

Cannon, W. B. 1939. *The Wisdom of the Body.* New York: Norton.

Cantin, Marc, and Jacques Genest. 1986. The heart as an endocrine gland.
Scientific American. Feb. Vol. 254, no. 2:76.

Chamberlain, David. 1988. "Consciousness at Birth: A Review of the
Empirical Evidence." Available from Chamberlain Publications,
5164 35th St., San Diego, CA 92116.

———. 1989. "The Expanding Boundaries of Memory," Address presented at
The 4th International Congress on Pre- and Perinatal Psychology.
Amherst, MA. Aug. 5.

———. 1988. *Babies Remember Birth.* Los Angeles: Tarcher.

Changeux, J. P., and A. Danchin. Learning produces redistribution toward
synapses that are more frequently used. *Journal of Comparative
Neurology.* 266:478–94.

Cheek, David B. 1988. Prenatal and perinatal imprints: Apparent prenatal
consciousness as revealed by hypnosis. *Pre- and Perinatal Psychology Journal.* 1, Winter: 97–110.

Chatwin, Bruce. 1987. *The Song Lines.* London: Picador, Jonathan Cape.

Chugain, Harry. 1987. 50 percent more synaptic connections in children than
adults. *BMB.* Aug.

Chun, J. J. M. 1987. Fetal protobrain. *Nature.* 325:617–20; *BMB.* Aug. 1987.

Cloninger, Robert. Three brain chemical systems. *Science.* 236:410–16.

———. *Archives of General Psychiatry.* 44:573–38.

———. 1986. *Psychiatric Developments* 3:167–226; Reports in *BMB.* Sept.
1987.

Condon, William, and Louis Sander. 1974. Neonate movement is synchronized with adult speech: Interactional participation and language acquisition. *Science.* Jan. 11: 99–101.

———. *BMB.* Vol. 1 & 2, 1977. "More Evidence for Innate Language Concept." ". . . there might be a bond between human beings, who are
perhaps participating within shared organizational forms rather
than as isolated entities sending discrete messages."

———. Entries in *Child Development* 45:456–62.

———. *Science* 183:99–101.

———. *Journal of Autism and Childhood Schizophrenia* 5 (1) 37–56.

Cooper, Lynn, and Roger Shepard, 1985. Spatial rotation mimics real rotation
of objects. *Scientific American.* 256:106–14; *BMB.* Vol. 10, 1985.

Coren, Stanley, Joan Stern Girgus. 1979. *Seeing Is Deceiving: The Psychology of Visual Illusions.* Somerset, NJ: Halsted/Wiley.

David, Henry. Report to the 97th American Psychological Association meeting, on Czech studies of unwanted children. *BMB.* Nov. 1989. Dytrich David, Z., Z. Matejcek, and V. Schuller. 1988. *Born Unwanted: The Developmental Effects of Denied Abortion.* New York: Springer Pub.

Davidson, Richard, and Nathan Fox. Left hemisphere processes positive feelings, right, negative. *Science.* 218:1235–37; *BMB.* Vol. 8. *BMB* Themepack no. 15, 1983.

Davies, Paul. 1987. The creative cosmos. *The New Scientist.* Dec. 17.

De Chateau, Peter, and Britt Wiberg. 1977. Long-term effect on mother-infant behavior of extra contact during the first hour post partum. *Acta Paediatrix.* 66:137–43.

Desrochers, Allan, and Alain Desrochers. *Canadian Journal of Psychology.* 33:17–28; *BMB.* Vol 4, 1979

Dias, M. G., and P. L. Harris. Make-believe imagining increases ability to reason in young children. *British Journal of Developmental Psychology.* 6:207–21.

Eckhart, Meister. 1980. *Breakthrough: Meister Eckhart's Creation Spirituality.* Edited and with commentary by Matthew Fox. New York: Doubleday.

Edelman, Gerald. 1987. *Neural Darwinism: The Theory of Neuronal Group Selection.* New York: Basic Books.

Ellisman, Mark H., Darryl Erik Palmer, and Michael P. Andre. 1987. Diagnostic levels of ultrasound may disrupt myelination. *Experimental Neurology* 90:78–92.

Epstein, Gerald. Imagination-sense realm not subject to laws of time-space. *Advances.* 3 (1): 22–31.

Epstein, Gerald, and Patrick Fanning. 1989. Mental imagery may well become most dramatic tool for healing. *BMB.* Sept.

Epstein, Herman T. 1974. "Phrenoblysis: Special Brain and Mind Growth Periods." In *Developmental Psychology.* New York: Wiley.

Fantz, Robert L. 1961. The origin of form perception. *Scientific American.* May: 66–72.

———. 1958. Pattern vision in young infants. *Psychological Review.* 8:43–47.

Farber, Susan L. 1980. *Identical Twins Reared Apart.* New York: Basic Books.

Feinberg, Leonard. 1959. Firewalking in Ceylon. *Atlantic Monthly.* May.

Ferguson, Marilyn. 1980. *The Aquarian Conspiracy, Personal and Social Transformation in Our Time.* Los Angeles: Tarcher.

Feynman, Richard P. 1985. *QED The Strange Theory of Light and Matter.* Princeton, NJ: Princeton University Press.

Finke, Ronald. 1987. Imagery and vision. *Scientific American.* Mar.

Fisher, Charles, et al. A psychological study of nightmares and night terrors. *Journal of Nervous and Mental Disease.* 187 (2).

248

Flor-Henry, Pierre. 1985. Left hemisphere mediates positive states. *BMB*. Vol 10. *BMB* Themepack no. 15.

Foulkes, David. 1971. "Longitudinal Studies of Dreams in Children." In *Dreaming Dynamics*, edited by Masserman. NY: Grune and Stratton.

Fox, Matthew. 1983. *Meditations with Meister Eckhart*. Santa Fe, NM: Bear & Co.

Frank, Ian, and Harold Levinson. 1976–1977. Non-conscious knowing: Mediated by cerebellum. *Academic Therapy*. Winter. 12 (2): 133–53.

Furth, Hans G. 1973. *Deafness and Learning*. New York: Wadsworth.

———. 1970. *Piaget and Knowledge*. Englewood Cliffs, NJ: Prentice-Hall.

———. 1966. *Thinking without Language*. New York: The Free Press.

Gackenbach, Jayne, and Jane Bosveld. 1989. *Control Your Dreams: How Lucid Dreaming Can Help You Uncover Your Hidden Desires, Confront Your Hidden Fears, Explore the Frontiers of Human Consciousness*. New York: Harper & Row.

Gardner, Howard. 1985. *The Mind's New Science*. New York: Basic Books.

———. 1983. *Frames of Mind*. New York: Basic Books.

Gazzaniga, Michael S. 1988. *Mind Matters: How Mind and Brain Interact to Create Our Conscious Lives*. Boston: Houghton Mifflin.

———. 1985. *The Social Brain*. New York: Basic Books.

Geber, Marcelle. 1958. The psycho-motor development of African children in the first year and the influence of maternal behavior. *Journal of Social Psychology*. 47:185–95.

Giorgi, D.. How the brain wraps up. *New Science*. 112:26, 486.

Goleman, Daniel. 1989. Doctors find that surgical patients may still "hear" despite anesthesia. *The New York Times*. Oct. 26.

Gould, Gordon. 1988. "Inventors on Art, Intuition, Overcoming Resistance." *BMB*. June: 4.

Gould, Stephen Jay. 1987. *Time's Arrow, Time's Cycle*. Cambridge, MA: Harvard University Press; quoted in *BMB*. Dec. 1987.

Grosvernor, Donna, and Gilbert Grosvernor. 1966. Ceylon. *The National Geographic Magazine*. 120 (4).

Hales, D., B. Lozof, R. Sosa, and J. Kennell. 1977. Defining the limits of the maternal sensitive period. *Developmental Medicine and Child Neurology*. 19 (4): 454–61.

Harlow, Harry F. 1959. Love in infant monkeys. *Scientific American*. June.

Harlow, Harry F., and Margaret Harlow. 1962. Social deprivation in monkeys. *Scientific American*. Nov.

Harwood, A. C. 1940. *The Way of a Child: An Introduction to the Work of Rudolph Steiner for Children*. London: Rudolph Steiner Press.

Harwood, W. S. 1904–1905. A wonder-worker of science: An authoritative account of Luther Burbank's unique work in creating new forms of plant life. *The Century Magazine*. (69): 838.

Hasted, John. 1981. *The Metal Benders*. London: Routledge & Kegan Paul.

Haviland, Jeannette. 1988. Effects of mood on adolescent intelligence. *Society for Research in Adolescence.* Mar.

Hayes, Donald, and Dana Birnbaum. 1980. Mixing sound and video tracks unrecognized by young children. *Developmental Psychology.* 16 (5): 410–16. *BMB.* Vol 5. *BMB* Themepack no. 9.

Healy, Jane M. 1990. *Endangered Minds: Why Our Children Don't Think.* New York: Simon & Schuster.

Heit, Gary, Eric Halgeren, et al. 1988. Memory. *Nature.* 333:773–75; *BMB.* Sept. 1988.

Hepper, Peter. 1990. Effect of heartbeat on Infants. *British Journal of Psychiatry.* 155:289–93; *BMB.* June. 1990.

Herman, John. 1984. Dreaming affected by daytime experience. *BMB* Themepack 9.

Hilgard, Ernest R. 1976. Two separate cognitive systems. *BMB.* Vol. 1. *BMB* Themepack no. 9, Mar. 15.

———. 1965. *Hypnotic Susceptibility.* New York: Harcourt Brace.

Holden, Janice Miner, and Charlotte Guest. 1991. *Journal of Transpersonal Psychology* 22:1–16; *New Sense Bulletin (BMB)* Vol 16, no. 12. Sep. 1991.

Hubel, David. 1988. Vision and the brain. *Los Alamos Bulletin* 16.

———. 1983.

Hudspeth, William J., and Karl H. Pribram. 1992. "Psychophysiological indices of cerebral maturation." *International Journal of Psychology.* 12:19–29.

Hull, David, Marshall Klaus, and John H. Kennell. 1976. Parent-to-infant attachment. *Recent Advances in Pediatrics.* No. 5.

Jacobson, Bertil, Karin Nyberg, Gunnar Eklund, Marc Bygdeman, and Ulf Rydberg. 1988. Obstetric pain medication and eventual adult amphetamine addiction in offspring. *Acta Obstet Gynecol Scand.* 67:677–82.

Jahn, Robert G., and Brenda J. Dunne. 1987. *Margins of Reality: The Role of Consciousness in the Physical World.* San Diego: Harvest Books, Harcourt Brace Jovanovich.

Jamieson, David. 1988. Teacher image affects students. *Journal of Educational Psychology.* 79:461–66; Listening, speaking, and the brain. *BMB.* Vol. 13. *BMB* Themepack no. 7, Apr. 1988.

Jay and Sparks. 1984. Auditory receptive fields change with eye position. *Nature.* 309:345–47. May 24.

Jenny, Hans. 1984. Sound and viscous liquids forming geometric patterns. *BMB.* Vol. 9. *BMB* Themepack no. 5.

Jensen, Adolf E. 1963. *Myth and Cult among Primitive Peoples,* Chicago: University of Chicago Press.

Jindrak, Kare, and Heda Jindrak. 1988. *Medical Hypotheses.* 25:17–20; Listening, speaking, and the brain. *BMB.* July. 1988.

Johnson, Marcia. Perception and imagination. *Journal of Experimental Psychology*. 117:390–94.

Johnson, Roger. 1980. Address to the meeting of American Psychological Association in New York. *BMB* Themepack.

Jones, Blurton N. 1972. *Ethnological Studies of Child Behavior*. New York: Cambridge University Press.

Josephson, Brian. 1975. Possible connections between psychic phenomena and quantum mechanics. *The Academy*. 14, no. 4 (Dec.).

Kafatos, Menas, and Robert Nadeau. 1990. *The Conscious Universe: Part and Whole in Modern Physical Theory*. New York: Springer-Verlag.

Katz, Richard 1982. *Boiling Energy: Community Healing Among the Kalahari !Kung*. Cambridge, MA: Harvard University Press.

Kaufman, C., and L. Rosenbloom. 1967. Depression in infant monkeys. *Science*. Feb.

Keeton, William. 1977. Maybe "birdbrain" is a misnomer. *BMB* Themepack 16:2.

Keltikangas-Jarvinen, Liisa, and Paula Kangas. Inability to imagine alternative behaviors is a cause of aggression in children. *Aggressive Behavior* 14:255–64.

Kennell, John H., and Marshall H. Klaus. 1979. "Early mother-infant contact: Effects on breastfeeding." In *Breastfeeding and Food Policy in a Hungry World*. New York: Academic Press.

Kennell, John H., Mary Anne Trause, and Marshall H. Klaus. 1975. Evidence for a Sensitive Period in the Human Mother. Parent-Infant Interaction: CIBA Foundation Symposium 33.

Klaus, Marshall. 1972. Maternal attachment: Importance of the first post-partum days. *New England Journal of Medicine*. 9:286.

———. 1970. Human maternal behavior at the first contact with her young. *Pediatrics*. 46, (2): 187–92.

Knudsen, Eric, Sascha duLac, and Steven D. Esterly. 1987. Computational maps in the brain. *Annual Review of Neurosciences*. 10:41–65.

Lacey, John, and Beatrice Lacey. 1977. "Conversations Between Heart and Brain." Rockville, MD: Bulletin, National Institute of Mental Health. Nov.; *BMB*. Mar. 1987.

Laird, James. 1983. Strong link between emotion and memory. *Journal of Personality and Social Psychology*. 42: 646–57; *BMB*. Vol 8. 1983

Landau, Barbara. 1981. Brain maps. *Science*. 213:1275–77; *BMB*. Vol 6. 1981.

Langer, Susanne K. 1942. *Philosophy in a New Key*. Cambridge, MA: Harvard University Press.

Laski, Marghanita. 1962. *Ecstasy, A Study of Some Secular and Religious Experiences*. Bloomington: Indiana University Press.

Levi-Montalchini, Rita. 1988. *In Praise of Imperfection: My Life and Work*. New York: Basic Books (Sloane Research Series).

Levine, Seymour. 1960. Stimulation in infancy. *Scientific American*. May, 80–86.

Liedloff, Jean. 1987. *The Continuum Concept: Allowing Human Nature to Work Successfully.* Reading, MA: Addison-Wesley.

Lippin, Richard. Methadone and injuries. Reported by Michael Holden on endorphin system. *Journal of Primal Therapy* 4:117–39; *BMB.* Vol. 3. 1977.

Lorber, John. 1980. Is the brain really necessary? *Science.* 210: 1232–34.

Lozoff, B. 1978. The mother-newborn relationship: Limits of adaptability. *Pediatrics.* 71 (1): 1–12.

Luria, A. R. 1977. *The Neuropsychology of Memory.* New York: Halstead/Wiley; *BMB* Themepack no. 9. 1977.

———. 1961. *The Role of Speech in Normal and Abnormal Behavior.* New York: Liveright.

Lusseyran, Jacques. 1988. *And There was Light.* New York: Parabola Books.

Lynch, James. 1987. *The Language of the Heart.* New York: Basic Books.

McDermott, Robert A., ed. 1984 *The Essential Steiner: Basic Writings.* San Francisco: Harper & Row.

McFarland, Richard, and Robert Kennison. 1988. *Journal of General Psychology.* 115:263–72.

McKellar, Peter. 1957. *Imagination and Thinking, A Psychological Analysis.* New York: Basic Books.

MacLean, Paul D. 1985. Brain evolution relating to family, play, and the separation call. *Archives of General Psychiatry.* Volume 42. Apr.

———. 1978. A mind of three minds: Educating the triune brain. Offprint from the *Seventy-seventh Yearbook of the National Society for the Study of Education.* Chicago.

———. 1977. "The Triune Brain in Conflict." In *Psychotherapy and Psychosomatics,* edited by P. O. Sifneos. Switzerland: S. Karger, Basel.

———. 1976. "The Imitative-Creative Interplay of our Three Mentalities." In *Astride the two Cultures: Arthur Koestler at 70,* edited by H. Harris. New York: Random House.

———. 1975. "Sensory and Perceptive Factors in Emotional Functions of the Triune Brain." In *Emotions—Their Parameters and Measurement,* edited by L. Levi. New York: Raven Press.

Magid, Ken, and Carole McKelvey. 1988. *High Risk: Children Without a Conscience.* New York: Bantam Books.

Mander, Jerry. 1977. *Four Arguments for the Elimination of Television.* New York: Morrow.

Manning, Mathew. 1975. *The Link.* London: Van Duren Press.

Marcel, Anthony, and Emmanuel Conkin. 1984. Recent studies show strong role for unconscious in everyday life. *BMB.* Vol. 9. *BMB* Themepack no. 11.

Maturana, Humberto R., and Francisco J. Varela. 1987. *The Tree of Knowledge: The Biological Roots of Human Understanding.* Cambridge, MA: New Science Library.

Maunsell, John H. R., and William T. Newsome. 1987. Visual processing in monkey extrastriate cortex. *Annual Review of Neuroscience.* 10:363–401.

Mikulak, Marcia. 1991. *The Children of a Bambara Village.* Santa Fe, NM: Santa Fe Research.

Mitchell, Gary. 1975. What monkeys can tell us about human violence. *The Futurist.* Apr.

Mitford, Jessica. 1990. Teach midwifery, go to jail. *This World.* Oct. 21: 7–12.

Monroe, Robert. *1971. Journeys Out of the Body.* Garden City, NY: Double-day.

Montagu, Ashley. 1971. *Touching: The Human Significance of Skin.* New York: Columbia University Press.

——. 1964. *Life Before Birth.* New York: New American Library.

——. 1962. *Prenatal Influences.* Springfield, IL: Charles C. Thomas.

Muktananda, Baba. 1978. *The Play of Consciousness.* San Francisco: Harper & Row.

Muller-Ortega, Paul Eduardo. 1989. *The Triadic Heart of Siva: Kaula Tantracism of Abhinavagupta in the Non-Dual Shaivism of Kashmir.* Albany, NY: SUNY.

Nathans, Jeremy. 1987. Molecular biology of visual pigments. *Annual Review of Neuroscience.* 10:163–94, esp. 181.

Nazario, Sonia L. 1990. Midwifery is staging revival as demand for prenatal care, low-tech births rises. *The Wall Street Journal.* Sept. 25.

Odent, Michael. 1986. *Primal Health: A Blueprint for Our Survival.* London: Century Pub.

——. 1981. The evolution of obstetrics at pithiviers. *Birth and the Family Journal.* 8, no. 1 (Spring).

Olds, James. 1958. Self-stimulating of the brain. *Science.* Vol. 127, no. 3294. Feb. 14.

Ounce of Prevention: Toward an Understanding of the Causes of Violence, An. 1981. Preliminary report to the people of California published by the State of California Commission on Crime Control and Violence Prevention. Stanley M. Roden, Chairperson.

Patizzi and Robertson. 1988. Tuning in the mammalian cochlea. *Physical Review.* 68:100. Oct.

Pearce, Joseph C. 1985. *Magical Child Matures.* New York: Dutton.

——. 1983. Nurturing intelligence: The other side of nutrition (address at 1982 Oxford University, World Health Organization and MacCarrison Medical Society Conference on Nutrition and Childbirth). *Nutrition and Health.* London: A. B. Academic Publishers. 1:143–52.

——. 1977. *Magical Child.* New York: Dutton.

——. 1971. *The Crack in the Cosmic Egg.* NY: Julian Press.

Pearse, Innes H. 1979. *The Quality of Life: The Peckham Approach to Human Ethology.* Edinburgh: Scottish Academic Press.

Penfield, Wilder. 1977. *The Mystery of the Mind.* Princeton, NJ: Princeton University Press.

Peterson, James W. 1987. *The Secret Life of Kids: An Exploration into Their Psychic Senses.* Wheaton, IL: Quest.

Pettit, Thomas. 1981. Report on Anna Mae Pennica, Jules Stein Eye Institute, UCLA, Los Angeles. *BMB.* Vol. 6. *BMB* Themepack no. 9.

Piaget, Jean. 1951. *The Child's Conception of the World.* New York: Humanities.

Power, Roderick. 1981. *Perception.* 10:29; We believe what we see over other sensory input. *BMB.* Vol 6. 1981.

Prescott, James W. 1975. Body pleasure and the origins of violence. *The Futurist.* Apr.

———. 1974. Touching. *Intellectual Digest.* Mar. 6–8.

Pribram, Karl. 1982. "What the Fuss Is All About." In *The Holographic Paradigm,* edited by Ken Wilber. Boulder, London: Shambala.

———. 1977. Primary reality in frequency realm. *BMB.* Vol. 1 & 2.

Prigogine, Ilya. 1984. *Order out of Chaos.* New York: Bantam Books.

Prose, Francine. 1990. Confident at eleven, confused at sixteen. *The New York Times Magazine.* Jan. 7.

Rakic, Pasko. 1986. Overproduction of neural systems in development and elimination of large population of cells. *Science.* 232:233–35; Developing brain full of surprises. *BMB.* Aug. 1987.

Ramamurthi, B. 1988. "The Challenge of the Internal Universe." The Sir C. V. Raman Centenary Lecture at the Anna University. Dec. 9.

Restak, Richard. 1984. *The Brain.* New York: Bantam Books.

Richardson, Rick. 1986. State-bound recall. *Animal Learning and Behavior.* 14:73–79.

Ringler, Norma, Mary Trause, Marshall Klaus, and John Kennell. 1978. The effects of extra post-partum contact and maternal speech patterns on children's IQs, speech, and language comprehension at five. *Child Development.* 49:862–65.

Rochlin, Gregory. 1961. "The Dread of Abandonment: A Contribution to the Etiology of the Loss Complex and to Depression." In *The Psychoanalytic Study of the Child,* vol. 16. New York: International University Press.

Rosenberg, Martin. 1983. Tinitus may exaggerate ear's normal sounds. *BMB.* Vol. 8.

Rosenfield, Isaac. 1988. *The Invention of Memory.* New York: Basic Books; *BMB.* July 1988.

Ross, Elliott. 1982. Depression as disorder of brain. *The Sciences.* 22 (2): 8–12.

Ross, John. 1977. Unconscious interpretation precedes "seeing." *Scientific American.* Mar.

Sacks, Oliver. 1984. *A Leg to Stand On.* New York: Harper & Row.

Saltz, Eli. 1979. Imaginative play and learning. *BMB* Themepack no. 11.

Sandman, Curt. 1987. Influence of heart on brain/mind. *BMB*. Mar.

Schatz, Carla. 1989. Pioneer cells in early neural networks. *Science*. 245:978–82.

Schell, Orville. 1984. *Modern Meat: Antibiotics, Hormones and the Pharmaceutical Farm*. New York: Random House.

Sergent, Justine. 1983. Human Perception and Performance. *Journal of Experimental Psychology*. 8:1–13, 253–58; *BMB*. Vol. 7. 1983.

———. 1988. Split-brains. *Brain*. 109:357–69. *BMB*. May. 1988.

Shapely, Robert, and Peter Lennie. 1985. Spatial frequency analysis in the visual system. *Annual Review of Neuroscience*. 8:547–83.

Sheldrake, Rupert. 1982. *A New Science of Life, The Hypothesis of Formative Causation*. Los Angeles: Tarcher.

Sheppard, Kenneth. 1983. Multiple personalities and vision. *BMB*. Vol. 8.

Shields, Eloise. 1976. *Research in Parapsychology*. Metuchen, NJ: Scarecrow Press.

Shimony, Abner. 1988. The reality of the quantum world. *The Scientific American*. Vol 258, no. 1. Jan.

Siegle, Ron. 1980. Universal forms of hallucination aid brain research. *BMB*. Vol. 5. *BMB* Themepack. no. 7.

Sky, Michael. 1989. *Dancing with the Fire: Transforming Limitation Through Firewalking*. Santa Fe, NM: Bear & Co.

Smith, Carlyle, and Gina Kelly. 1988. *Physiology and Behavior* 43:213–16.

Solomon, George. Early handling increases immunity. *Journal of Neuroscience*. 18:1–9.

Sperry, Roger. 1987. *Perspectives in Biology and Medicine*. 29:413–22; Sperry sees mind at top of hierarchy. *BMB*. Mar. 1987.

Spitz, Renee. 1965. *The First Year of Life: A Psychoanalytic Study of Normal and Deviant Development of Object Relations*. New York: International Universities Press.

Staley, Betty. 1988. *Between Form and Freedom: A Practical Guide to the Teenage Years*. Stroud, U.K.: Hawthorne Press.

Sternberg, Saul. 1975. The brain as supercomputer. *Quarterly Journal of Experimental Psychology*. 27; *BMB* Vol 1 & 2. *BMB* Themepack no. 11. 1977.

Stewart, David. *The Five Standards for Safe Childbearing*. Available from NAPSAC International, Box 646, Marble Hill, MO 63764.

Storfer, Miles. 1990. *Intelligence and Giftedness: The Contributions of Heredity and Early Environment*. San Francisco: Jossey-Bass.

Tart, Charles R., ed. 1969. *Altered States of Consciousness, A Book of Readings*. New York: Wiley.

Tart, Charles, Harold Puthof, and Russel Targ, eds. 1980. *Mind at Large*. New York: Praeger.

Taubes, Gary. 1989. The body chaotic. *Discover*. May: 62ff.

Tomatis, Alfred. 1991. "Chant, the Healing Power of Voice and Ear." In

Music, Physician for Times to Come, edited by Don Campbell. Wheaton, IL: Quest.

Towbin, Abraham. 1968. Birth spinal injury and sudden infant death. *The Spartanburg, South Carolina Journal.* Mar. 2.

Transmitters in heart tissue. 1983. *New Science.* July 14, p. 99.

Treffert, Darold. 1989. *Extraordinary People: Redefining the "Idio-Savant."* New York: Harper & Row.

Truth Seeker, The. 1989. (Entire edition relating to routine hospital circumcisions of newborn males and to other atrocities.) July/Aug.

Tweedie, Irina. 1986. *Daughter of Fire: The Diary of a Spiritual Training with a Sufi Master.* Nevada City, CA: Blue Dolphin Pub.

Ullman, Shimon. 1986. Artificial intelligence and the brain. *Annual Review of Neuroscience.* 9:1–26.

Vasiliev, Leonid. 1977. Unusual long-distance vision. *BMB* Vol. 1 and 2. *BMB* Themepack no. 15.

von der Heyt, R. 1984. Visual illusions in higher brain centers. *Science.* 224:1260–62; *BMB.* Vol 9. 1984.

von Senden, M. 1960. *Space and Sight: The Perception of Space and Shape in the Congenitally Blind before and after Operation.* London: Methuen.

Wald, George. 1988. Cosmology of life and mind. *Los Alamos Bulletin* no. 16.

Wallach, Charles. 1990. Infant telepathy. *BMB.* Vol 15. no. 5. Feb.

Weinberger, Norman. 1984. Unconscious Learning. *Science.* 223:605–7.

West, John Anthony. 1979. *Serpent in the Sky: The High Wisdom of Ancient Egypt.* New York: Harper & Row.

White, Burton. 1975. *The First Three Years of Life.* Englewood Cliffs, NJ: Prentice-Hall.

Whittlestone, W. G. 1978. The physiology of early attachment in mammals: Implications for human obstetric care. *The Medical Journal of Australia.* Jan. 14. 1:50–53.

Wickes, Frances. 1968. *The Inner World of Childhood.* New York: Appleton-Century-Crofts.

Wikswo, John, John Barach, and John Freeman. 1980. Magnetic fields. *Science.* 208:53–55; *BMB.* Vol 5. 1980.

Wilber, Ken, ed. 1982. *The Holographic Paradigm: And Other Paradoxes.* Boulder, CO: Shambhala.

Williams, Robert W., and Karl Herrup. 1988. The control of neuron number. *Annual Review of Neuroscience.* 2:423–53.

Williamson, Scott G., and Innes H. Pearse. 1980. *Science, Synthesis and Sanity: An Enquiry into the Nature of Living.* Edinburgh: Scottish Academic Press.

Windle, W. F. 1969. Brain damage by asphyxia. *Scientific American.* Oct.

Winson, Jonathan. 1985. *Brain and Psyche: The Biology of the Unconscious.* Garden City, NY: Anchor Press/Doubleday.

Wong, Robert, and Richard Miles. 1984. Single neuron entrains populations. *Nature* 306:371–73; *BMB.* Vol 9. 1984.

Woods, Bryan, and Susan Carey. 1980. Age 8 threshold of vulnerability in language recovery. *Annals of Neurology.* 6:405–9; *BMB.* Vol 5. 1980.

Zihl, Josef. 1980. *Neurophysiologia.* 18:71–77; Blindsight: Training an alternative mode of vision. *BMB.* May 1980.

Zimmler, Jerome, and Janice Keenan. 1983. Visual images and spatial configuration of images in congenitally blind. *Journal of Experimental Psychology.* 9:269–82; *BMB.* Vol 8. 1983.

Zuccarelli, Hugo. 1981. Holophonic sound. *BMB.* July 15.

Zurek, Paul. *Scientific American.* 244 (5): 96–97.

Index

259